DATE DUE

"Rearing Wolves to Our Own Destruction"

SLAVERY IN RICHMOND, VIRGINIA, 1782–1865

Carter G. Woodson Institute

Series in Black Studies

Reginald Butler, *Editor*

"Rearing Wolves to Our Own Destruction"

SLAVERY IN RICHMOND, VIRGINIA, 1782–1865

Midori Takagi

University Press of Virginia

Charlottesville & London

THE UNIVERSITY PRESS OF VIRGINIA
© 1999 by the Rector and Visitors of the University of Virginia
All rights reserved
Printed in the United States of America

First published 1999

∞ The paper used in this publication meets the minimum requirements
of the American National Standard for Information Sciences—Permanence
of Paper for Printed Library Materials, ANSI Z39.48-1984.

Library of Congress Cataloging-in-Publication Data

Takagi, Midori, 1962–
    Rearing wolves to our own destruction : slavery in
Richmond, Virginia, 1782–1865 / Midori Takagi.
        p.   cm. — (Carter G. Woodson Institute series
in Black studies)
    Originally presented as author's thesis (Ph. D.)—
Columbia University, New York
    Includes bibliographical references (p.   ) and
index
    ISBN 0-8139-1834-0 (cloth : alk. paper)
    1. Slavery—Virginia—Richmond—History—18th
century.   2. Slavery—Virginia—Richmond—
History—19th century.   3. Slaves—Virginia—
Richmond—Social conditions.   4. Afro-Americans—
Virginia—Richmond—Social conditions.   5. Richmond
(Va.)—History—18th century.   6. Richmond (Va.)—
History—19th century.   I. Title.   II. Series.
F234.R59N4   1999
306.3'62'09755—dc21   98-35770
                                                            CIP

For Asaye Takagi, and to the
memory of Shigeo Takagi

Contents

Illustrations

Tables

Acknowledgments

MANY PEOPLE helped me during the process of writing this book. First and foremost I wish to thank my adviser, Eric Foner, for his sharp analysis, guidance, and patience. Without his help, my Ph.D. would have remained a dream, and this book, a mere wish. I also would like to thank the Center for Black Studies at the University of California, Santa Barbara, and the Mellon Post-doctoral Fellowship Program at Bryn Mawr College, Pennsylvania, for their support, which was crucial to completing this study. Both the Virginia Historical Society in Richmond and the Huntington Library in San Marino, California, generously opened their archives to me and sponsored my travel to their collections.

I also would like to extend a hearty thanks to Conley Edwards, Minor Weisiger, and other members of the staff at the Library of Virginia in Richmond. Their expertise, knowledge, and guidance helped me through the many months I spent searching through boxes of Hustings Suit papers, wills, and estate inventories.

Lee Furr also deserves credit; her careful research in tracking down references, selecting artwork, and handling important paperwork helped find errors in my manuscript.

My family also played an important role in this process. Their emotional, financial, and culinary support was immeasurable. Finally, I especially wish to thank my husband, Jonathan Hamilton, without whom this could not be.

Introduction

THE IMAGE of slaves tilling the soil of a large plantation under the watchful eye of an overseer has been indelibly printed on American minds as the North American slave experience. To a great extent this image is accurate given that 90 percent of African-American slaves lived in rural areas. But the remaining 10 percent—a small but significant segment of the slave population—worked and lived in urban and industrialized areas of the South. During the antebellum era as many as 400,000 slaves lived in cities such as Charleston, St. Louis, New Orleans, and Richmond.

Slavery in these southern urban centers, and particularly in Richmond, differed from rural slavery in its location, working and living conditions, and character. In Richmond slave men and women worked in tobacco factories, iron foundries, flour mills, and a number of manufacturing businesses producing goods such as chewing plugs, locomotive engines, milled wheat, shoes, and candy. But perhaps more unusual than their jobs were the conditions under which urban slaves worked. In an effort to adapt slave labor to the urban industrial setting, employers turned to the unusual practices of hiring out and living apart. Bondmen who were hired out were temporarily employed away from their owners as skilled artisans, house servants, firefighters, road pavers, and factory hands. Although most hiring negotiations were handled by professional slave brokers, there were instances in which slaves "hired their own time," needing neither owner nor broker to negotiate agreements.

Wages generally were paid in cash, and in many cases slaves were able to keep a portion of what they had earned. The practice of living apart permitted many slaves, especially those who were hired out, to reside outside their owners' household. As a result, it became common for urban slaves to live with their own families in separate communities that included slave and free black residents.

To slave owners and employers these practices constituted a breakthrough in city slavery because the traditional slave system had proved far too rigid for the rapidly changing labor demands of emerging industries. Hiring and living out helped make slavery more flexible and adaptable to the city and factory setting. For slave owner and employer alike, urban industrial slavery was a resounding success. It was slave labor that made tobacco manufacturing (the backbone of Richmond's antebellum economy) a multimillion-dollar industry by 1860 and greatly contributed to the growth of a range of other industries.

Many slave residents also found that hiring out and living apart offered benefits, such as the ability to decide where they worked and lived. Furthermore, city life offered advantages over the rural environment; Richmond's large, dense population (nearly 12,000 by 1860) provided bond men and women with anonymity and the ability to travel unnoticed, to socialize with white, free black, and other slave residents, or simply to relax over a brandy in an illegal grogshop.

Through its very success, however, the use of bond workers in industries altered the character of slavery in Richmond so that it only loosely resembled its counterpart on plantations. The result was a system that brought tremendous profits but relinquished a degree of slave owners' control and weakened the bond between slave and owner. The practices and privileges used to adapt slavery to the city factory system also enabled bond men and women to build a community organized around family and kinship networks, segregated neighborhoods, all-black churches, mutual aid organizations, secret fraternal and financial societies, and shared work experiences. Through these institutions slave residents educated and politicized themselves and in all likelihood acquired expectations of full control over their labor and lives. At the very least these developments provided slave residents with economic, psychological, and emotional support to combat the oppressive nature of slavery; at most, urban conditions threatened to undermine the slave system by refuting the moral and ideological foundations supporting the "peculiar institution."

This book, then, is as much a human drama as it is the history of a city and slave system. Although it takes a chronological approach to the intertwined development of urbanization, industrialization, and slavery,

I made a concerted effort to keep the focus on the human forces that created Richmond's antebellum society and its institutions. Keeping such a focus proved difficult at times because human nature and life often defy logical, progressive patterns; but I remain convinced that black and white Richmonders, slave and free residents, continually used the battles, the successes and losses of the previous generations as building blocks for the future, but with glaring differences. While white Richmonders used the past to strengthen the urban industrial economy and slave system, black slave men and women workers used previous experiences to build larger and stronger forms of resistance for each new generation.

This book examines the city of Richmond and its slave system from 1782, when the city was first incorporated, to the end of the Civil War in 1865. I chose to focus on this one location and for such a lengthy period of time in order to see the larger changes in population, occupation, and economic growth. By scrutinizing this eighty-three-year period, I also was able to chronicle the lives of the slave residents and how those factors affected them and the development of their community. I believe such a case study is important because it furthers the discussion of urbanization in the "backward" South, further demonstrates the diversity of North American slavery, and shows the African-American experience as an integral part of urban industrial history. Furthermore, this study helps to demonstrate the long tradition of urban black communities, for nineteenth-century urban black residents were not ghetto dwellers but city residents, factory workers, families, friends, church members, and political leaders, and their lives need to be examined within those contexts.

For all of the factors mentioned above, Richmond was, without a doubt, an anomaly in the predominantly rural antebellum South. Yet it was not unique. As studies by Richard Wade, Robert Starobin, Claudia Goldin, Barbara Fields, and Mary Karasch demonstrate, elements of Richmond's experience, such as the hiring systems, factory employment, and cash payments, existed in other southern cities as well as more rural factory towns. The ten southern cities Wade examines in his work, *Slavery in the Cities: The South, 1820-1860*, for example, all featured the systems of hiring out and living apart. Yet the very fact that so few cities and urban slave systems emerged in the South strongly indicates how exceptional Richmond became. And it is on this point that much of the historical debate about city slavery has pivoted: the compatibility of slavery and urbanization.

With a few exceptions, most historians agree that the overall number of southern urban slave residents declined during the late antebellum era. The causes for this change, however, have been greatly debated. Some observers, such as Wade, believe city living and working conditions "struck at the very heart of the [slave] institution" and caused its rapid decline.[1] As this argument goes, city slave conditions created a "twilight zone" between slavery and freedom within which bond men and women took a "step toward freedom" and became "quasi-free" or "quasi-wage-laborers."[2] This argument is not without precedent. Frederick Douglass, who lived in Baltimore for a short time before escaping north, believed that slavery did not work in urban areas precisely because city conditions made slaves more like free people. In his autobiography Douglass explained: "A city slave is almost a free citizen, in Baltimore, compared with a slave on [a] plantation. He is much better fed and clothed, is less dejected in his appearance, and enjoys privileges altogether unknown to the whip-driven slave on the plantation."[3] More recent observers have expanded on these beliefs and have found additional causes for urban slavery's decline stemming from larger economic and political trends. Claudia Goldin, for example, concluded that market forces, not incompatibility with the urban milieu, caused the decline. She argues that city hirers did want slave laborers, but that high prices and the availability of low-cost immigrant workers dampened urban slave employment. Barbara Fields in her work on Maryland makes an even more persuasive argument that many, if not all, southern urban centers were inhospitable to slavery because they lacked the necessary economic foundations on which to base slavery. According to Fields, this was especially evident in Baltimore, where a wheat-based economy and a plentiful supply of immigrant labor prevented the city from becoming economically "subservient to the slave system."[4]

Although I support many of the arguments raised by Richard Wade and Barbara Fields, I am less emphatic that slavery and urbanization were incompatible. For all intents and purposes, slavery in Richmond did work. Because of its location, the type of crops grown in the surrounding area, the products manufactured and the high dependence on slave labor in the industries, Richmond was a slave city. But I also believe that Richmond's slave system was fraught with terrible problems and tensions that, had the Civil War not erupted, probably would have led to a slow, inexorable decline. Urban industrial conditions did alter slavery in the city, and they did threaten the integrity of the system. My interest, however, is less in the question of compatibility than the opportunities this problem-filled slave system gave to black bond men and women. It is my belief that it was not city living and social conditions per se that compromised the system, but how they increased slave residents' ability to resist slave owner control. To demonstrate how Richmond's dependence on slave labor unwittingly sowed the seeds for its (potential) demise, this book traces the development of the city's economy, its slave system, their intertwined relationship, and how the two matured over time. Chapters 1 through 3, which begin in the late eighteenth century and end in 1840, follow the city's initial steps toward industrialization and demonstrate how slavery became linked to the city's economy from the very start as the major source of labor. Although slave workers were largely concentrated in the tobacco-processing industry, their presence in other businesses, such as flour milling and boat towing, grew over time and proved as important. Quickly, many business owners came to see slaves not as ancillary laborers to free men but as the principal work-force. As a result, slavery became as much a determinant of Richmond's growth as did the city's geographic location and the type of crops grown nearby.

Moving away from an institutional perspective, chapter 3 centers around slave workers and the impact of Richmond's development on their emerging community. Among the most notable effects of industri-alization on city slaves was the creation of a large pool of highly skilled workers. Richmond slaves were not ordinary field hands but craftsmen, ironmakers, blacksmiths, tailors, and of course, tobacco processors. As a result, Richmond's slave community was unlike many of those found on plantations in terms of its diversity of experience, collective ability, individual skills, and knowledge. Many of these workers were accus-tomed to traveling alone, negotiating their work contracts, and receiving cash payments for their labor. Additional evidence suggests that many also were literate. These privileges and abilities had significant ramifi-cations for the development of the slave community that flourished be-tween 1840 and 1860.

Chapters 4 and 5 continue examining the intertwined relationship among the urban industrial economy, the slave system, and the slave community as they matured during the late antebellum years. By 1850, for example, annual production by the tobacco industry reached more than $4 million, thereby making Richmond the premier tobacco man-ufacturer in the country. At the same time the city won recognition as a major flour-milling center and the home of a notable iron factory, the Tredegar Iron Works. Crucial to the economic success of Richmond's businesses was none other than slave workers. The labor of thousands of bondmen, and to a smaller degree bondwomen, allowed the factories to become multimillion-dollar industries. For slave residents, however, the real achievement was the success not of the tobacco industry but of their community. The increased number of urban and industrial slave laborers—all with varying degrees of privileges and benefits—enabled members to fund, build, and create institutions to help them survive. Most notably black Richmonders were able to build not one but three independent, all-black churches, which gave parishioners spiritual guidance and a venue to develop crucial political, judicial, and leadership skills. Extra cash also helped purchase members from bondage or buy them a ticket on the Underground Railroad to freedom. Aware of the "liberating" effects of the city slave system, and fearful of slave rebellion and escape, owners, employers, and city authorities attempted to curb the "freedoms," the unusual practices of hiring out, living apart, and cash payments. This atmosphere of fear prompted residents to blame the lax city slave system for encouraging slaves to rebel. Critics charged that by allowing slaves some measure of autonomy and self-control, Richmonders had been "rearing wolves to our own destruction."[5] Citizens' efforts to reverse these trends, however, proved ineffectual. Laws and tightened security measures were useless so long as slave residents continued to hire themselves out, live apart, and socialize without supervision. Furthermore, it became clear that these practices had become as much a part of the slave system as it was an integral part of the urban industrial economy. On the eve of the Civil War, then, Richmond authorities, owners, and other white residents found themselves in a kind of stalemate with regard to slave workers: to tighten the lax slave system would threaten the success of the economy, while failing to do so might encourage resistance and rebellion.

The advent of the Civil War, the focus of chapter 6, broke this impasse by eliminating the numerous privileges and benefits Richmond slave workers enjoyed and by providing the necessary soldiers and patrols to enforce the new laws. On the surface, it appeared that the Confederate government through martial law accomplished what white Richmonders had been attempting to do for the past sixty years: secure the slave system and closely monitor slave activities. City authorities, owners, and employers had little to celebrate, however, as the demands of the war of the Confederacy altered the slave system so that it gave few benefits to them. For example, many city slaves were summarily appropriated for wartime use. For slave workers and free black Richmonders, the consequences were even graver. Slaves experienced the total loss of privileges, and free blacks lost their freedom. Wartime life presented even greater hardships for the free and enslaved black Richmonders as food and clothing shortages made survival more difficult and harsh working conditions severely compromised their health and safety. In spite of the terrible conditions, opportunities to live and be free continued to present themselves to slave workers. Hundreds of workers slipped away in the night and made their way toward Federal lines. Although listed as having been "carried away by the enemy," few actually received assistance from Union soldiers, other than prompting from the Federal troops. In most cases their desire to be free, their knowledge of the terrain, and their survival skills were the only aids slaves had to help them escape. For a smaller group of slave residents, the opportunity to escape bondage came not from the Union troops but from the Confederacy itself through its decision to arm bond-men for battle with the tacit understanding that they would be freed in exchange for their services. No doubt many of those who volunteered believed they had nothing to lose; should the Confederacy win, they would gain their freedom, and should the Union army win, they would still be freed. No city slave resident ever saw battle as a Confederate volunteer, however, as the Union army's successes preempted the use of Richmond slave soldiers. On April 4, 1865, as members of the Confed-erate government fled the burning city, the first of the Federal troops entered Richmond and declared slavery to be over.

One

Inauspicious Beginnings

In 1782 when Richmond received its formal recognition as a city, it had only a thousand inhabitants and hardly resembled a bustling metropolis; incorporated or not, it was little more than a small port town. But Richmond's newly conferred status did portend the greatness the city would achieve within the next eight decades. During those years Richmond would evolve from a sleepy town to one of the most important political and economic centers of the South.

Many factors contributed to this change. One was the relocation of Virginia's capital in 1780 from Williamsburg to Richmond, a city less vulnerable to enemy attacks during the Revolutionary War. The arrival of the state government acted as an early catalyst for population growth. One study estimates that Richmond's prewar population of 640 increased by 63 percent to 1,031 by 1782.[1]

Politicians, society figures, office seekers, and their entourages were drawn to the new capital, as were a number of businesses hoping to supply this new wealthy populace with goods and services—as evidenced by the sudden availability of silver and gold items, plush coaches, European fashions, and exotic wines and foods. Any doubt that the influx of wealth and people was caused by the city's newfound political status can be removed by looking at Williamsburg. The relocation sounded the death knell for that once bustling town, which, lacking politics, was left with little more than "grass, and several cows, pigs, horses, mules and goats."[2] But for Richmond, being the capital of Virginia or even, as it would later become, the capital of the Confederacy had less impact on the city's growth than several other factors, among them its geographic location.

Situated on the James River just below the rapids, Richmond had access to the ocean and the interior of the state. The river snaked through the upcountry and into the hinterlands, providing planters and small farmers with a means to transport their goods on rafts and bateaux. Richmond was a natural stopping point because of its location just below the fall line. The rapids prevented ships from sailing beyond Richmond either up or downstream. As a result, Richmond, like other river cities such as Alexandria and Fredericksburg, became an ideal spot for commerce and for shipping goods to and from the interior of Virginia.[3] Once their goods were in Richmond, farmers traded or sold them to merchants and European agents who then transferred the goods to larger ships bound for the eastern coastline or England.

Richmond's location close to the rapids also gave it the distinct advantage of being able to harness the energy that flowed from the rushing waters. The falls provided residents with a cheap, dependable source of power that helped them mill wheat and corn and in later years run machinery. This energy source would prove crucial to the many emerging factories in Richmond during the antebellum era. Later, when the Kanawha Canal was built around the James to allow navigation, two sources of waterpower became available. With this increased energy, factory owners were able to expand their businesses and production greatly.

Crucial to Richmond's development were the staple crops grown in the surrounding countryside. The two major ones, tobacco and wheat, greatly influenced the nature of Richmond's growth by requiring certain kinds of processing, packaging, and shipping. In the eighteenth century tobacco had been picked, dried, and stemmed on the plantation before being sent to Richmond by cart or bateaux in large wooden hogsheads. Once in Richmond the tobacco was stored in warehouses, its quality inspected by state officials, and its price negotiated with European agents. But by the late eighteenth century, market changes, stricter inspection laws, and increased European demand changed the method of processing and shipping.

The stringent tobacco inspection laws passed during the nineteenth century required that all tobacco exports be reviewed and graded by state-appointed officials on the docks.[4] This was an attempt to upgrade the quality of exported tobacco by eliminating trash (lower-grade) weeds. These laws also precluded the more informal tobacco trade among small farmers, country merchants, and ship captains. And because all export tobacco was required to be lodged in warehouses prior to shipment, tobacco agents and ship captains congregated at these sites. As a result, Richmond became an important center for inspecting, negotiating, and selling the lucrative leaf.

In addition to the inspection process, other tobacco-related businesses and services flourished in Richmond. Attendant industries such as coopering and stave making set up near the wharves and tobacco warehouses to meet the demand for hogsheads and boxes used to ship tobacco. Hotels, boardinghouses, and taverns appeared to lodge the inspectors, ship captains, and agents.

The changes in European tastes had an additional effect on Richmond's economic development. By the turn of the century European preference for a smoother, more refined tobacco product encouraged greater processing of the leaf. Tobacco growers and later tobacco manufacturers—who had little to do with the growing process—began to stem, boil, press, flavor, and twist the leaves into licorice-flavored plugs. As shops providing such services sprang up, more craftsmen and laborers came to Richmond seeking employment. The earliest manufacturing census of Richmond illustrates the industrial growth: in 1820 twenty tobacco manufactories employed a total of 760 workers. By 1850 there were nineteen manufactories employing 1,406 workers. During the next decade, the number of tobacco-processing factories and tobacco workers nearly tripled.

The growth of tobacco manufacturing was fairly steady even though the counties surrounding Richmond turned to other crops, such as wheat. Many local farmers diversified their crops because of soil exhaustion and wildly fluctuating tobacco prices, causing the nation's major source of raw tobacco to shift toward the lower piedmont region of Virginia during the late eighteenth and early nineteenth centuries. Despite the increasing distance to tobacco farms, Richmond continued to receive large shipments of raw tobacco for processing. By 1820 the city was firmly established as a hub for tobacco processing and shipping, and it retained that position throughout the antebellum era.

The other staple crop that affected Richmond's development, though to a lesser degree than tobacco, was wheat. Wheat cultivation in the tidewater area throughout the eighteenth and nineteenth centuries encouraged the growth of flour milling in Richmond, which was a prime location for such an industry because of its abundant waterpower. Although wheat never commanded the prices or profits of tobacco, wheat processing and exporting proved an important industry for the city.

The increase in European demand for flour, the steady rise in grain prices in comparison to unstable tobacco prices, and the rapid exhaustion of soil from tobacco growing encouraged many farmers to grow more wheat. Most of this wheat was for export and required a certain amount of processing and storage prior to shipping. To meet this need, the flour and gristmill industry moved from quaint riverside grinding shops to large, bustling mills.[5] By 1860 Richmond possessed the second and third largest flour mills in the country (the largest mill was in Oswego, New York), producing, respectively, 190,000 and 160,000 barrels of flour per year.[6]

In addition to tobacco and wheat there was another "crop" that greatly affected Richmond's urban and industrial growth: coal. The city was located only miles from the eastern Virginia coalfields, which made the area one of the few mining centers with access to coastal vessels.[7] More important, coal was essential to the production of iron, a product with even greater economic implications for the city. Bituminous coal and its by-product, coke, were needed to heat the furnaces that made iron. Without them, iron could not be melted or cast into products. Iron foundries in Richmond were first established during the American Revolution to produce goods for the war, such as shells, castings, pikes, nails, and cannonballs. After the war the iron industry became an integral part of other Richmond businesses, providing them with parts for coaches, carts, machinery, tools, and most important, the railroad.

The city's three major products, combined with iron manufacturing, further stimulated industrial and commercial activity by creating a need for numerous attendant industries and businesses. New businesses that supported the tobacco, wheat, and iron industries quickly arose, producing goods such as barrels, tobacco boxes, machine parts, wagons, tobacco cutters, grain-grinding machines, sheet iron, and farm tools. In addition, a number of businesses and services appeared to serve the growing population. Among businesses that flourished were those producing clothing, shoes and boots, soap and candles, guns, hats, sashes and blinds, and furniture. There also was explosive growth in the service sector with the arrival of lawyers, doctors and hospitals, auctioneers, commission merchants, and slave traders.

Together, tobacco, wheat, coal, and ironmaking contributed greatly to Richmond's status within the eastern Virginia region. And because of these crops and products, Richmond did not remain merely a shipping or trading port. The tremendous volume of processing, marketing, and shipping of these goods, as well as the extensive development of attendant industries and services, allowed Richmond to diversify and become a commercial, industrial, and political center.[8]

Essential to Richmond's development was the system of slavery. Slaves provided the labor for nearly all aspects of Richmond's economic, urban, and industrial growth, from cultivating and manufacturing tobacco and wheat to building supporting industries and creating the physical structures of the city.

Tobacco, for example, could not have been cultivated in such high volume without slaves. Their labor was crucial at every juncture in the growing, harvesting, and manufacturing of the plant. From the painstaking activities of planting, picking, and drying to stemming, pressing, and twisting the brown leaves, slaves constituted the majority of the workforce throughout the antebellum years. As a result, at every stage of cultivation and production slavery and tobacco became intertwined.[9]

Slavery and tobacco cultivation became linked initially during the late seventeenth century when the numbers of white immigrant laborers who earlier performed these tasks began to decline rapidly. Several factors precipitated this decline, including improved employment opportunities in Europe and in northern colonies that proved more enticing than a stint of indentured servitude in Virginia. As a result, planters in need of a cheap source of labor began to substitute African slaves for white servants.[10] By the turn of the eighteenth century, most large tobacco farms were fully manned by slave labor.

By the early to middle nineteenth century, slave labor had become equally important to the processing of the leaf. As tobacco production moved from plantations to factories, so did the labor force. Slaves frequently were purchased or hired by tobacco manufacturers to process the dried leaves into flavored chewing plugs. Manufacturers, like planters, employed slaves because they were viewed as a cheaper and more tractable source of labor, because many slaves already were skilled at processing tobacco (having been trained on the plantations), and because there were few white laborers willing to do such labor.[11] For all of these reasons, there was little resistance to the use of slave labor in tobacco factories.

Slaves also played a major role in the harvesting and processing of grains, both in the countryside and in the city of Richmond. Not only did they manage the wheat fields surrounding the city, they were responsible for turning the grain into flour. In the water-powered mills beside the James River, slaves could be found grinding the wheat into several grades of flour as well as making the barrels in which the product was shipped.

The increase in wheat cultivation in the immediate countryside had an additional impact on Richmond's slave system: the creation of a labor surplus. As more farmers began growing wheat instead of tobacco, they found themselves with more workers than they could use because the new crop was far less labor-intensive. Rather than keeping idle hands on the farms, planters began to hire out their slaves to other farms or to

Richmond businesses, including the tobacco manufactories. This trans-
fer of surplus slave labor was an important part of Richmond's industrialization. The intermittent labor demands of wheat cultivation and the
resulting release of slave labor greatly encouraged practices such as hiring out.

A third important factor that influenced the development and growth
of slavery in Richmond was the prior use of slaves for industrial tasks
beginning in the Revolutionary War. Although bondmen had been working for ironworks and other craft shops across Virginia as early as 1721,
it was not until the 1770s and 1780s that industrial slave employment
took hold in the city.[12] During those decades slave workers from the city
and nearby counties were forcibly moved from households and crafts
shops to state-owned industries. The public ropewalks in Warwick and
in Richmond were manned entirely by slave workers who spent long
hours "manipulating the dressed hemp [and twisting] the strands into
rope."[13] A major portion of the workforce at the lead mines run by the
government during the Revolutionary War was slave labor with duties
that included chipping the lead from the earthen walls, removing the
gravel from the shaft, and separating ore from rocks through coarse
grinding. Construction of the capital also was based on slave labor. Most
if not all of the government buildings such as the State Capitol, the
governor's mansion, and the new arms manufactory were built by slave
workers.

The extensive use of slave labor in the various wartime industries and
public projects was hailed by the state government as a resounding success. Encouraged by this, the Virginia government not only continued
to purchase and employ slaves but demanded that all public development projects of the late eighteenth century do the same. The James
River Company was quick to respond to the governor's wish; in 1791 its
directors wrote that "having been instructed to make the purchase of
negroes for the use of the Company, & wishing to comply therewith at
a sale shortly to be made in the county of Gloster, we have to request of
your Excellency & the Hon'ble Board for supply of money, or tobacco
at the present value, as will enable [us] to make the purchase."[14]

The use of slaves in war-related industries—and later public projects—set an important example that encouraged other employers to
consider slave labor. A range of documents indicate the private sector's
response was enthusiastic. Colonel Davies, who was in charge of the state
ropewalks, was approached by several businesses interested in hiring the
slave rope makers. In a letter to the governor in 1782, Davies informed
the executive council that a local rope-making company presented such
an offer: "Drawing attention to the condition of the Public works at

Warwick, little or nothing is done there at present, and yet there are 'the hands kept there' belonging to the state, who could be hired out to advantage, most of them are Rope-makers, but as the public rope-walk is burnt, the proprietors of the private rope-walks near Richmond are very anxious to hire these negroes and will give high wages for them."[15]

The ropewalk was not the only company interested in hiring state slaves. During that same year the original lead mine owners petitioned Governor Harrison, through Thomas Madison, for the return of the mines and specifically asked to hire the state slaves who had been working there since the war. Harrison gave his reply to Madison and specified the terms of his agreement: "Sir, I am ready to receive proposals from the proprietors of the lead mines for delivering up the said mines to them, and hiring the public negroes provided they will furnish the state with one hundred tons of lead."[16]

From these few documents it is clear that government use of slave workers during the war did help city employers and slave owners see the potential of slave labor for a variety of nonagricultural businesses. By providing solid evidence that slaves could be used effectively and efficiently in industries that brought profits to both the owner and employer, the state helped open the door to large-scale employment of slave workers in the industries during the antebellum era.

Many historical works have played up the drama and romance of Richmond's history. They have highlighted events such as the arrival of Captain Christopher Newport, who in the seventeenth century reportedly claimed the area for England by planting a wooden cross at the falls and shouting, "For our King and our prosperous success in this his action." This history instead focuses on typical city residents and the less romantic factors that created this urban industrial center in the South.[17] Such an approach seemed more sensible, given that the development of Richmond's industries and slave system had little to do with the actions of larger-than-life individuals and much to do with geography, economics, politics, greed, racism, and fear.

Two

The Road to Industrialization and the Rise of Urban Slavery, 1800–1840

RICHMOND in the early to mid–nineteenth century began to lose much of its provincialism. The various shops, taverns, and hotels that filled the main thoroughfare greatly popularized the commercial area and drew crowds of residents and visitors alike. The opening of the Bank of Virginia added a sense of financial strength to Richmond, while the Roman-style brick and stucco Capitol (designed by Thomas Jefferson and completed just before the turn of the century) gave the city a certain air of permanence and importance.[1]

The quaintness that remained following the Revolutionary War disappeared as the city continued to expand, incorporating areas that once had been countryside. Farmers living on the outskirts of Richmond were now counted and taxed as city dwellers, and their vistas of the river and valleys were interrupted by newly built homes and businesses. In the heart of the city, numbered wardships assumed the more dignified names of Jefferson, Madison, and Monroe. Within each district emerged neighborhoods with colorful names such as Libby Hill, Shed Town, Church Hill, Screamersville, and Butchertown.

An increase in population forced the city to expand. The original square village lots could no longer accommodate the influx of newcomers to the city. Between 1800 and 1840 the number of black and white residents grew 350 percent, from 5,737 to 20,153 (table 1). Although Richmond was no Baltimore or New Orleans (both of which had populations exceeding 102,000 by 1840), its citizenry did surpass those of

Table 1. Breakdown of Richmond's population, 1800–1840

Year	Slave	Free black	White	Total
1800	2,293	607	2,837	5,737
1810	3,748	1,180	4,807	9,735
1820	4,387	1,235	6,445	12,067
1830	6,345	1,960	7,755	16,060
1840	7,509	1,926	10,718	20,153

Source: U.S. Bureau of the Census, Population, 1800–1840.

other notable cities such as Savannah (11,214) and trailed only slightly behind Louisville (21,210).[2]

Creating new roads to, from, and through Richmond topped the city council's list of priorities during these years. To ease travel and to lessen the inconvenience of dust and mud, local officials banned the rolling of tobacco hogsheads through the city. They also were less inclined to create narrow, picturesque streets, opting instead to carve out wide boulevards.[3] Later, to further improve travel conditions, the major thoroughfares were paved with cobblestones and flagstones. But the greatest improvements in travel came with advances in transportation technology. During these years the city became linked with the rest of the country by eight turnpikes, several ferries, a large canal, and by the 1840s, two railroads.

The most significant and conspicuous change to Richmond during these years, however, was the emergence of industry. Between 1800 and 1840 Richmond shifted its focus from commercial to manufacturing activities. Alongside the many shipping and trading houses, new factories began to appear, producing goods for the local market, such as shoes, clothing, saddles, wheels, carts, bricks, nails, and other building supplies. The most lucrative industries, however—chewing tobacco and flour—supplied markets as far away as Europe and South America. Of these two key products, tobacco proved more important to Richmond and more dependent on slave labor.

Tobacco always had been an integral part of Richmond's economy and in many ways was the very basis for the city's existence. Because of its location near tobacco-producing farmlands, and because of its access to the ocean, Richmond became an important transshipment point for tobacco exportation to Europe, feeding that continent's appetite for the brown leaves. But starting in 1800, Richmond's role in the tobacco economy expanded to include the processing of tobacco. High market demand for the processed leaf encouraged city entrepreneurs to combine shipping with tobacco manufacturing, which became one of Virginia's fastest-growing industries and dominated Richmond's economy throughout the early nineteenth century.

Crucial to the growth of tobacco manufacturing was slave labor (table 2). In hindsight, there is little reason to believe the industry would have succeeded without slave workers. Census materials indicate that slaves played an important role from the very start; in the early 1800s, when tobacco processing took hold in Richmond, the industry consisted of three rooms, a handful of benches, a few tools, and some twenty-two slave men. Even as the facilities, processing techniques, and tools changed over the years, slaves remained the main source of labor. Furthermore, it was the labor of slaves that helped build the industry from its modest beginnings to the most lucrative business in the city and state. Between 1800 and 1840 the industry grew from three workshops employing 22 laborers, to thirty or so manufactories with 981 workers, 73 percent (716) of whom were slaves.[4]

Although tobacco factories engaged the highest number of slave workers, these businesses were not the only ones to seek slave labor. Increasingly slaves could be found in a variety of locales including flour mills, coal mines, river docks, cotton-weaving factories, and in private homes as domestic servants.

Predictably the increased use of slave labor in the various industries encouraged a rise in the number of city slave residents. Between 1800

Table 2. Tobacco and flour industries, Richmond and Henrico County, 1820 and 1840

	No. of employees		1840	
Product	1820	1840	Capital invested	Value of manufactured item
Tobacco	655	981	$429,250	$629,340
Flour	24	106	$467,200	$402,570

Source: Richmond, Manufacturing Census, 1820; Compendium of the Enumeration of the Inhabitants and Statistics of the United States, 1840.
Note: Statistics for 1840 reflect totals for Henrico County.

and 1840 Richmond's slave population grew from 2,293 to 7,509 (table 3), a rate of increase that kept slaves at about one-third of the total population through those years. This growth is remarkable even in comparison to other nearby Virginian cities with rapidly growing slave populations. Petersburg's slave community, for instance, increased 250 percent, from 1,487 in 1800 to 3,637 in 1840. The slave population of Norfolk increased 130 percent between 1800 and 1840, from 2,724 to 3,709.[5]

Industrial employment of bondmen also influenced the gender and age distribution patterns of Richmond slave residents by bringing a large influx of male slaves. As a result, between 1820 and 1840 there were nearly equal numbers of slave men and women, a pattern not seen in other southern urban centers where women typically were in the majority (tables 4 and 5). In Baltimore, for example, slave women outnumbered men in 1840 by a ratio of 100 to 57. This pattern also was evident in Charleston, Louisville, New Orleans, and Washington, D.C., which suggests a high demand for female domestic servants in those cities. Although Richmond also had a significant demand for such servants, the growing need for industrial slaves during the early nineteenth century assured a more balanced sex ratio.

Table 3. Urban slave populations in Virginia, 1800–1840

	Richmond	Norfolk	Petersburg
1800	2,293	2,724	1,487
1820	4,387	3,261	2,428
1840	7,509	3,709	3,637

Source: U.S. Bureau of Census, Population, 1800–1840.

Table 4. Sex distribution of slave population, 1820–40

	Male	Female	Ratio
1820	2,171	2,150	101:100
1830	3,134	2,844	110:100
1840	3,816	3,347	114:100

Source: U.S. Bureau of Census, Population, 1820–40.

Table 5. Age distribution of slaves, 1820–40

1820	Under 14	14–26	26–45	45+	
Male	724	653	604	190	
Female	726	628	571	221	

1830	Under 10	10–24	24–36	36–55	55+
Male	713	1,092	33	496	54
Female	725	941	634	544	213

1840					
Male	685	1,320	1,190	621	137
Female	724	1,215	685	206	3

Source: U.S. Bureau of Census, Population, 1820–40.
Note: Age distribution for 1800 and 1810 is not available.

Industrial demand for male slaves is further reflected in the age distribution of Richmond's bondmen. Throughout the period the majority of black males held in bondage were between fourteen and forty-five, the prime years for industrial and factory workers. This indicates that city owners did not send able-bodied bondmen to plantations in the Deep South for work but kept them in the city (see table 5).

Slave labor demands during the early nineteenth century also affected slaveholdings by maintaining a sizable minority of owners with four or more slaves—a pattern that originated in the post–Revolutionary War era. Although the majority of Richmond owners held three or fewer slave workers (and continued to do so throughout the antebellum era), nearly one-third of the city's slaveholders possessed a greater number of workers, indicating healthy business demands for bondmen. As table 6 demonstrates, 244 households (69%) in 1800 owned between one and three slaves, and 111 (31%) households held between four and thirty-three slaves. These percentages remained the same over the next forty years. By 1840, 69 percent (785) of all households with slaves held three or fewer slaves, and roughly 31 percent (298) held four or more slaves.

Table 6. Slaveholding patterns, 1800 and 1840

Slaves per household	1800 and (1840)				
	No. of households	%	Total no. of slaves	%
1	121 (286)	34 (29)	121 (386)	10 (9)
2	80 (238)	23 (24)	160 (476)	13 (11)
3	43 (161)	12 (16)	129 (483)	11 (11)
4+	111 (298)	31 (30)	789 (2,892)	66 (69)
Total	355 (983)	1. (1.)	1,199 (4,237)	1. (1.)

Source: Richmond, Personal Property Tax Lists, 1800 and 1840.
Note: Percentages have been rounded to the nearest whole number.

Although these are but a few of the many statistics available for Richmond, they clearly show a region that had become markedly different from other places in Virginia.

During the first few decades of the nineteenth century, Richmond grew up. With new residences and businesses, cobblestone thoroughfares, a major banking facility, and the State Capitol, it began to resemble a city of importance. The most significant development, however, was the rise of industries, which greatly shaped both the landscape and the community to fit the needs of a manufacturing center. By 1840 tobacco manufactories and flour mills crowded the banks of the James River, and hundreds of workers, particularly male slave laborers, filled its stemming, pressing, and grinding rooms. These facts alone set Richmond apart from any other city south of the Mason-Dixon Line and any industrial center farther north. Of greater importance than how Richmond fared in comparison to other cities, however, was how the emerging industries and slavery became intertwined and affected the development and character of each other. The result was the creation of a city, an industrial center, and an urban slave system unlike any other in the South.

Origins of Urban Industrial Slavery

In the early decades of the nineteenth century, the use of slave workers as the main source of labor in craft shops and preindustrial factories was rare, and in some business circles practically unthinkable. Richmonders were used to seeing individual slave workers hired to shoe a horse, build a table, or hem a garment and knew that slave artisans provided a wide range of craft services on most large plantations. But the idea of a workshop manned entirely by bondmen would have been considered radical and dangerous.

Much of the trepidation concerning industrial slave labor came from the popular belief among whites that free white laborers were best suited to skilled positions and factory jobs. As the argument went, not only were free workers more capable of performing highly technical jobs, but they needed fewer incentives to do good work. Furthermore, to replace white artisans with slaves or to "put liberty and slavery side by side" would "degrade" and "depress" the former and encourage them to leave the state in search of better employment opportunities. Finally, to employ slaves as artisans in shops was considered folly because it would give them a great deal of freedom and inspire them to demand more— perhaps even by force.[6]

The strength of this belief did not deter all Richmond business owners. Some city residents were willing to experiment with slave labor in their emerging factories and workshops. Moreover, slaves already had been performing some of the rudimentary steps of processing tobacco on plantations.[7] Other businessmen received encouragement from the examples of slave employment that occurred during the Revolutionary War. During that conflict the war industries in Richmond employed slave workers extensively to produce much needed items such as sails and ropes. An equally persuasive factor, and one that became key to adapting slavery to the urban and industrial milieu, was the use of unusual labor practices. These practices included leasing slave labor (also known as hiring out), requiring slaves to secure their own lodgings (living apart), rewarding workers with a portion of the money earned (cash payments), and providing opportunities to earn overtime bonuses. Of the four practices, hiring out had by far the greatest effect on city businesses.

The hiring-out system entailed leasing slave workers to individuals or businesses for cash or payment in kind. In some areas wealthy plantation owners had been known simply to lend their slave workers to poorer neighboring farms during harvest periods as an act of noblesse oblige.[8] Hiring-out transactions in Richmond, however, generally involved some form of payment. During the American Revolution, for example, the Virginia war industries hired slave workers and paid owners in specie and in tobacco leaves.

Hiring out made slave labor extremely flexible, attracting businesses that never would have considered purchasing slaves. Contracts typically lasted one year, but businesses could hire workers for periods as short as one month, one week, or even a single day. This flexibility was enormously attractive to business owners who needed an extra hand or two to complete a specific job or task. The hiring system also appealed to larger employers because it allowed them to adjust their labor force to meet market demands, although there is some question as to whether hiring slaves on a long-term basis, that is, for several years, was actually less expensive. This feature was particularly helpful to tobacco manufacturers, whose businesses were vulnerable to dramatic fluctuations in the market caused by droughts, fires, and at the other extreme, bumper crops. No doubt tobacconists valued the flexibility that hiring out offered in 1843 when prices plummeted because of "too many having been engaged in the business last year, which has thrown more [tobacco] into the markets than can be disposed of."[9] To cope, manufacturers simply chose not to rehire slave workers when their contracts had ended.

Hiring also gave city businesses the ability to secure a stable slave workforce with far less capital than would have been required to purchase such workers. According to data gleaned from local newspapers, personal papers, court suit papers, and deed records, between 1800 and 1840 the average annual cost of hiring a slave in Richmond was approximately $34 for a female and $70 for a male. In contrast, the cost of purchasing an adult slave ranged from $100 to $600 for females and $250 to $900 for males. Hiring allowed a resident like J. S. Ellis to hire skilled hands such as John Prosser's slave George for a fraction of the purchase cost. According to court records, George was valued at $325 in 1811 but was hired out for $70 per year.[10]

Accompanying the slave-hiring system was the practice of living out, which allowed slaves (predominantly factory hands) to secure lodgings apart from both owner and employer. This system evolved because employers commonly lacked space and funds to build housing for hired slave workers. Instead, employers gave bondmen money to pay for room and board. Employers preferred these living arrangements because the system released them from any responsibilities for slave workers once the working day was over.

The flexibility that hiring out and living apart offered quickly won over owners, employers, and slaves themselves. By 1840 businesses were openly enthusiastic about hiring slave workers and believed them essential to economic success. Although it is not clear if the approach produced higher profits than free labor, in cases such as the tobacco industry it offered manufacturers a way to control costs during economic downturns. The unusual labor practices also offered employers the opportunity to experiment with, and make adjustments to, the workforce by using black and white, slave and free labor until they assembled a group of laborers that best suited their needs based on cost, but also on age, sex, and even class.

Factory, Mill, and Beyond

Around the turn of the century Colonel Samuel Jones opened one of the first shops devoted completely to tobacco manufacturing.[11] With the assistance of four male slave workers, Jones planned to stem and twist the brown leaves into chewing plugs and sell them for consumption. Little did Jones know that he was starting a new business trend; not long after his shop began production, other Richmond residents embarked on similar ventures. David Barclay, for example, soon began processing tobacco with one slave assistant, as did Daniel Triplett once he was able to find "two negro fellows" to help him.[12] These small manufactories required little initial investment. All that was necessary were a few workers and a screw press. The raw tobacco generally was purchased on credit and repaid after the finished product was sold. Once profits from selling the processed tobacco accumulated, the manufacturers who were able to survive during the first lean years expanded their businesses by employing more workers and purchasing more presses. Although the process seems straightforward now, Jones, Barclay, and Triplett were taking a substantial risk by entering a new industry with an untried type of labor. Before that time nearly all raw tobacco was shipped out of Virginia for processing. But that would change with these entrepreneurs, who succeeded in launching a major industry for Richmond and a major source of employment for hired slaves.

Over the next few decades, the small shops grew into large manufactories, and the link between slavery and tobacco manufacturing only became stronger. As production increased and facilities expanded from one-room shops to two-story buildings, the number of tobacco slave workers grew. During the first decade of the nineteenth century, fewer than 100 slave hands worked in a small number of shops. By 1820 there were between 370 and 480 tobacco slave workers at fifteen to twenty businesses, and by 1840 between 600 and 700 slaves worked at some thirty manufactories processing about 100,000 pounds of tobacco per year.[13]

Hundreds of workers were needed because of the high labor demands of tobacco processing. Manufacturing tobacco was a labor-intensive, hand-mechanized system that required varying levels of skill and training, depending on the specific task. Raw tobacco packed in large wooden hogsheads (which resembled huge barrels), weighing roughly 1,400 pounds each, would arrive at the factory daily. If the leaves were dry and brittle, they would be wrapped in cloth and moistened with water. Once softened, the leaves would be wiped carefully, and a worker would re-move the "backbone" of the leaf with a knife or razor, a process known as stemming. The leaves were then twisted into lumps and plugs and sent to be prized (pressed) using a large iron screw press. At this point some manufactories would air or fire dry the twists for a day or two before a second prizing. The final step was to return the tobacco to the stemming rooms to be retwisted and packaged for shipment. This pro-cess remained basically unaltered throughout the antebellum era, though a few extra steps were added over time to enhance the flavor and quality of the chewing plugs. In 1839, for example, manufacturers began storing lower-quality tobacco in fire- or sun-heated rooms to "sweat" before being prized a second time. This seemed to improve the flavor and consistency of lesser-quality leaves, thereby raising their value on the market.[14]

The numerous stages of processing coupled with the increasing size of most facilities encouraged the use of an assembly-line production system. As a result, by 1840 slave workers performed each stage of pro-cessing in a different room and sometimes even on a different floor. Under this labor system slave workers were placed together—side-by-side—for expediency and efficiency even though the tasks they per-formed were individual, not group activities. This labor system was in-troduced during the Revolutionary War in the state-owned industries and continued in the newer factories of the early nineteenth century. As a result, workers who stemmed the leaves worked apart from the hands, in the twisting rooms. There, while seated on long benches ar-ranged in rows, they would stem the tobacco using a knife and part of the bench as a cutting board. To manipulate the leaves into chewing plugs, workers used a variety of tools including shaping mills, lump shapes, and tobacco bands. Although young boys increasingly filled the ranks of stemmers, it was considered semiskilled, not unskilled, labor, requiring dexterity, agility, and some training.[15]

The finished plugs were sent to another part of the manufactory to be prized. There, slave men squeezed the tobacco into compact cakes using a press made of two large stones with a metal screw on top. In order to apply sufficient pressure to the leaves, two to three men gen-erally manned each press. Once prized, the tobacco cakes were sent to a third area where another group of workers packaged the product and prepared it for shipping.

The numerous time-consuming tasks involved in processing tobacco make it clear why tobacconists needed so many workers. But the tasks do not explain why bond workers rather than free were selected. That answer can be found by looking at the priorities of tobacco businessmen and their experiments with various forms of labor. These businessmen were most concerned with obtaining a workforce that was cheap, abundant, efficient, and manageable. As a result, during the early decades of the nineteenth century tobacconists tried different types of labor—including slave—in order to find one that best suited their needs.

Attempts to find laborers based on those criteria resulted in a tobacco workforce integrated by race, class, and gender. Census figures and tax returns indicate that before 1830 tobacconists employed workers including free blacks, white women, and slave women, boys, and girls, in addition to bondmen. Richard C. Gilliam, for example, hired both slave and free men as well as women and children. Fellow tobacconist Richard Anderson employed a similarly diverse workforce consisting of 30 men, 16 women, and 15 boys. Of the 61 workers, 25 appear to have been slaves. Mansfield Watkins, on the other hand, hired only 6 workers, all of them white. The peak of workforce experimentation may have come in 1820. According to the manufacturing census for that year, there were 112 women and 256 girls and boys working in the tobacco industry. The census does not specify workers by race, sex, or age, but a comparison of the manufacturing and population census returns along with the personal property tax lists suggests that a handful of firms were integrated by race and class. P. Cantor (or Cotton) is listed in the manufacturing census as employing 8 men, 3 women, and 5 boys and girls. According to the other sources, however, he owned (or paid taxes on) no more than 6 adult slaves. It appears, then, that the other 5 adult workers were free blacks or whites.[16]

Surprisingly, data on slave tobacco workers were a little easier to find than information on their free black or white counterparts. A sample based on twelve tobacco manufactories yielded composite portraits of the different slave tobacco hands. As table 7 indicates, slave women comprised nearly 25 percent (70) of the workforce, and children under ten years old constituted 39 percent (121).

While the census does not reveal whether this was the first decade in which so many women and children entered the tobacco factory workforce, it does indicate it was the last; after this time period male slave workers overwhelmingly dominated the factory rolls.[17] By 1840 tobacconist Samuel Myers hired exclusively male slave workers, as did Samuel and Thomas Hardgrove, William Greanor, and James Fisher, Jr., among others.[18]

Precisely why Myers and the rest chose to hire only male slaves will never be known; company and personal records from the various firms no longer exist. It appears, however, these men made the switch partly because of increased availability of male slave workers, the ease of em-

Table 7. Age and gender distribution of tobacco slave workers in selected tobacco manufactories, 1820

Manufacturer	Ages of males				Ages of females			
	0– 10	10– 24	24– 36	36– 55	0– 10	10– 24	24– 36	36– 55
Anderson, R.	0	0	1	0	4	5	3	0
Barclay, D.	41	37	6	0	7	8	0	0
Cunningham, E.	3	1	3	0	5	2	3	0
Enders, J.	17	16	0	1	0	1	1	0
Gibbon, J.	0	1	2	1	1	3	0	0
Harris, B.	5	25	3	1	0	1	0	1
Harris, T.	4	9	2	1	0	0	0	0
Johnson, J.	1	3	2	1	1	0	0	1
Jones, S.	14	14	9	0	0	5	0	1
Rutherfoord, T.	4	2	2	2	5	3	2	0
Warwick, D.	2	2	0	0	5	0	2	0
Weisigar, J.	0	1	1	0	2	0	1	0
Total	91	111	31	7	30	25	12	3
Percentage	29	36	10	2	10	9	4	.2

Sources: U.S. Bureau of Census, Population, 1820; Richmond, Manufacturing Census, 1820.

ploying them through the hiring system, and a distinct preference for male rather than female laborers. Between 1820 and 1840 the number of slave workingmen (between the ages of ten and fifty) increased and narrowly exceeded the total number of free white workingmen (table 8). This increase was important to tobacconists because it helped stabilize the price of purchasing and hiring bondmen by the mid to late 1820s, thereby making slave hiring affordable. Cost, however, was not the only factor that led to the predominance of male slave workers. It appears that high slave employment may have discouraged white males and females from working in the factories because they began to view tobacco manufacturing as "slave work." But it remains unclear whether employers stopped hiring white laborers because they felt it inappropriate for the two to work together, or because white workers voluntarily

Table 8. Workingmen in Richmond, 1820–40

Age	1820		1830		1840	
	Slave *<14–45*	*White* *10–45*	*Slave* *10–55*	*White* *15–50*	*Slave* *10–55*	*White* *10–50*
	1,981	2,498	4,605	4,479	3,131	3,921

Sources: U.S. Bureau of Census, Population, 1820–40.

withdrew from the workforce. In any case, the number of white laborers in the tobacco industry significantly declined by 1830, and by 1840 there were almost none.

The decline of slave women and girls in the tobacco workforce is more difficult to explain. It was cheaper to hire an adult female worker than a male, and the cost of hiring children was even less. Given the widely fluctuating costs of hiring and purchasing adult male slave labor during the early 1820s—because of the competition for workers among the canal and mining companies—hiring bond women and children would have seemed a logical economic decision.[19] But in spite of the fact that women and children could perform some of the unskilled and semi-skilled tasks, tobacco manufacturers overwhelmingly chose to hire only male slave workers.

To some extent this is unsurprising; tobacconists shared owners' ideas about female differences and generally believed women unsuitable for, and largely incapable of, factory work. There were certain tasks, such as operating the screw press, that required more upper-body strength than most women possessed. So tobacconists may have preferred male slaves because these workers could be switched at a moment's notice from tasks requiring strength to less demanding jobs. What is surprising, however, is the tenacity of such gender-based notions in the face of a growing need for more workers and compelling evidence that women were as capable as men in most jobs. On plantations slave women frequently worked alongside men out in the fields, performing many of the same tasks.[20] In those locales slave owners generally assigned jobs according to the "availability and strength of slaves," not based on their sex.[21] In the city, however, factory employers selected workers on the basis of gender, rather than ability, even though there were jobs that slave women could perform for a lower cost than free or enslaved men. In the tobacco industry, for example, there were several tasks that required little upper-body strength and relatively little skill. One such task involved stemming tobacco leaves, which one Richmond tobacco manufacturer described as a job that "a good apt boy [c]ould learn in about two months."[22] No doubt a grown woman could learn it in less time. Indeed, women were employed full-time in the tobacco manufactories after the Civil War. But during these years such reasoning apparently escaped the industry. Given the growing demand for labor, the large supply of slave women available, and the cost benefits gained by hiring women, tobacconists should have eliminated illogical and inefficient gender-based divisions. Instead, they quickly replaced the women and girls with men and boys as soon as male slave labor prices returned to affordable levels. Clearly gender rather than cost concerns prevailed. It would be another twenty years before slave women entered the halls of industry again—and they would find a place in the cotton mills, not in tobacco manufactories.[23]

Perhaps what most persuaded tobacconists to employ male slave labor almost exclusively was the integral role bondmen came to play in creating the industry. Slave male workers not only provided the main source of labor for the factories, over time they also helped define the manufacturing process itself. In some cases employers required them to become involved; frequently manufacturers selected older "seasoned" slave workers to train the younger hands and to monitor the quality of their work. Tobacconists preferred this arrangement because it reduced their day-to-day responsibilities, which expanded steadily as the facilities grew larger and the number of workers increased.

In other cases slave tobacco hands clearly took the initiative in defining aspects of the manufacturing process such as controlling the pace of production. Stemmers and twisters, for example, typically set the speed at which they worked by rolling and lumping the leaves in a unified motion and by singing songs to keep the tempo. Employers chose not to interfere, realizing that hastening the workers could have resulted in sloppy work and costly damage to the leaves. William Cullen Bryant, who visited a tobacco factory in Richmond during the 1840s, was quick to note the use of song among stemmers and twisters: "In another room were about eighty negroes . . . who received the leaves . . . rolled them into long even rolls, and then cut them into plugs. . . . as we entered the room we heard a murmur of psalmody running through the sable assembly, which now and then swelled into a strain of very tolerable music."[24] A more observant visitor, however, noticed that songs provided a way to set the pace of production: "In one very large room there were 120 negroes at work. . . . those who were rolling the leaf, performed with a regular see-saw motion, all in concert, not only of action, but of voice, singing in parts, a hymn, or sometimes an impromptu chant."[25]

Slave prizers similarly maintained a degree of control over the work because it was their labor that kept production going. The pressers managed to set their own pace using "deep-drawn groans" and grunts to help unify their efforts while turning the "long iron arms" of the screw.[26]

The integral role that slave workers came to play in the manufacturing process became the final, and perhaps most important, link between slavery and tobacco processing—a link that was initially forged by tobacconists' employment preferences, the slave hiring system, and custom. The combination of these factors convinced tobacconists that it was not only advantageous but necessary to use slave labor. By 1840 slave workers no longer were viewed as an experimental labor force but had become the only group of laborers tobacconists would consider for the job.

Tobacco manufacturing was not the only industry that found slaves an attractive labor source. Following in the footsteps of the tobacco industry were the flour and cotton mills, dock and canal companies, and even the state government—all eager to experiment using slaves as a part of their workforce because of their low cost and ready availability. Millowners, for example, found hired slaves best suited their rapidly changing labor demands.[27] Even though flour milling was the second most profitable industry in Richmond, stiff competition and frequent flour fires caused the closing of many mills. Between 1800 and 1840 the number of mills steadily declined from five to two as old mills burned or went bankrupt.[28] As a result, slave flour hands often found themselves looking for new jobs.

As the number of mills fluctuated, so too did the number of slave workers. In the first decade of business, the entire milling industry consisted of twenty male slaves responsible for cleaning, milling, shoveling, and delivering the flour for shipping.[29] During the next decade the number of workers peaked with seventy slave hands spread out among five mills, including ones owned by Gallego, Haxall, Bragg, and Warwick. The closure of one of the mills in the early 1830s, however, reduced the total number of slave hands to fifty-six. And by the end of this time period, 1840, only two mills remained, employing just thirty-five slave workers.[30] The dramatic changes in the mill industry made hiring slaves rather than purchasing them or employing free labor the easiest method of securing workers who could be let go if conditions worsened.

The hiring system brought slaves into a number of other unusual businesses. In 1830 a crew of thirty-five slaves began hauling coal for

Smith and Govern. Not long afterward thirty-three new slave sailors took the helm for the Richmond Towing Company and began guiding ships along the James River.[31] Slaves also helped develop the city's physical landscape by building government offices and the arms manufactory, as well as roads, bridges, docks, the canal, and later the railroad.

Like the flour mills, Smith and Govern, the Richmond Towing Company, and the individual city improvement projects depended on an exclusively male slave labor force. But at businesses such as the Richmond Dock Company and the Richmond Manufacturing Company (also listed as the Richmond Cotton Factory), slaves worked with free blacks and whites. Slave dockworkers, for example, moved cargo on and off ships alongside white laborers. Slave weavers at the Richmond Manufacturing Company, which opened around 1835, found themselves working in a labor force integrated by both race and sex. Although company records no longer exist, census materials and travelers' journals hint at the extent of integration that existed within the factory. In 1835 Joseph Martin visited the cloth factory and noted that there were 70 white and 130 black employees working side by side producing osnaburg, the coarse cloth generally used for slave clothing.[32] Five years later a second visitor noted that the workforce consisted of "100 whites and 150 blacks as spinners and weavers."[33] Although neither account specifies whether the black operatives were free or enslaved, men or women, the 1840 census indicates that 36 percent (99 of 276) of the factory's workers were slaves and that the majority of slave workers (65 percent) were women between the ages of ten and twenty-four (table 9). But like the tobacco manufactories, the mill did not allow its female slave hands to remain long. In 1850, after a devastating fire, the mill closed its doors. Although another cotton and wool factory took its place shortly thereafter and may have rehired some of the Richmond Cotton Mill hands, it appears slave women were not among them.[34]

The firm in charge of building the James River canal—the prized water route that provided inland farmers and planters a cheap method of conveying goods and materials to and from the city—also employed a mixed labor force. In fact, it may have been the first large industry to do so. According to the records of the James River and Kanawha Company (JRKC), between the late 1780s and early 1800s, the canal company employed as many as 350 laborers, of whom 150 were slaves. Company records do not indicate why JRKC initially used both free and slave labor; but it appears company officials preferred this arrangement and continued to hire a mixed labor force throughout the antebellum era. The number of slave workers fluctuated greatly, and there is evidence to suggest such shifts depended on the availability of hired bondmen. By 1830,

Table 9. Slave women employed in the tobacco and cotton industries, 1820 and 1840.

Industry	(Year)	0–10	10–24	24–36	36–55	Total
Tobacco	(1820)	30	25	12	3	70
Cotton	(1840)	6	51	7	0	64

Source: U.S. Bureau of Census, Population, 1820 and 1840.
Note: Age distribution for women in tobacco factories is based on a sample of eleven companies. In 1840 there was only one cotton mill.

for example, slaves made up 67 percent (300 of 450) of the workers employed by the canal company. In the fall of 1836, however, only thirty-eight slaves had been secured because of the great demand for slave labor by other canal, coal, and gold companies. As a result, JRKC hired immigrant laborers to supplement its workforce.[35] Between 1836 and 1837 the company sent agents to Europe who returned with nearly 300 contract workers, dramatically altering the racial balance of the workforce. And by 1837 two-thirds of the canal workers were white men.

From the outset the company's only concern was to secure a large labor force, whether free or enslaved. This pragmatic approach was necessary because the initial phases of work were arduous and required a huge number of workers. Before digging could begin, the canal path had to be cleared of trees and logs, and all rocky areas had to be blasted with explosive powder. Hundreds of workers were needed to perform tasks such as excavating the canal and digging its many drains and puddle ditches. After each portion of the canal was excavated, the men had to level the canal floor with "carts drawn by horses, oxen or mules." Then, stone walls were built along the edges and banks of the canal to prevent erosion.[36] Finally, locks, dams, and bridges had to be built.

With no machines and only a few animals to help, the work was strenuous and unrelenting. Laborers, both free and slave, worked long hours in all weather conditions. Although there is little documentation indicating how labor was organized, it is likely that most workers labored in traditional gangs under the close supervision of canal officials, overseers, and managers. Slave and free black and white canal workers apparently were used interchangeably, except in highly skilled positions such as quarrymen, stonemasons, carpenters, and blacksmiths, which were generally filled by free laborers.[37] These skilled positions, however, were relatively scarce, with the vast majority of jobs being unskilled manual labor.

The influx of free canal workers from Ireland and Scotland in the late 1830s should have amply met the company's needs, given that the work did not require great skills and slave labor was expensive. But their experience with immigrant laborers confirmed the belief of James River and Kanawha Company officials that slaves were crucial to the completion of the canal.

By the late 1830s the company's efforts to secure a stable workforce by recruiting white immigrant laborers had proved unsuccessful. To the chagrin of JRKC officials, immigrant workers refused to accept the poor working conditions and wages. On two occasions in 1837 they struck, demanding higher pay. In 1838, when workers were informed their wages would be delayed because of the national economic crisis (the panic of 1837), "not less than one half of the whole white force, and a much larger proportion of the masons . . . left the line."[38] Company officials also were disturbed by white immigrants' hostility toward slave workers. The project's chief engineer said in a written report that he lacked patience for the immigrant laborers, "who war against our institutions, and refuse to work with our slaves."[39]

In its annual report the company announced its intention to increase "the proportion of black labour on the work [due to] the inaptitude of the still preponderating mass of foreign labourers."[40] And by late 1838 the company successfully secured more slave laborers and changed the proportions of the workforce to "two third blacks and one third whites," which was, according to the board of directors, "more manageable and stable."[41]

The advantages of using slave instead of free workers (for reasons other than cost) were noted by other industries as well. George Cooke, the agent at Busby's mine (a Richmond coal mine), frustrated with the white employees, wrote to the company's president complaining, "You have no idea. . . . I am plagued by the worthless white men who pretend to labor about here."[42] As a solution, Cooke recommended replacing white workers with slaves. The Richmond Dock Company apparently reached a similar conclusion about its mixed workforce and replaced all wage laborers with slaves. In 1819 the company employed thirty-six white, three free black workers, and twenty-five slave hands. The following year, however, company officials reported a workforce made up of sixty-four slaves only.[43]

Industrial interest in hiring a predominantly slave workforce obviously did not extend to women workers largely because of the factors mentioned earlier, including notions of female differences. As a result, the majority of the 2,000 to 3,000 slave women in Richmond worked as household domestics, laboring as cooks, nannies, personal servants,

chambermaids, seamstresses, and laundresses. While most female domestics were expected to perform any job assigned to them, owners and
employers acknowledged that some women excelled at certain tasks and
sought after them for those skills. This is most evident in the newspaper
advertisements featuring slave women for sale or hire that touted them
as "good cooks" or "excellent maids," and by the fact that cooks generally commanded higher prices than maids.[44]

In contrast to the men, however, the differences in positions and skills
women held had little impact on their working conditions and environment. The dramatic differences in the labor systems under which canal
hands and tobacco stemmers worked did not exist in domestic servitude.
Whether they were cooks or maids, female slave domestics working in
the "Big House" were on call twenty-four hours a day and spent a great
deal of their time under the watchful eye of their owners and employers.
Although most of the jobs that slave domestics performed allowed them
a degree of latitude in the pace of their work, the fact that their working
and living arrangements were housed under one roof meant they had
little privacy or independence. In further contrast to the men, slave
women, regardless of their skills and jobs, were vulnerable to being sex-
ually exploited and oppressed by their owners and employers.

Richmond slave owners and employers did not experiment with the
domestic workforce as they had with its industrial counterpart. Throughout this period household servants were mostly slaves and generally
women. Although a few households had slave and free laborers under
the same roof, typically all the workers were black. Few, if any, households mixed black and white domestic workers—with the exception of,
perhaps, the craftshop households. There were a number of slave men
working as domestics alongside the women, but their jobs were distinct
from those performed by females. Servants within their master's home
were assigned tasks on the basis of sex. Male slaves often were chosen to
act as butlers, valets, carriage drivers, gardeners, or stable boys.[45] The
separation of duties by sex was fairly commonplace, and rarely did servants perform the duties of the opposite sex. Advertisements for slave
labor indicate a strong division of tasks based on gender as owners and
employers called for female maids and male gardeners. An exception
was when there was a shortage of servants. Then, female slaves would
assume certain "male" jobs such as that of dining room servant. There
also are a few instances in which a male slave would be selected and
trained as a cook. These instances, however, were quite rare, as both
slave owners and male slaves generally followed gender conventions
that prevented men from performing "female" jobs such as doing the
laundry.[46]

Although it may appear that the emerging urban industrial system had little impact on slave women's working and living conditions, what went on outside of the "Big House" did affect what happened inside. The rapid increase in slave male hiring costs, for example, had the dramatic effect of pulling women out of the kitchens and into the tobacco and cotton factories for a brief period. Although they never entered the industries that way again, slave women briefly experienced the "liberating" effects of the unusual working and living conditions brought by the emerging urban slave system.

Tobacconists and other industrialists initially used slave workers because of cost, availability, and perhaps custom. But by 1840 slavery had become an important, if not vital, tool to continue the city's industrial development. In the case of the tobacco industry, slave hands became essential to production; not only did they supply the labor, they also helped shape the system of processing, supervised themselves, and set the pace of production. For a handful of other businesses, such as the canal and dock companies, there appeared to be no viable alternative; slave workers proved more efficient and less costly than free laborers.

By the mid–nineteenth century the status of urban slavery had changed dramatically from the Revolutionary and postwar eras. Male slave workers, once considered questionable for factory jobs, had established themselves as part of the permanent workforce and in some cases helped to define the production process itself. In spite of earlier reservations, Richmond elites came to see urban slavery as a superior labor system that was more efficient, economical, flexible, and manageable than free labor. In the words of one canal engineer, "There is no portion of the work which cannot be executed by slaves."[47]

As employers struggled to define the role of slaves within the workplace, owners, local authorities, and—within certain limits—slaves themselves searched to define bond labor's position within urban society. The discussion among these latter groups was not, however, whether slaves should reside in the city, but in what manner. As owners quickly discovered, aspects of slave management and organization such as accommodations, discipline, and moral guidance needed to be reexamined and renegotiated because the system used on plantations did not fit the city environment. Urban slave quarters, for example, could not be a series of small shacks within sight of the "Big House." Instead, owners and employers made a variety of arrangements, including placing slaves in boardinghouses and rented tenements. Methods of slave discipline and control commonly used on plantations also needed to be reviewed. It was clear the system of overseers, drivers, and slave patrols would not work in the city with its network of alleyways, hidden grogshops, and corner stores, which defied attempts to monitor workers at all times. In short, owners and employers came to realize that slavery in Richmond required methods of slave management and organization that would accommodate the unusual demands of urbanization and industrialization. As a result, slaves worked and lived under a vast range of conditions, ranging from brutal to permissive. Those fortunate enough to enjoy the latter conditions found the greatest opportunities for "control" over their lives. For some bondmen this "control" was simply the ability to choose where they lived and what they ate. For others it was the opportunity to challenge slavery by helping define their working conditions and their relationships with owners, employers, and other white Richmonders and to take a step toward creating their own community.

Three

Behind the Urban "Big House"

AT THE END of the workday, long after the sun had set, George, Richard, Manuel, and John left Hezekiel Wight's tobacco factory and walked through the dock and warehouse area toward their respective homes. As hired slaves they did not have to live with their owner, John Prosser, and were not required to stay with their employer because there was no housing for workers on the premises. Instead, each man received a small amount of cash with which to secure his own food and lodgings.[1] With the small sums, these men had several housing options: they could sleep at Prosser's house if he had room, they could rent rooms in a boardinghouse, or each could live with a family member. By the late antebellum era, their options also would include renting a house or a tenement near the tobacco manufactories. Although severely limited in their choices, these men and many other tobacco hands were free to select their lodgings.

Where George, Richard, and the others lived had a great impact on other aspects of their lives, including what they ate. If their lodgings came with a fireplace, the workers could prepare a simple meal of meat and vegetables at home. If cooking facilities were not available, they could grab a hot meal at one of the local cookshops or simply dine on cold bread and butter.

After supper, the hired tobacco hands could have stayed at home, visited friends, or—if they had the funds—gone to a local grogshop for a brandy and a game of billiards. In any case, they had to be careful making their way through the city because even with passes it was illegal for slaves to be "going at large." After a short night of rest, George and the others would be expected back at the tobacco factory.

In comparison to plantation slaves, and even to most other urban slaves at the turn of the century, George, Richard, and the others who lived and worked apart from their owners were anomalies. But by 1840 the jobs they worked and their sleeping arrangements became more commonplace as hiring out and living apart evolved into standard features of the urban slave system. The process by which George and the others came to work at Wight's tobacco factory, for example, became a standard practice among Richmond slaves, owners, and employers. Most commonly, hiring negotiations were held directly between employers and owners. Typically an employer would approach an owner proposing to hire his or her slaves, or an owner would indicate to certain businesses that his slaves were available for hire. Frequently employers and owners found one another through newspaper advertisements such as one placed by J. P. Shields, who "wanted to hire 25 black slave males to work on Manchester Turnpike Road." A recent study on hiring arrangements during the 1850s and 1860s indicates that employers and owners frequently knew each other through either family ties or close working relationships.[2] But during these early decades this pattern did not hold; owners and employers typically were strangers.

As hiring out became widespread, professional slave brokers began to handle the transactions.[3] For a percentage of the hiring fee, these traders would serve as a liaison between owners and employers, often brokering deals between parties in different counties, thus relieving both groups from having to travel and meet one another. By the 1840s slave brokers played a prominent role in hiring negotiations.

Some slave-hiring transactions were handled by slaves themselves, a practice that became known as "hiring one's own time." Under this system owners allowed slaves to go to Richmond to find work for a specified period of time, ranging from one day to one year. This system became popular among owners who cared little for paying an agent or for the hassles of finding employment for their slaves. According to this practice slaves were required to "pay their masters a stipulated sum of money . . . but whatever they could earn above that amount was theirs to do as they wished." As the practice became more common, slaves would arrive from neighboring rural counties and roam the streets of Richmond in search of work. Some came as soon as the harvest season was over, but the majority arrived in Richmond during the Christmas holidays—a time when most employers were looking to hire help for the new year. During the week between Christmas and New Year's Day, the streets of Richmond came "alive," as Nehemiah Adams once described, "with the negroes, in their best attire, seeking employment for the year to come, changing places, and having full liberty to suit themselves as to their employers."[4]

Some slaves arrived holding notes of introduction from their owners to facilitate hiring negotiations. Bob carried this crudely written message from his owner, Thomas Woodson, while searching for work: "If any person may be inclinable to hire [Bob] to drive a wagon I can recommend him to be as good a wagoner as any in Richmond, he is honest & cherfull felow. . . . the price I have not made menchend of but gentle men that wishes to hire the sade felow I make no dubt but will give him worth his laber." Other notes were simply passes giving slaves permission to travel, such as this one that slave worker Will held: "Will has lief [leave] to pass to Richmond without any interruption as long as he care to stay. . . . James Gary."[5]

Although it appears that male slaves made up the vast majority of those allowed to "hire their own time," a handful of women also enjoyed this privilege. Sarah Clayton from Charles City County, for example, allowed her slave Nancy Read to find work in Richmond by herself.[6]

Where slaves worked and whether they were self-hired or directly owned dictated where they lived. Housing options available to workers such as George, Richard, and the other tobacco hands were greatly determined by their occupation and position, the wealth and generosity of their owner, the budget constraints on their employer, and the physical layout of the city. As a result, slave living conditions varied widely and were subject to constant change.

Even living in the "Big House"—which meant a place in the master's residence for rural slaves—had a slightly different connotation for urban domestic slaves. For some, such as Edmund Randolph's eight adult slaves, it meant any corner in Randolph's modest two-story brick and wooden house, which measured 50 by 20 feet.[7] For Carter Braxton's slaves, however, it meant sleeping in a separate one-story building about ten paces from the main house. And for Cyrus, Smith, Ford and Jerry, four of John Wickham's eight slaves, living in the "Big House" meant sleeping in the wooden barns across the yard.[8]

Homes in Richmond generally were much less spacious than plantation mansions because city lots were small and the cost of building an urban home was high. As a result, it was common for domestic slaves to sleep wherever space was available. Some were lucky: Claiborne and his wife Nancy, for example, were fortunate enough to share a private room below their employer's chambers.[9] And no doubt Henry, who lived with his owner Nancy Ellert, was pleased that he did not have to share his bedroom with any other servants.[10] More commonly, however, domestic slaves did not have private rooms and had to sleep in parts of the house that served other functions during the day. Martha Hill's servant Lucy spent her nights in front of the fireplace in the kitchen and would roll up her bed linens in the morning. Another Lucy, a domestic hired to John Chevallie, had to sleep in the cellar among the many preserved foods and stored clothing and furniture.[11] In rare instances domestic slaves were given the opportunity to live apart. Charlotte was one of those lucky individuals able to live with her husband and children even though she was a servant in a private household and her husband ran errands for a nearby druggist.[12]

If domestic slaves found their choice of living quarters limited, then slaves working on construction projects, such as the canal workers, probably found their arrangements unbearable. These laborers had to live under the most uncomfortable conditions, often sleeping in "crude, poorly constructed dirt-floored cabins, without shutters or doors." Meals were "usually cooked . . . in an open pit at the center of the shack; smoke rose through a hole in the roof, since few dwellings had chimneys or fireplaces." Not all slaves working on construction projects lived in such rough quarters, but those working on "temporary" projects often endured brutal conditions. As a rule, the shorter the job, the poorer the facilities. Canal building, though it took years, was considered a temporary job because once the canal was completed, slave labor was no longer needed. As a result, housing for canal laborers tended to be hastily built shacks made from leftover lumber. Many of these dwellings were no more than propped-up rooftops that kept the rain off workers while they slept.[13]

In contrast to either domestic or construction slave workers, most factory (or nondomestic) slave hands had enormous choice of and control over their living quarters. Slaves who were hired out to businesses generally were allowed to secure lodgings apart from both owner and employer. This meant bondmen living apart resided in a variety of dwellings such as boardinghouses owned by white or free black proprietors, or they rented small shacklike houses behind wealthier white residents' homes. Sometimes they stayed with family members who worked as domestic servants. Through this system Pleasant, who was hired to Mr. Smity, was able to live with his mother, who lived in her owner's house.[14] And Ned, who belonged to Robert Greenhow, stayed with his wife Lucy, a slave nurse owned by Robert Scott. Each night after work, Ned returned to Lucy's room in Scott's home.[15] Later as the system of living apart became more standard, slave workers found they could use their board money to move even farther away from owners and employers by renting houses and tenements, by themselves or with family members. The ability to live apart and stay with relatives was of great importance to many city slaves because it allowed them to be with their loved ones and helped them keep their families together.

Other aspects of life, such as diet, also were determined by a slave's working situation and place of residence. Domestic servants often ate the leftovers from their owner's meal or were fed a separate meal specially prepared for them by the cook. As one slave maid explained, "I worked in de house for old Miss, and we had plenty to do and plenty to eat. When de white folks was through eatin', I got a pan and got de grub, and set on de floor and eat it."[16] Because they shared meals with their owners, household slaves probably ate a fairly good mixture of meat, grains, and vegetables. Account books and shopping lists for a typical middling white household during the nineteenth century frequently included coffee, sugar, meat and poultry, vegetables, fresh fruit in season, and bread.[17] Although no slave was guaranteed such a diverse and steady diet, a domestic servant was fairly likely to receive some of these foods, while a factory bondmen probably would receive much more limited rations from his employer or overseer.

Slaves working in construction were among those who frequently ate a much less varied diet. Companies generally served their slaves simple meals consisting of pork or fresh beef, when available, and cornmeal. In comparison to a "typical" nineteenth-century slave diet, as described by historian Sam Hilliard, company meals lacked the usual supplements of sweet potatoes and other vegetables.[18] Fresh vegetables, fruits, and coffee were rarely available to these industrial slaves. In fact, company records indicate that some slaves received a diet that offered little more than subsistence. The Richmond Mining Company fed its workers only dried beef and cornmeal. Slaves working for the canal company ate a similar diet, although its sick workers received fresh bread in addition.[19] Records from the late antebellum era show that rations for slave workers—at least those working for the city government—eventually became standardized, though hardly diverse. The rations city slave workers received were laid out clearly in the contracts between the city council and the firm of Burwell and Sampson. These workers were to receive "3 lbs of bacon, one & half pecks of corn meal, one quart of molasses . . . quarter of a pound soap, and one gill of salt" at unspecified intervals.[20]

Slaves who lived apart were expected to fend for themselves when it came to food. Though some factories provided their workers with one meal a day, hired slaves generally had to purchase and prepare their own meals with their board money.[21] While this ostensibly gave slaves greater choice, the small sums given by employers typically limited purchases to foods that were cheap and filling, such as bread, cabbage, and potatoes. Some slaves with extra cash earned from overtime bonuses were able to supplement their diets with meals from local cookshops. These establishments, run by free black and white proprietors, offered anyone, including slaves, a ready-cooked meal for a few pennies. Mary Wright, a free black woman, sold a variety of prepared "snacks" to workers from her house on Eighth Street. And for those in search of something headier than food, Wright also kept a full bar, "with all the fixtures," in the back of her house.[22]

The nutritional value of the meals and the amount of food given to slave workers varied depending on their working situations and how much opportunity they had to supplement their diets.[23] Adult slave workers who had extra funds to buy meals or had access to their owners' pantries probably ate better than slave hands without such advantages, such as those working on the canal. Young children and elderly workers probably had a more difficult time securing enough food. In fact, company books and court records of the early antebellum era indicate that young slave children often did not receive adequate food or care, which is clearly demonstrated in the court case of Daniel and Sam, two young slave boys who worked at William Patterson's tobacco manufactory.[24]

Daniel and Sam, who were thirteen and eleven, respectively, worked as tobacco stemmers at Patterson's factory in 1822. During that year both boys complained to their owner, Richard Carter, that they were being mistreated at the factory. In response, Carter removed the boys from the factory and hired them to another business. Patterson, in retaliation, sued Carter for breach of contract. During the trial it became evident that Daniel and Sam not only were treated badly but also were underfed. Although the company served the workers a meal a day, the boys were forced to fight for their food against larger children. Furthermore, it seems that Patterson rarely provided enough food. Joshua Goode, who worked at the tobacco factory and even hired out his own slaves to the same establishment, acknowledged that young slave workers frequently complained they were not fed enough. Goode admitted this while being cross-examined by the defendant.

> Question: What was the reason that you took your boys away was it not because they complained that they had not enough to eat?
>
> Goode: I took them away because I was about to leave Mr. Patterson & they did not like to stay behind. As to their not having enough to eat tis sure that they did complain that they did not have enough.

Question: Did you not hear my boys Sam & Daniel complain that they had not enough to eat?

Goode: I heard them complain but boys in Manufactories are very much in the habit of complaining.

Question: Did you not alwas give out as much provisions for the boys as you thought was necessary for them.

Goode: I alwas gave out as much as I used to give out at Price's factory where I lived, which I though was sufficient but the boys used to grumble there.[25]

Sam and Daniel were not the only ones who went hungry. It appears that many industrial slaves did not receive enough food. Court records suggest that those who could not afford to buy extra food often stole it. Throughout these decades slaves were brought to court on charges of stealing food or purchasing stolen food. In 1822 David Russell, a slave, was convicted of buying "one piece of dried beef = $1.00 [and] one peck of meal = 50 cents" from another slave. In 1825 John Bailey, another slave, was charged with stealing corn and oats from a local shop.[26]

In contrast to living arrangements and diet, the clothing provided to slave workers varied little by occupation and locale. Slaves generally received two sets of clothing (one for summer and the other for winter), a pair of stockings and shoes, and a blanket. Men received shirts made of osnaburg (coarse cotton material), two pairs of pantaloons (one of osnaburg and the other possibly made of wool), a jacket, and a hat. Women received two dresses, also made of osnaburg, and a jacket.[27] Sometimes slaves were given just the material to make their own clothing; but by the mid–nineteenth century owners increasingly hired seamstresses to sew the items or purchased clothes from local shops. By the 1840s buying ready-made slave clothing was quite common in Richmond as evidenced by the numerous advertisements for such items in the local newspaper.

Nondomestic slaves, particularly hired factory slaves, frequently possessed basic work clothing and little else.[28] And some lacked even these items. Antebellum court books are filled with charges against employers for not furnishing slaves with clothing and other goods. Catherine McCall, for example, sued employer George Ingles several times for refusing to clothe her slaves while in his service.[29]

Urban slave workers found many ways to supplement their wardrobes. Domestic servants, for example, often owned—in addition to their work clothes—outfits of "colorful cast-off finery" from their masters and mistresses. Sy Gilliat, a well-known slave fiddler, was known to perform at barbecues and other outings dressed in a "silk coat and vest of faded lilac . . . silk stockings . . . terminating in shoes fastened . . . with large buckles," which he inherited from his owner. James Hamilton and Peter Woolfolk, two domestic slaves, had wardrobes with a variety of suits that they had received from their deceased owner Nathaniel Dunlop. Proud of their wardrobes, slaves prominently displayed their finery on Sundays and holidays, thereby brightening the usually dusty drab streets on those days. As traveler J. S. Buckingham described, "On Sundays . . . the females [slaves] wear white muslin and light silk gowns, with caps, bonnets, ribbons and feathers; some carry reticules on the arms and many are seen with parasols, while nearly all of them carry a white pocket-hand-kerchief. . . . the young men, among the slaves, wear white trousers, black stock[ing]s, broad-brimmed hats and carry walking-sticks." During the working week, though, nearly all slaves wore coarse cotton clothes to perform their duties.[30]

Like food and shelter, medical care for slaves also varied depending on their working situation. Domestic servants, for example, might treat themselves or be treated by their master or the owners' family physician. Although few records exist concerning Richmond slaves' home remedies, legislation banning the sale or administration of any "medicine, domestic or foreign," to slaves suggests that such a practice did occur in the city. Evidence of remedies administered by owners is more commonplace. Masters and mistresses often treated their servants in hopes of curing a variety of ailments, including smallpox and pneumonia, using ingredients such as castor oil, magnesia, and Peruvian bark. Not all slave owners, however, showed such concern. One owner, a Mrs. Taylor, left her sick slave Rachel in the hands of a free black nurse for several weeks. Taylor literally abandoned Rachel, failing to clothe her slave or pay the nurse, Evey Jones, for her services.[31]

Many Richmond slave owners summoned private physicians to treat their slaves. Mrs. Mary Williamson often called upon Dr. William Foushee Sr. to examine and treat both the enslaved and free members of her household. Court records show that Dr. James Currie frequently visited Peyton Randolph's household to treat "the old lady's negro maid" and his "negro Diane."[32]

Slaves hired to small businesses were more likely to receive medical attention from private physicians than home remedies from their employers. Owners, concerned about their property, did not want employers to be administering home formulas, and many specified that a professional physician be summoned should their slaves fall ill. John Walker of King and Queen County demanded that his slave Daniel, who was hired to a business in Richmond, be examined by "no other physician but a Tomsonian doctor[,] they being my preference." James Martin made a similar demand for his slave Sally, who he insisted should "be attended by Doctors R & R Cabbles [and that] any other [will be] at the expense of the hirer." Such stipulations meant that employers most often summoned private physicians to examine their hired workers. Dr. Lewis Chamberlayne, a local physician, was one such practitioner frequently called to visit hired slaves, as his accounts indicate:

> 1835
> Mr. George P. Crump,
> May 11: To visit . . . Billy belonging to Frank Smith, $1.25.
> July 14: ditto . . . $2.00
> Mr. Edmund Brown
> April 1: To advice . . . to Sam belonging to Dr. Richardson
>   of James City, $1.00.[33]

Slaves working on the canal and in the mines usually saw the company-employed physicians who visited the worksite several times a week or went to company-run hospitals. When Robert, a slave canal worker hired out for a year, fell ill, he was treated at the factory hospital for eleven days. Both free and enslaved canal workers who collapsed from heat exhaustion were placed in the small hospitals set up by the James River Company.[34]

Slave patients also received treatment at the city hospitals. These facilities concentrated more on nursing and quarantining than curing persons with infectious diseases. In the early 1800s when cases of smallpox first appeared in Richmond, city officials established a public health facility to separate victims from other city residents. Another public hospital was opened during the early 1830s to treat cholera victims.[35] Slaves in need of treatment for non-life-threatening afflictions, however, could not depend on the hospitals because they were temporary facilities that closed once an epidemic passed. It was not until the late 1850s that permanent public health facilities were established to serve both free and enslaved patients with a variety of injuries and illnesses.

The preceding discussion of slaves' diet, clothing, medical care and housing suggests the wide range of material conditions under which city slaves lived. It also indicates the degree to which urbanization, industrialization, employers' budgets, and even the size of an owner's home affected working and living conditions, and how those circumstances prevented owners from using one common method of slave management. Given the diverse working conditions, a uniform slave system would have been impossible. What emerged, as owners and employers sought to shape urban slavery to meet their needs, was a set of control methods that varied as much as the working conditions themselves. Sometimes the controls of owners and employers proved redundant, sometimes they conflicted. But more often than not, the urban industrial milieu created a gap between the reach of owner and employer—a space where neither proved able to control certain elements of slave life. It was in this space that slaves found opportunities to shape their own working and living conditions.

For some slaves this gap provided an opportunity to choose their own lodgings and their meals. For others, such as hired factory hands, it allowed them to accumulate small sums of cash from their wages and to spend these funds at their own discretion. The gap also gave slaves the chance to live with their families and friends and to create a separate, insulated space away from owners and employers. While these privileges may seem small, they significantly aided slave residents in their attempts to gain more "control" over their lives and to defy absolute owner control.

THE PRIVILEGE OF "LOSING TIME"

By law and custom every free person, particularly white residents, had power over slave workers. Owners held ultimate control and could discipline, hire out, or sell a bond laborer at any time. Under hiring contracts, hirers shared some of this authority and were able to discipline slave hands in their employment. Shopkeepers, manufacturers, and city watchmen all enjoyed privileges and power denied slaves (and many free blacks), such as the right to vote, own property, testify in court, and sue. Furthermore, according to the political and racial ideology that supported slavery, slaves were powerless, mentally less capable than, and subservient to, every free person. Richmond slave residents, however, like slaves elsewhere, acted in ways that belied such ideas and continually fought attempts at full control or domination. Most of the methods and weapons in this struggle were borrowed from the plantation setting, where disgruntled slaves had long practiced techniques such as feigning sickness, breaking tools, or escaping. But over time, urban slave workers discovered a few new tactics made possible by their new environment.

Slave workers soon discovered that city working and living conditions often left them "unattended to." Frequently there were periods of the day and night when no authority appeared to govern their actions. Naturally the opportunities to evade one's owner depended on a slave's occupation and position; but they existed for nearly every slave, from the female domestic who slipped away from the owner's house late at night, to the slave drayman who stopped to chat or share a brandy while making deliveries. Constant, strict control was not possible. The city offered an increasing number of places a slave worker could blend in and hide, such as a corner shop, a crowded marketplace, or even a busy intersection. In 1800 when there were about 2,000 slaves it might have been more difficult to go unnoticed. But by 1840 when there were more than 7,000 slave residents and 20,000 Richmonders altogether, a slave could hide temporarily with little effort. Monitoring slaves' activities would have required constant supervision, something few owners were willing to provide.

Given these circumstances, then, it is not surprising that slave workers took to "losing time," that is, they simply walked away from their jobs when no one was watching. One hired slave laborer, Carter, made it a frequent habit to "lose time" when running errands.[36] Isham similarly took advantage of the working hours he spent alone to hide from his employers, but for almost two weeks.[37] Some slaves seized the opportunity to "lose time" permanently. Lewis, a slave worker from Goochland County, ran away during the year he was hired to the Washington Tavern in Richmond. Ned Robinson, also a slave, waited until he was lodged in the city—far from his owner—before running away.[38] And these men were not the only ones to take advantage of their time as hired slaves to escape; Richmond newspapers throughout the antebellum years were filled with advertisements offering rewards for the capture of slaves who had run away from local businesses.

Owners were not oblivious to the effects of the city and devised a number of ways to thwart such ploys and to prevent runaways. Philip Nelson sent instructions to each new employer of his slave Carter, advising them to watch him constantly. Other owners sought employers who were known to monitor slave workers closely. Edmund Taylor, who was concerned about his slave William Giles, requested that Giles be hired to "a stranger; the *stricter* the manager the *better*." It appears Taylor believed that a stranger, rather than a friend, would be tough and uncompromising when dealing with Giles. Some owners went so far as to appoint acting masters whom they considered to be more conscientious than employers. Samuel Bailey of Hanover County, for example, allowed his slave Peter White to work in the city under the condition that Jesse Franklin of Richmond "act as master" during his stay. Sarah Clayton made similar arrangements for her slave, Nancy Read, when Read went to the city. Clayton asked David Hardy to "stand as master for her" while "she is at work in part of your house." Billy, a slave belonging to George Major of Charles City County, was similarly supervised while working in Richmond by Cornelius Crew, an old friend of Major's.[39]

Many other slave owners, however, recognized that no acting master or strict employer could prevent slaves from "losing time" or, worse, escaping; there were still too many opportunities for bond men and women to avoid supervision. So many owners attempted to gain control of slave workers by using rewards as incentives not to "lose time." A good number of owners, for example, tried to use hiring out and some of the unusual privileges to encourage slaves to work hard and not escape. Self-hiring was considered a significant privilege to most slaves because it gave them greater control over their labor. Bob and Will, two slave men described earlier, for example, were dispatched unsupervised to Richmond with few instructions other than to give their pay to their owners. Where they lived or what they did during their nonworking hours was up to them.

Court records indicate that owners also gave slaves the chance to pursue their own entrepreneurial ventures as incentives or rewards for good behavior. W. B. Mahan allowed his slave Lucy, while employed by John Chevallie, to sell fruit "out of the cellar that she now lives in" to earn extra money. Piter (Peter), another Richmond slave, was not only able to earn extra money but to run his own craft shop.[40]

Not all owners were so generous, but many tried to encourage good behavior by allowing slaves to have some role in the hiring process and to negotiate the terms. Frequently this meant accommodating a slave's employment preference. When Edmund Taylor sent his slave William to Richmond for work, he gave explicit instructions to hiring agents Hill and Dabney that they should heed William's request to "get a situation at the Exchange [Hotel]." Owner John Scott gave similar instructions to his agent demanding that Isaac, the slave to be hired out, should be "consulted" as to his "inclination." Maria, on the other hand, did not get to choose her employer, but her owner requested that her "happiness and comfort" had to be taken into account when placing her in a new job.[41]

Owners were not the only ones using incentives. Employers experimented with similar tactics, especially after learning that tough disciplinary action or coercion might not produce the intended effect. Although hiring contracts implicitly gave employers the ability to punish negligent workers, hirers were afraid of developing a reputation for being harsh taskmasters. Such a reputation would cause owners to cease leasing hands for fear their property would be in danger. James Brooks and Francis Markam, the two hirers who employed Isham—the slave who "lost" twelve days of work—certainly took no chances. Rather than disciplining Isham for running away, Brooks and Markam merely deducted the days missed from the pay owed to his owner.[42]

The courts added additional pressure on employers not to abuse hired workers. Slave owners' successful negligence suits, such as *Ran-*

dolph v. Hill in 1836, served as potent reminders that employers were liable for damages to hired slaves. In this case, physical abuse was not even the issue. The employer, Hill, was found guilty of improperly using Randolph's slave hand by sending him into a coal mine that was filled with poisonous gas.[43] This does not mean, however, that employers treated all slave workers well. Employers often beat and neglected workers. As the earlier example concerning the two young slave boys working in the tobacco factory indicates, industrialists often cared more about production than the welfare of their workers. But during this period there were relatively few reported cases of severe abuse.

Instead, employers increasingly chose to use incentives such as liquor and cash bonuses. The James River Company books often list rum among their grocery items, as did the books of the coal mines and other construction companies. Though much of this liquor probably went to sick workers (it was thought to be medicinal), it also was used as a reward for good work. Officials at the Dismal Swamp Company, for example, plied their slave workers with liquor in this fashion as company officer Richard Blow indicates in this letter: "I have sent up some spirits last week . . . some for the purpose of giving the hands a dram in the morning, this is contrary to former usage, but I wish them encouraged if they behave well, a gill a day in the winter, is not too much provided they behave well, but if delinquent in duty [they] should be debard of their allowance."[44]

Cash bonuses appear to have been even more common. Records from various companies show that employers paid their slave workers, most of them men, anywhere from 50 cents a week to $5.00 a month for working extra hours. Davidson and Garnett, a tobacco and wheat shipping firm, which included a warehouse, cooper's shop, and mill, often paid their hands for extra work. In their account books entries such as the following appear frequently between 1816 and 1822:

> 1818, August 1
> M[ill] Exp[enses] paid mill hands for extra work
>   this day $8.00
> 1818, September 4
> M[ill] Exp[enses] paid Ben, Sam & Dick
>   for extra work $1.25.[45]

Slave tobacco hand Lott Cary, who later became a preacher and one of the first Richmonders to emigrate to Liberia, often received five-dollar bonuses and "the privilege to sell the waste tobacco" for extra cash as a reward for good work.[46]

While owners and employers experimented with self-hiring and cash bonuses, slave workers devised new ways to gain greater control of their labor and lives. Often they took the privileges and rewards offered and used them to their advantage. For some slaves this meant asking to be hired out and clearly indicating their job preferences. Thomas Woodson's slave Bob, for example, let it be known that he wished to be reunited with his wife and work as a wagoner in Richmond. Amos, another hired slave, wanted to remain in the city for the following year and not to return to his owner's farm. To boost his chances, Amos persuaded his employer, Mr. Green, to write to his owner, Edward Garlick, before other plans had been made. Amos's plan worked well. According to Garlick's reply, it was not his "intention to have hired him [out] this year," but Green's offer persuaded him to do otherwise.[47]

Court records on a slave named Ambrose suggest how far some slaves went to get their way. Ambrose had been approached by Robert Brooke to work as a house servant but told Brooke he was too ill to work. As Brooke described their discussion, "Yesterday I saw your man Ambrose and asked him whether he wished me to hire him for the ensuing year or not. I often repeated this question to him, and he as often told me he was sick and could do no body any good. I therefore told him I would have nothing to do with him."[48] In spite of Ambrose's claims, his master forced him to work for Brooke. Ambrose responded four weeks later by running away from both Brooke and his master.

In comparison to the power that owners and employers possessed, slave workers had little leverage and few ways to effect their desires. Yet more often than not, owners and employers did heed slaves' requests, largely because ignoring them often proved costly. Although many owners voiced paternalistic concerns about slaves' welfare, having a slave mistreated or seriously injured also meant the owners lost revenue or saw their property's value diminish. It was chiefly for these reasons that Richard Carter, the owner of Sam and Daniel, immediately removed them from the factory and placed them in new jobs when they complained about the working conditions. Initially, Carter may not have had any reason to believe the two youths and could have easily rejected their claims. Yet he did listen to them and upon further investigation discovered the boys had indeed been neglected by Patterson.[49]

Sometimes, however, this method backfired. Isaac, who was hired to Curtis Carter, attempted to return to his owner, William Bowles, because he did not like the working conditions. Isaac complained that he was sick and that Carter had sent him home because an ill slave was of no use to him. Bowles doubted his slave's claim and sent word to Carter asking if Isaac's employment had been terminated. Carter replied no. "Having been informed," Bowles then "drove him [Isaac] off his plantation & directed him to return to the complainant." Moses suffered a similar fate when he left his employer, Meacon Green, and returned to his owner, Thomas Stanton. When Moses turned up at his master's shop, Stanton demanded to know why he had returned. Moses replied that "he had ranaway from Mr. Green [and] that he could not live with Mr. Green because he was too severe a task master, and required him to do more work than he was enabled to do." Stanton's response was to "reques[t] his brother Elihu Stanton to take Moses home to his then master."[50]

Perhaps the most common manner in which slaves took advantage of the city environment—with its attendant working conditions and privileges—was through social and leisure activities. After working hours and even during the day if time permitted, slaves met one another at places such as Mrs. Sydner's corner store for conversation and perhaps a hand of "five corns . . . at two cents a game."[51] Jamerson's grocery was another popular spot until he was charged with "harboring and entertaining in his shop . . . an unlawful assembly of slaves nine in number . . . without the knowledge or consent of their respective masters or owners." Those with some extra money were able to patronize local taverns and grogshops. One popular spot among slave, free black, and white residents was a tavern run by Mrs. Mary Martin. In fact, several of her more famous clients helped Gabriel Prosser plan his famous revolt in 1800.[52]

Not all slaves drank or gambled. Instead, many went visiting when they had the chance. Depositions from court cases indicate that slaves often went to one another's home (or the owner's home) to chat, share a meal, or exchange goods or services. Historian U. B. Phillips indicated that this was a popular form of entertainment among slaves within the cities: "The home of a . . . well-to-do townsman was likely to be a 'magnificent negro boarding house,' at which and from which an indefinite number of servants and their dependents and friends were fed. In town the tribe might increase to the point of embarrassment."[53]

Although owners were concerned about the times slave workers went unattended, they apparently believed it not to be a significant problem and viewed it as one of the many growing pains of the new urban and industrial slave system. Nor does it appear that owners were overly anxious about the gambling games or social parties—so long as these activities did not interfere with work. Perhaps their relative lack of concern over these activities was justified; the social parties did not pose a major threat to the daily work routine, and the number of slaves who could "lose time" were few in 1800. Furthermore, owners knew if they did try to discourage their slave workers from socializing without supervision, their warnings would have been taken lightly.

What owners did not realize, however, was how these activities—influenced by the unusual privileges—sowed the seeds for future resistance by enabling certain slaves to gain skills and nurture beliefs that would threaten the ideological foundations of slavery. With the ability to self-hire, live apart, voice employment preferences, and even pursue independent economic activities, slaves were placed in a position to judge their own working situations based on cash payments, tasks, and exertion required, and even safety standards. In these cases, slaves' opinion had a direct impact on their lives and offered them a few of the fruits of their labor. In essence, they gained a small amount of leverage. Although slaves' power was minuscule compared with that wielded by an owner or employer, it held great importance to them. On a practical level this leverage enhanced slaves' bargaining position when negotiating employment or dealing with merchants, tavern keepers, and landlords. They could reject potential hirers and exercise certain rights as customers and consumers. Of greater significance, however, the privileges and the activities they encouraged opened the door to slave self-determination. The ability to set the terms of employment and secure living necessities provided some tools to defy owner domination. In the early 1800s this newfound power posed only a small threat because so few slaves had the opportunity to explore the full potential of their privileges. Owners and employers remained confident that they held a fairly tight rein on slave workers. But by 1840, when thousands of city slaves had secured privileges as well as new skills, ideas, and ambitions, the threat became more evident and left many owners wondering if they had somehow helped slaves launch a sort of rebellion.

Not all Richmonders were as shortsighted. Some residents were considerably more concerned about slave activities and the threat they posed in the short and long term and worked hard to control and eliminate them. Instead of using physical coercion or privileges and benefits as incentives, however, these residents offered spiritual salvation. Armed with sermons, catechisms, and the promise of equality in God's eyes, Richmond clergymen, particularly Baptists, struggled to stop slave workers from drinking and gambling and sinning altogether. But pastors, like owners and employers before them, quickly discovered they could not dominate slave congregants. And ironically, the very tools used to control slaves became weapons in slaves' battle for religious freedom.

"CHRIST'S FREEMEN . . . CHRIST'S SLAVES"
While fear, arrests, or religious apathy may have slowed the spread of organized religion and "visible" churches among black Virginians during the late eighteenth century, such forces did not stop black Richmond

residents from receiving the Word of God.[54] In fact, even the hint that the new evangelical religions possessed radical messages of equality and may have encouraged a group of slaves—led by a young man named Gabriel—to plan a revolt in 1800 did little to stop clergymen's rigorous efforts to bring city slaves into the fold.[55] The desire to Christianize and "civilize" bond men and women ran strong and deep among the religious leaders of the city. As a result, by the turn of the century black Richmonders, slave and free, had an enviable choice of religious services to attend, including those at Anglican, Methodist, Presbyterian, Catholic, and Baptist churches, as well as a Jewish temple.[56]

During the early nineteenth century, the most popular and fastest-growing church among black residents was the First Baptist.[57] Initially about 200 residents (150 blacks and 50 whites) joined the church in 1800. By 1824 Baptist membership had increased to 800, and by 1840 there were more 2,000 members, (1,708 blacks and 387 whites).[58] No other church could match these membership figures; few black residents joined any other institution. Records from the Catholic and Episcopal churches, for example, show only a minuscule number of slave Richmonders as members during the nineteenth century. And the First Presbyterian Church had only about 60 black members on its rolls by 1843.[59]

Key to the popularity of the Baptist religion among slave and free blacks was the church's liturgical message of egalitarianism. Because the Baptist religion stressed the individual's efforts for rebirth and conversion, rather than infant baptism, black and white, slave and free members were equally reproached for the sins they committed and were offered an equal opportunity to be saved. It comes as no surprise, then, that among the members of the church were "not many wise . . . not many mighty."[60] Because Baptist preachers had little doubt of slaves' capacity to understand and embrace the conversionary experience, slaves found themselves taken as seriously as free black and white members.[61] In God's eyes they were the same, or as one pastor described it, if slave they were "Christ's freemen,—if free, as Christ's slaves."[62]

Bond men and women also were attracted to the Baptist religion because of its accessibility, even to those who could not read. Baptist preachers expressed sin and salvation in physical terms: the weight of sin, the burning fires of hell, and the cleanliness and purity of conversion. As a result, literacy and education were not necessary. Even the Reverend John Courtney—the church's first full-time minister—was known to have "lacked the advantages of [an] education."[63] Anglican and Catholic churches, by contrast, were far less visual and tended to impart religious values by way of a written discourse that included the Ten Commandments and the Lord's Prayer.[64] Even if these churches ceased to depend on the written text, it is doubtful slave men and women would have found these religions appealing. According to Luther Porter Jackson, the nonevangelical religions' "greatest handicap" was their "lack of emotionalism and a spirit to fire the masses."[65]

The popularity of the Baptist church was further enhanced because of the leadership opportunities it offered. The church selected a committee of black deacons to administer to black congregants and regularly ordained free and enslaved blacks and allowed them to preach to both black and white congregants. Although other separatist sects appointed black preachers, historians find that a large portion of selected speakers were from the Baptist church.[66] This is largely because Baptist churches, unlike the Presbyterians or the Methodists, were autonomous and did not have to abide by a larger governing authority; as a result, members of an individual church could appoint or remove preachers without approval from any external organization.[67] This flexibility encouraged members of the First Baptist in Richmond to ordain free black and slave members such as Lott Cary, Colin Teague, Joseph Abrams, and John Jasper, all of whom became important religious figures precisely because of those opportunities.[68]

For these reasons, among others, the Baptist church was considered an oddity and was watched by the Richmond public with great curiosity. The outdoor baptisms on the riverbank drew gawking visitors, as did the large associational meetings that were held in Richmond on occasion. Even the pastors were followed with interest. Within his first few years of service, John Courtney was dubbed by white critics as a "haranguer among Negroes."[69]

While the general public saw the Baptist church as flashy and wildly attractive to overly emotional dissenters, a panderer to blacks and poor whites, and a possible instigator of slave rebellions, members of the First Baptist saw themselves as part of a serious organization dedicated to saving souls. To carry out their evangelical mission, local Baptists made extraordinary efforts to attract and convert Richmonders from all walks of life. In the early 1800s prayer meetings run by and for women were established under the guidance of the Female Missionary Society. In 1815 the Richmond African Baptist Missionary Society was formed, marking the beginning of the church's efforts to "aid [the] unhappy kindred in Africa." By the 1820s the church could boast of missionary efforts in India as well as among various Native American tribes.[70] The same year missionary efforts to Africa were started, Deacon William Crane, a shoemaker by trade, opened a school within the church to teach reading, writing, arithmetic, and the Bible to anyone interested, including free black residents. In the 1820s members of the First Baptist

Church became involved in the Virginia Colonization Society, designed to help free black residents relocate to Africa.[71]

The First Baptist's efforts paid off, and church membership increased rapidly in spite of the widely fluctuating range in pastors' skills. The church's pastors ranged from "old and feeble . . . slow [and] persever-ingly plodding," to young, "brilliant . . . rapid of speech" and "exul-tantly soaring."[72] Between 1800 and 1840 black Richmonders came in droves.

In spite of the missionary efforts, the church school, the egalitarian principles professed by the Baptist liturgy, and the potential it held for slaves to control their own religion, black Richmonders found them-selves being squeezed into a restrictive confining role and physically squeezed out of the church by their fellow white members. It appears that the small minority of white First Baptist members had strong ideas about the position of black congregants in the church and who should control and spiritually guide black Richmonders.

One of the most blatant ways the white minority asserted control was by creating a strict code of moral behavior that applied more to black members than to whites. Because white members dominated the upper echelons of church authority as pastor, deacons, and committee leaders, they were able to create and enact such restrictions unilaterally. Even when black deacons were appointed to administer to black congregants, few bond men and women could escape scrutiny. White deacons often called upon their black counterparts to investigate rumors of impropri-ety among the black members and severely punish the violators.

Black residents were required to adhere to this code in order to be accepted into, and remain a part of, the church. Any infraction of the code meant immediate exclusion. Activities banned included adultery, "improper conduct and language," gambling, intoxication, stealing, ly-ing, fighting, and running away from one's master.[73] While some of these prohibitions, such as adultery, raised few objections, other targeted ac-tivities probably caused slave members to chafe; stealing and escaping, for example, were tactics that slaves commonly used to protect them-selves against the conditions of bondage.

Neither black nor white deacons, however, took into account the mo-tivations behind such activities. As a result the church records are filled with lists of black members called before the deacons to answer charges of impropriety. Between 1825 and 1830 there is only one case against a white member noted in the records, compared with fifty-seven cases against black congregants. It is clear the deacons singled out and pe-nalized black male members for drinking and gambling. This was the fate of Henry, a slave who was caught gambling in 1828. Henry had the misfortune to be seen by fellow church member Brother Myers "in a room with three other men, at a table with cards, dice and money upon it."[74] Henry, however, was not any more prone to gambling than most Richmond men. Gaming, going to the racetrack, playing billiards, and drinking were among the most popular forms of entertainment for the majority of Richmond males. It seems highly unlikely that white male congregants shunned such activities.[75] But it is clear they rarely, if ever, had to face the consequences of such actions in church.

Deacons also singled out black female congregants, most often for sexual behavior deemed improper. Of the thirty-three adultery charges between 1825 and 1830, just eight involved black men; the rest were against slave and free black women. Again, few white male or female congregants faced such charges during this period. The deacons even saw fit to scrutinize the behavior of black women who were experiencing marital problems. In a number of cases black women were excluded for "withdrawing from [their] husbands and refusing to live with [them] again" or for displaying "conduct unbecoming a wife and a Christian."[76]

The white minority further attempted to maintain control over black congregants by limiting their access to church leadership positions. A black parishioner seeking to become a deacon had to be accepted by the white congregation. Although black church members initially chose the candidates through a voting process, their choices were subject to the white congregation's approval. Ordination of black preachers and those who desired to "speak in the pulpit" was decided in an even less democratic way. In this case congregants did not vote. Instead, the church committee—made up largely of white members—designated which laymen could publicly preach. In 1826 the committee chose five black members to preach and seven black laymen to "speak in public by ways of exhortation but not to take texts." But these twelve men enjoyed their status for only a brief period. In an effort to demonstrate the authority of the committee, in 1829 all preaching privileges were revoked, and all black speakers were forced to reapply.[77]

In addition to the aforementioned powers, the church committee had the authority to appoint congregants to various ad hoc committees. The result was that in spite of the overwhelming number of black church members, few blacks were appointed to these committees. In 1827, for example, a committee to take collections for the pastor's salary consisted of "ten white male members, five white female members and [five] coloured male members."[78] Not only were blacks outnumbered, but, as was often the case, slave and free black women were excluded completely.

Finally, white church members sought to maintain control in a manner that blatantly violated the spirit of the Baptist religion; they tried to limit the number of black members who could attend services. By requiring slaves and free blacks to sit in the galleries of the church, white members in effect capped the number of black congregants and made religion inaccessible to many.[79] Black members unable to find seats were turned away from the services and forced to attend a different sermon later that day or week when space was available.

Although church records indicate that white members held enormous power over their black brethren, they also show that black congregants did not passively accept the treatment they received. Slave and free black parishioners strongly resisted the forced standards of moral behavior, the undemocratic methods of choosing preachers, and the restrictive seating arrangements, thereby ending any illusions that black congregants could be easily controlled. An example of this can be found in the lengthy lists of slave exclusions for gambling and drinking; on the one hand the lists suggest "inappropriate" behavior and mayhem, and on the other hand, they clearly indicate that a portion of the congregation refused to adhere to the bans and did not find the deacons' threat of exclusion a deterrent. Another good example is the 1829 revocation of preaching certificates for black members. By forcing black preachers to reapply for licenses, the committee appeared to be demonstrating its power to confer such a privilege. The events leading to that incident, however, suggest that power was tenuous at best. According to church records, the committee revoked the licenses not because the certified preachers were doing poorly but because other black members were preaching without church approval and did not bother with the certification process.[80]

Slave and free black members attacked white congregational control in more fundamental ways than just breaking moral codes. Black congregants managed to assert their interests by integrating their interpretation of the Baptist religion into the church services, which included, among other things, a form of music, movement, and speech. During services slave and free black parishioners shouted, sang, moved their bodies, and clapped their hands as if possessed by the spirit of God. When the pastor's words struck a chord within them, they did not hesitate to punctuate the particular phrase or moment with "loud ejaculations and groans."[81] Black Baptists also gave their own slant to the hymns and psalms sung in church, with "long and loud bursts of praise" that reminded the pastor of the "sound of many waters."[82] Although there had been cases of white congregants who responded similarly to services in other churches, overall black and white Baptists at Richmond's First Baptist Church received the Word of God in vastly different ways.[83]

The difference between black and white congregants reflects more

than a contrast in worshiping styles; it is indicative of distinctive theological approaches. Black Baptists in Richmond, as in the rest of the
South, practiced a form of evangelicalism that brought together elements of both African and European-American beliefs, or what Mechal
Sobel calls "the melding of the African and Baptist Sacred Cosmos." As
Sobel describes it, black Baptists took evangelicalism and redefined it as
a uniquely Afro-Baptist religion by incorporating aspects of the African
cosmology and culture.[84] The melding of the two helped make evangelicalism more responsive to slave and free black residents' daily lives by
bringing "within this world all the elements of the divine"—a distinct
component of the African faith systems.[85] In this interpretation, God
exists not only in heaven but on earth as well, is compassionate, restores
justice, responds and rescues those in need, and holds "the ultimate and
final power over the visible and invisible creations."[86] And since God was
omnipotent and omnipresent, black Christians could speak directly to
him and did not need white Christians to mediate. This view of God gave
bond men and women the strength to reject a white Christian theology
that stressed black subordination to white slave owners as part of being
a good Christian because slaves knew that only God—not their owners—
could determine whether they went to heaven.

The Afro-Baptist view also allowed for stories of the sacred world to
be discussed in terms of daily events of the secular world. The eviction
of Adam and Eve from Eden, for instance, became a lesson to men who
did not look after their families. Had Adam been with Eve, as the tale
was once told, she would not have been tempted by the devil. But, la-
mented John Jasper, a resident of Richmond who became one of the
most famous nineteenth-century black preachers, "Adam worn't wid her;
doan know whar he wuz—gorn bogin' orf sumwhars."[87] Adam's failing
was a clear warning to slave and free black men: stand by your family at
all times. Adam was not the only biblical figure portrayed as a member
of the community and recognized for his or her good deed or evil doing. As Sobel describes, "Adam was next door, Jezebel was a present
danger, Jesus a friend to share burdens with and Moses the ever-expected
emancipator."[88]

Other elements of the African cosmology, such as metaphysical beliefs, also entered the First Baptist Church with slave membership.[89]
Much to white congregants' horror, black members maintained a strong
belief in spirits and witchcraft in addition to their unshakable faith in
God and saw no conflict or contradiction between the two.[90] Although
the Reverend Jeremiah Jeter (1836-41) admitted that a belief in witchcraft should not be a barrier to church membership, he struggled hard
to eliminate what he referred to as the "dread of imaginary beings or

evils."[91] Jeter's successor, Robert Ryland, also made a concerted effort to "preach out their dreams and fancies, their visions and revelations, and all their long cherished superstitions."[92] Black parishioners, however, held fast to their "superstitions"; from laymen to deacons, black congregants continued to consult fortune-tellers and tell stories about "witches, hags, [and] giants."[93] Simon Bailey, one of the few black deacons, revealed the strength of such beliefs when he leaped to the defense of a church applicant who held views unacceptable to white congregants. The incident occurred during a membership interview when one of the white deacons, Archibald Thomas—who was known to be a strict disciplinarian—asked the elderly black applicant if he believed in witchcraft. The old man quickly replied that he did. The deacon then asked, "Did you ever see a witch?" The man thought for a moment and answered, "Did you ever see the devil?" These responses displeased Thomas, and the applicant's chances for membership appeared in jeopardy. It was at this point that Bailey came to the old man's defense. An eyewitness described what happened next: "This altercation brought to his feet one of the colored deacons, Simon Bailey. . . . He stated that he had lived in the country, and that, with his own eyes, he had seen the manes and tails of horses twisted into stirrups. He was wary, in the presence of Deacon Thomas, of expressing any opinion of the cause of this entanglement, but it was the common opinion that the horses were rode by witches, and, for his own part, if these stirrups were not made for them he could not tell what they were made for."[94]

Whether Simon Bailey's animated response helped the applicant's chances will never be known; the records do not indicate if the old man was accepted. But if Deacon Thomas and the Reverend Mr. Jeter had entertained any hopes to keep supernatural ideas out of their church through the interview process, this incident no doubt shook their confidence. Belief in spirits was widespread and deeply embedded within the black congregation, even among those whom white congregants considered to be the most responsible and most pious.

Further evidence of the melding of African and Baptist worldviews can be seen in the conversionary experiences of black Baptists. Though elements of black conversions were similar to those of white Baptists, such as having feelings of worthlessness and "eternal damnation," visions and dreams played a significant role in the conversions of black Baptists. Studies indicate these visions generally involved certain distinct themes: the existence of two selves—a "little me" and a "big me"; a sense of traveling to heaven and hell; the appearance of a guide who assists during the travels; and clear, detailed images of heaven and God. As the studies further indicate, these aspects were not products of

European-American cosmology but elements drawn from African faiths and an "integral part of the black Christian cosmos."[95]

The pervasiveness of these themes in black Baptists' conversionary experiences is clear from personal accounts. In *God Struck Me Dead,* a compilation of black religious narratives, nearly all converts saw themselves as two bodies, traveled through space and time, or found themselves being led by a person or voice up to heaven. Members at the First Baptist Church anticipated conversion through these visions as well. Slave Richmonder Fields Cook, who struggled hard to embrace, and be embraced by, God, fully expected to travel as part of his conversionary experience. In his diary he stated that to be converted was "to see heaven & hell and not only to see them but actually to go to both places and see all the departed souls those which was in heaven were to make me welcome home and those in hell were to be laid on a gridiron boiling and unless I could bring this news to the elders of a christian church I was none of his."[96]

Fellow slave Richmonder John Jasper apparently did travel. While standing in the middle of the tobacco factory where he was working, Jasper felt "de light broke" and had the sensation of being weightless with his feet no longer planted on the floor but "on de mount'n."[97]

When Jasper converted he found himself surrounded by hundreds of other black members who shared his joy and understood the journey he had taken. His fellow white church members, however, could not empathize in the same way. White congregants did not experience these conversionary visions, nor did they sway, shout, sing, or dance in the same way as their black brethren. Even though white members may not have recognized the African influence on the black Christian faith, it was clear to them that the two groups did not share the same spiritual attitude. Black Baptists, they realized, worshiped God in "their own language and idiom."[98] Even the Reverend Jeremiah Jeter had to admit—in retrospect—that his black and white parishioners required different "instruction" and that the "style of preaching demanded by the white congregation" was not appropriate for black members.[99] But whether or not white congregants liked it, the Afro-Baptist view played a more prominent role in the First Baptist Church than their own vision—a role that grew larger as black membership increased. Ironically, the predominance of the Afro-Baptist view gave black members the control in spiritual matters that they lacked in institutional decisions. While black congregants could not define the moral standards (though they certainly could evade them) or choose committee members, their religious interpretation—not the white Christians' view—reigned within the First Baptist Church.

White Baptists greeted black membership and the Afro-Christian religion with mixed feelings. Large black enrollments testified to their success in bringing the Word of God to black residents. But the predominance of the Afro-Baptist view presented a challenge to their power to define black spiritualism and the role of blacks within the church. Uncomfortable with the competing visions, the crowded facilities, and the obviously different worshiping styles, white Baptists chose to withdraw. Starting in 1820 black and white members no longer shared services; the morning sermons were reserved for white members, and black congregants attended afternoon sessions.[100]

Separate church services constituted a major victory for black congregants. In an immediate and visible way, the separate services gave black church members a physical and spiritual forum to express themselves and to practice their brand of Christianity without inhibition. It also gave black congregants greater self-rule within the church and more control over their religious lives. The separation of the two congregations was a physical manifestation of the deep fundamental differences between black and white Baptists. Black Baptists demanded a religion that could respond to their particular needs. As Albert Raboteau describes it, "Slaves did not simply become Christians; they fashioned Christianity to fit their own peculiar experience of enslavement in America."[101] In a less visible way, the separation of the congregation signified the end of a lengthy war.[102] Although the battle for an independent all-black church still lay ahead, the retreat of white congregants to different services suggested that resistance to separate churches was weakening. Emboldened by this success and spurred by a rapid increase in black converts—particularly after the revivals of 1831—black Baptists pressed for a separate church. They won their holy war in 1841, with the organization of the First African Baptist Church.

In church, as in the larger city setting, slaves struggled with owners, employers, and white residents to gain greater control over their lives. In the Baptist church this conflict surfaced as a fight over whose vision would determine the religious culture. Black residents won a resounding victory thanks to the egalitarianism of the Baptist liturgy, the numerical strength of black congregants, and the popularity of the Afro-Baptist view. The result was a church that allowed slaves and free blacks an unprecedented opportunity to shape their own religious culture and establish systems of self-rule.

GABRIEL'S LEGACY
Slave owners, employers, and ministers all had concerns about illicit conduct by slaves. But the ultimate responsibility, and job of controlling

such behavior, fell to city and state authorities. Unlike owners worried about their property or ministers concerned about their congregants, government officials were responsible for all slaves and for repelling all threats to the slave system or to private property. Lawmakers' interest in illegal slave activities during the early nineteenth century was hardly new. Since the 1780s city officials had been cracking down on crimes by slaves and other poor residents. From the 1800s onward, however, local authorities felt a more pressing need to address slave control because of the actions of a man named Gabriel. His aborted rebellion in 1800 shook city and state officials and caused them to consider how slave discipline had failed and how they could reassert control. They would soon find, however, that a solution lay beyond their control.

On August 30, 1800, Pharoah and Tom, two slaves on the Sheppard farm, cautiously approached Mosby Sheppard, the brother of their owner, Philip Sheppard. They had news that the slaves in the area were preparing "to rise" that night. When pressed as to who organized the slave rebels, the two confessors replied: "Prosser's Gabriel."[103] Sheppard immediately set out to alert other slave owners and urged the local militia to investigate. William Mosby, a neighbor of Sheppard who was rumored to be among the first intended to be slain during the uprising, accompanied the militia on a raid of the alleged meeting place at Brook Bridge outside of Richmond. A number of slaves did meet that night at the appointed site. But a tremendous rainstorm prevented most followers from reaching the brook; the rising water had washed out many of the bridges leading to the meeting place.[104] Oddly enough Gabriel and a few of the organizers who waited did not see the militia men, nor were they spotted by them. Gabriel and his cohorts, however, decided to wait until the next day, Sunday, to start their attack because of the low turnout. They hoped the storm would be over by then and that recruits from neighboring counties would arrive.

When word that the conspiracy had been exposed reached their ears, Gabriel and the men who remained with him immediately fled the area, hoping to escape the armed white patrols that were closing in fast. Their escape routes, however, proved as ill-fated as their planned rebellion; in the days following August 30, various slave rebels including Gilbert, Ben Woolfolk, Solomon, Martin, and Sam Bird (or Byrd) were captured by the militia and brought to the public jail. Gabriel eluded the authorities for a week or so but finally was caught aboard a schooner in Norfolk.

Gabriel's ability to remain at large for nearly two weeks can be attributed to his familiarity with the landscape. Though his primary residence was on the plantation of his owner Thomas Prosser, which was six miles outside of Richmond, Gabriel traveled extensively between the city and the surrounding countryside attending religious meetings, barbecues, and market days. And because many of these social occasions occurred with little or no white supervision, Gabriel was able to meet with his cohorts and plan this rebellion as well as recruit participants without detection.

The mobility that Gabriel enjoyed was but one of many privileges he received as a hired slave blacksmith and carpenter. He was also able to find work, live apart from Thomas Prosser, and keep some of his cash payments. While the young, literate, highly skilled Gabriel stood out among most other slaves, he was not unique. Many of his friends and family members were like him: highly skilled artisans and house servants, with the ability to self-hire and travel between the countryside and city. Gabriel's brother Solomon, for example, was a blacksmith. His friend Moses worked at the coalpits in Tuckahoe. Another of his cohorts, Stepney, was a bateauman hired out for the year.[105] Each of these men frequently hired their own time or were hired out, received cash payments, and evidently had free time to do what they liked. Even though they worked for different employers in separate locations, they still had ample opportunity to meet and socialize with one another and to plan their attack on Richmond.

Their plan was to first kill Thomas Prosser, Gabriel's owner, and several other slaveholders in the neighborhood. Afterward, they would enter Richmond in three groups. One group was to "sett all the Wood houses on fire at the other end of the town and when the people were going to the fire they could take possession of the brik stores."[106] While Richmond residents were attending to the fire, the second group was to seize the Capitol and kidnap the governor. On the other side of town, the last group was to take over the arsenal at the penitentiary. At this point, Gabriel and his men were supposed to capture or indiscriminately kill the white residents, with the exception of Quakers, Methodists, Frenchmen, and poor white women, until the city surrendered. The planners agreed to spare these groups of people, according to Ben Woolfolk, "on the account as they conceived of their being friendly to liberty," and in the case of poor women, because they were not slave owners. Then Gabriel was supposed to raise a white flag as a signal for slaves outside the city to join and issue a proclamation declaring themselves and all slaves free.[107]

Given the nature of the attack and its intentions, the sentence given to Gabriel and twenty-six of his cohorts by the court was predictable: death by hanging.[108] With Gabriel's execution, slave owners, employers, and other Richmond elites breathed a sigh of relief. City and state officials, however, knew that the "slave problem" was far from over; in fact it was just beginning. As the details of Gabriel's plot became known, the difficulties of monitoring and controlling slaves in Richmond became more evident, and one of the major obstacles was the city environment itself.

Richmond's transition from a small port town to an urban industrial center left local officials scrambling to bring order and stability to the emerging city. This was not an easy task; as the city grew in population and size, so did its problems with sanitation, health, poverty, and crime. City authorities, however, probably were most alarmed by the growing crime rate; Richmond was becoming a violent city.[109] Visitors to the city around the turn of the century were astonished at the amount of blood shed at taverns, around gaming tables, and at the racetrack.[110] Newspapers were filled with incidents of gambling, drinking, fighting, and dueling in the streets involving members from all segments of the population, black and white, free and enslaved. Even law enforcement officers were not exempt. As early as 1782 the guards of the local jail had to be replaced because they were "either principals or accesaries in almost every robbery which has of late been committed among us." Because the challenges to the law came from all walks of life, there appears to be no one reason why the crime rate increased except, as Harry Ward and Harold Greer explain, that "the many new faces in the area fostered an atmosphere in which 'disorderly houses,' and thievery thrived."[111]

City and state officials' response to the seeming disorder and instability of city life included passing a wide-ranging set of laws that attempted to protect residents and property and to establish a standard of acceptable moral behavior. Before 1800 a crude system of fire control was established by requiring all homeowners to keep fire buckets on hand and have their chimneys inspected. To prevent epidemics, officials appointed a superintendent of quarantine and opened a hospital for diseased sailors. To reduce the market for stolen goods (and further increase the city and state treasury), all hawkers and peddlers were required to purchase special licenses.[112] Activities such as gambling, the selling of spirits and liquor, and horse racing were strictly regulated. "Disturbers of religious worship and sabbath breakers" could now be punished under the law, as could strangers and vagrants found loitering in the city.[113] Additional regulations passed during the late eighteenth century targeted slave activities and banned certain practices such as self-hiring. Slaves were required to carry a pass at all times or face being publicly whipped. They also were prohibited from playing cards, rolling dice, or gambling or attending horse races and cockfights. Slave residents caught participating in "riots, routs, unlawful assemblies, trespasses, and seditious speeches" would be punished with thirty-nine "stripes" or burned on the left hand with a poker.[114]

Overall the new regulations passed just before 1800 were designed to clamp down on the lower classes, both free and slave, within the growing urban environment. Although Richmond authorities recognized slave residents to be potentially more threatening than white residents, they did not display a particularly heightened concern toward them. In fact, Richmond authorities were somewhat more concerned about the white male population; prior to 1800 white men appeared before the court for alleged criminal activities more often than anyone else. During the last decade of the eighteenth century, it appeared the law enforcement efforts were working because the number of arrests decreased.[115] But if city officials developed a sense of confidence, it was a false one. The discovery of Gabriel's plot in the summer of 1800 revealed the flaws of their approach and the potential for much worse problems in the urban environment. There was an inherent difficulty in trying to maintain a secure, tightly controlled slave institution within a loosely monitored city setting. It was this problem that plagued city officials not only during the early nineteenth century but throughout the antebellum era.

City authorities were not entirely clear on how to secure slavery in the city. Unlike slave owners and employers, local officials had few ways to reward slaves to promote good behavior. Worse yet, punishments meant little in an environment in which detecting illicit slave activity was difficult, if not impossible. As a result, the period between 1800 and 1840 was spent restricting and eliminating the activities and practices believed to have enabled Gabriel to plan his plot and, later, to have helped Nat Turner carry out his rebellion in Southampton County in 1831.

Once again, ordinances and laws banned many of the unusual working and living practices. The ban on self-hiring, for example, was reaffirmed in 1801 and 1808 and sporadically throughout the antebellum era.[116] Other regulations prohibited slaves from meeting one another in groups of five or more and from gambling and drinking. In addition, slaves could not meet for religious purposes without a white person present. In direct response to Nat Turner's rebellion, authorities additionally banned black Richmonders (free and enslaved) from "preaching, exhorting, conducting or holding any assembly" under any circumstances, including performing burial rituals.[117] Furthermore, at least once a month, slave homes were subject to inspections by local guardsmen to prevent any type of illegal activities and "unlawful assemblies of slaves." Slaves caught roaming the streets after 9 P.M. received a lashing administered by the night watchmen unless their owners rescued them first. The new laws further limited slave mobility by prohibiting bond men and women from riding on railroads or horse carriages or crossing bridges without written permission and threatened slaves found on board boats without owners' consent with an immediate "39."[118]

In addition to attacking these activities, city council members and state legislators attempted to limit interaction between the free and enslaved populations—particularly slave and free black inhabitants—because they believed such associations only led to danger. Authorities contended—based on little concrete evidence—that free blacks enticed slaves to rebel and escape. As proof, lawmakers looked no further than the rumors implicating several free black residents and two Frenchmen as participants in the aborted revolt of 1800.[119] For additional "proof," lawmakers pointed to the discovery of David Walker's *Appeal*—a pamphlet written by a northern black resident calling on slave workers to rise and kill their owners—in the possession of certain slave Richmonders.[120] But even though there was evidence that free persons had not assisted Gabriel or Nat Turner, the mayor and his council were convinced that any contact with free blacks planted in "their weak minds a spirit of discontent, tending to insurrection."[121]

State and city legislation passed between 1800 and 1840 attacked slave–free black associations from a variety of directions. Some of the new laws sought to separate the groups by preventing them from meeting. Unsupervised gatherings between the two, for example, were prohibited. Free black workers who traveled into slave-populated areas were required to keep their distance. Black watermen or bateaumen had to stay close to their boats when traveling the river and could not to venture into the center of the city or visit friends. A more severe measure required all black persons freed after 1806 to leave the commonwealth within twelve months of their emancipation or else face reenslavement.[122]

While these laws may have prevented certain transactions from transpiring between free black and slave residents, they could never completely separate the two. Free black and slave residents continued to worship, celebrate, and raise families together in spite of the increasing restrictions against such interaction. The new ordinances passed after Gabriel's aborted rebellion, for example, did little to hinder free black barber Reuben Morton from marrying Clara, a slave woman, and raising four children.[123] Nor did the new restrictions squelch all impulses for the two to meet. Christopher McPherson, one of Richmond's more colorful free black residents, purposefully flaunted the new laws when he advertised the opening of his new school for the "people of colour" offering classes in reading, writing, and arithmetic, among other subjects. But McPherson's institute never opened as promised; white residents immediately brought charges against him for being a "nuisance" to the white community.[124]

Other state and local ordinances appeared to acknowledge that slave and free black residents would meet and simply sought to defuse the dangers of such interaction. Free blacks were prohibited from selling or giving ardent spirits to slaves, writing passes, or teaching any literacy skills (religious or otherwise).[125] To prevent slaves from obtaining guns and goods, the new laws also banned free blacks from keeping firearms without a proper license or loading any goods onto or off boats without written certification from some "respectable white person."[126]

While the dangers of slave–free black associations weighed heavily on legislators' minds, they were not blind to the potential problems that slave and white resident interaction presented. Among those most aware of these dangers was the mayor of Richmond. In his court, on a daily basis, the mayor was presented with cases involving theft, gambling, and selling and receiving stolen goods between slave and free white inhabitants. These cases included the charges against John McKenna, a white resident, for knowingly purchasing a cart of stolen iron pipes from two slaves, Nelson and Spencer Burch. And the case against white resident Thomas Stubbs, for writing passes for Richard Cooper, a black slave, thereby allowing him to pass as a free man. And the case concerning Oakly Philpotts, another white resident, and Harry, a black slave laborer, who were charged with conspiring to revolt. Both parties were brought up on charges of insurrection after three witnesses swore they had overheard plans for rebellion. Although none of the witnesses heard any specific details of an attack, one witness swore he heard Philpotts say to Harry "that he came of Adam & Eve, & he knew not why they should not have their freedom & drink their wine too."[127] Philpotts and Harry were subsequently found innocent of any wrongdoing, but the incident likely confirmed officials' belief that relations among the three groups needed to be limited and strictly supervised.

To limit interaction between slave and white persons who were not their owners or employers, authorities placed severe penalties on the latter should they assist the former to escape, to read and write, to gamble, to board a ship, or even to cross a bridge. Infractions of these laws resulted in high fines and jail time. Punishment for "counseling, advising, plotting or conspiring" with a slave or free black resident to rebel had even more dire consequences; free persons, black or white, found guilty of this crime would automatically "suffer death by hanging."[128]

Other activities banned even included trading and selling both illegal and legal goods. Slaves, for example, were prohibited from selling "eatables" to white, free black, or slave residents and were prohibited from owning shops.[129] Restrictions were placed on white merchants as well. In 1802 grocers and other residents were prohibited from purchasing or selling goods to free black and slave residents on the Sabbath day.[130] Later on, no merchant or resident was able to buy, sell to, give, or receive goods from a slave on any day without written permission.[131] Ostensibly these bans were to reduce the trade in stolen property, but they were also geared toward reducing contact between slave and free residents.

City officials anticipated resistance from slave and free black residents to these new regulations, but they did not expect resistance from white Richmonders. Much to their surprise, owners and employers willfully ignored many of the new regulations, finding them to be a nuisance and to conflict with their economic interests. The ban on slaves hiring themselves out and "going at large," for example, not only infringed upon the slave owners' authority over a slave but also hampered local businesses' ability to obtain slave laborers. Some owners were dependent on this labor system as a way to motivate slave workers while others needed it to generate income. Local businesses and individuals were equally dependent on this system to meet their short-term labor needs. Because the ban conflicted with owners' and businesses' economic interests, it was widely ignored. Slaves continued to hire themselves out with both owners' and employers' consent. In fact, this law produced an unlikely coalition of slaves, owners, and employers conspiring to actively resist slave laws.

Despite the ban on self-hiring, workers such as Iris, Titus, and Will continued to look for their own employment with their owners' written consent. Nelson Hylton received both his owner and his employer's consent to hire himself out. This was somewhat unusual because Hylton had already hired himself to Charles Holt for the year but was still looking for additional work.[132]

The slave laws created other unusual alliances as well. Slaves and the proprietors of small eating and drinking establishments frequently found themselves partners in crime as city officials attempted to ban slaves from consorting with free persons. Flouting the regulations, slaves with extra cash continued to patronize local grogshops and cookshops, and small shopkeepers continued to serve them. The new laws did not seem to bother the consciences of shopkeepers such as M. P. Shop or Jamerson who continued with business as usual. It was a common occurrence to see both slave and tavern keeper in court with the former charged with "going at large" and the latter charged with "selling spirits and permitting negroes to gamble in his establishment."[133]

Tavern keepers were not the only ones who continued to serve the slave clientele. Dozens of white Richmonders, including shoemakers and clothiers, refused to stop selling goods to, or trading services with, slave workers. Although many of these merchants probably agreed with lawmakers that slave discipline needed to be bolstered, few saw the harm in selling a pair of shoes or a hat to a bondman.[134]

The new regulations of the early nineteenth century and public response (that is, of slave owners, employers, shopkeepers, and slave workers) to the new laws reflect some of the confusion that residents felt about slavery and its role in the city economy and society. City businesses, owners, clergymen, local officials, and slaves themselves all struggled to determine exactly how and where slavery fit into the emerging urban and industrial milieu. Predictably, each group advocated practices that suited its needs best, and often these practices conflicted.

This confusion was not limited to the local level, however. During this same period representatives from across the state struggled to determine the future of slavery and its role in Virginia. Not surprisingly, the events of 1800 and 1831 (Gabriel's aborted plot and Nat Turner's Rebellion) sparked debates in the General Assembly and forced local residents to consider the future of the "peculiar institution."

Although the issue of slavery was no stranger to the halls of the assembly, these events encouraged legislators to discuss the institution in ways different from previous debates. Haunted by the fear of future slave insurrections and moved by the desire to protect the lives and property of white residents, state representatives turned from issues such as taxation and suffrage—topics that involved slavery—to slavery itself. Even though the participants in, and the contexts of, the two debates differed greatly, during both periods legislators seriously entertained proposals that would significantly alter the future of slavery either by slowing the growth of the institution or by abolishing it altogether. But the strength of conservative Virginians proved too great as moderates and abolitionists failed to rid the state of slavery. By 1840, despite the apparent risks and difficulties slavery presented, nearly all groups—except slaves themselves, of course—were determined to maintain the "peculiar institution" in Richmond.

The period of 1800 to 1840, then, was one of experimentation with, and adjustment to, slavery in order to fit the new urban industrial setting. In every part of the emerging city—in business, in church, in taverns, and within owners' homes—slaveholders, employers, and local authorities struggled to find a way for slavery and city life to coexist. The result was a set of legal, working, and living arrangements that often crossed purposes and at times created chaos. But where others saw disarray or incongruity, slave residents saw a golden opportunity. In the confusion, slave workers found room to work in their interests, push their demands, and help define the urban slave system. Their participation not only brought them more privileges and more "control" over their lives but allowed them to launch their greatest challenge to the slave system: the establishment of a strong, independent community.

Four

Maturation of the Urban Industrial Slave System, 1840–1860

BETWEEN 1840 AND 1860 urban industrialization and the city slave system reached a peak. During these years industries achieved their greatest output and their highest profit levels. By 1860 Richmond was home to fifty-nine tobacco manufactories, eight flour and corn mills, eleven iron and brass foundries, four soap and candle factories, and a variety of other plants producing machines, nails, iron and steel, saddles and harnesses, bottles, and boots. In fact, the city's industrial capabilities inspired a local newspaper to describe Richmond—in somewhat exaggerated terms—as "perhaps the most extensive manufacturing town south of Philadelphia."[1]

As in the past, Richmond's industries, particularly tobacco manufactories, were highly dependent on slave labor. About 80 percent of the tobacco workforce consisted of bondmen, and slave workers could be found in virtually all major segments of the economy. On the eve of the Civil War, slaves made up half of all adult male workers in Richmond.[2]

Industrial slave labor demands had a tremendous impact on the slave population; by the late antebellum period Richmond's slave community achieved a size and complexity unimaginable in rural areas. The population increased 56 percent, from 7,509 in 1840 to 11,700 by 1860, and consisted of thousands of workers united by strong kinship ties, independent churches, segregated neighborhoods, and secret fraternal and financial organizations.[3]

Urban industry and urban slavery appeared healthier and more successful than ever. But even as slavery ushered in a new era of prosperity, it began to encounter serious problems as a result of its interaction with the urban industrial economy. Industrialists' efforts to boost productivity combined with city living conditions generally proved antagonistic to a strong, tightly controlled slave system. The unusual labor practices and use of incentives to boost productivity, for example, encouraged slave workers to participate in the market economy, weakened bonds between slave and master, and made it easier for slaves to escape. The combination of these factors altered the slave system so dramatically that eventually it only loosely resembled the one that existed on plantations.

The implications of a less-than-traditional slave system did not escape the attention of white Richmond residents, for whom increasing incidents of slave resistance became clear signs of diminished control. In response, state and local authorities stepped up their efforts to fortify the system and reestablish control. And once again they attempted to eliminate slave privileges. But their efforts proved ineffective for several reasons. Officials severely underestimated the importance of the privileges to industries and businesses and found themselves in a divisive six-year battle against tobacco manufacturers over the practice of slave workers living apart. Local authorities also misjudged the relationship between slave workers and small merchants and threatened to cripple businesses by frequently arresting both customers and proprietors. But the most important reason authorities failed to assert total control was that Richmond slaves had become too "independent." Skills and knowledge acquired through jobs, churches, and social, political, and financial organizations allowed slaves to flagrantly disregard the laws and challenge the ideological foundations of racial slavery.

"ALL THE WORK IN RICHMOND IS DONE BY SLAVES"
During the late antebellum era, Richmond reached a level of industrial development and growth few southern cities could match. From the look of the spacious new factories, the countless numbers of billowing smokestacks, and the hundreds of workers going to and from work, it appeared that the captains of industry now resided in Virginia's capital. And based on various financial and manufacturing records, such an assumption was not so far-fetched. During the 1850s Richmond was the nation's largest manufacturer of tobacco and ranked second in flour milling.[4]

Not surprisingly, much of the city's economic prosperity was based on Richmond's tobacco industry, which was enjoying a high level of success. Between 1840 and 1860 the number of manufactories earning more than $500 in profits jumped from thirty to fifty-two firms, including three new firms that produced smoking tobacco.[5] Expansion in production triggered an increase in workers as well: between 1850 and 1860 the number of tobacco laborers leaped 58 percent, from 2,062 to 3,254. And on the eve of the Civil War, tobacco production values—totaling more than $4 million—exceeded the combined products of the flour and iron industries during 1860 (table 10).

The city's economic strength did not come from tobacco alone, however. Other industries also posted impressive gains. Between 1850 and 1860 the number of iron, copper, and brass manufactories increased from eighteen to thirty-five with a nearly 400 percent increase in the number of workers (413 to 1,601). Although statistics are available only for larger industries, it is clear that many smaller shops emerged and prospered as well. The manufacturing census returns during this period indicate the number of small workshops with annual products worth more than $500 increased 37 percent, from 191 to 261.[6]

Richmond's industries grew larger in size as well as in number. By the 1850s manufactories the size of city blocks replaced the one-room workshops that had predominated only a decade or two earlier. William H. Grant's factory, constructed in 1852, is a good example of this new industrial architectural style. Hailed by the *Daily Dispatch* as the city's largest

Table 10. Richmond tobacco, flour, and iron industries, 1840–60

Product	Year	No. of firms	No. of workers	Capital invested	Annual product
Tobacco	1850[a]	30	2,062	$370,471	$2,826,487
	1860[b]	52	3,254	$1,019,025	$4,583,495
Flour	1850[c]	2	80	$320,000	$1,090,000
	1860	2	248	$900,000	$2,530,000
Iron	1850	18	413	$382,970	$324,868
	1860	35	1,601	$1,333,650	$2,184,015

Source: Richmond, Manufacturing Census, 1850 and 1860.

[a] The 1850 Manufacturing Census figures include only those businesses that produced more than $500 annually and therefore are conservative estimates of the tobacco industry.

[b] The 1860 U.S. Manufacturing Census gives slightly higher amounts for Henrico County. In that report capital invested was $1,121,025; the annual product was $4,838,995 and the number of employees was 3,370 males and 34 females.

[c] The number of employees reflects only one firm. Haxall's mill did not list its number of workers in the Manufacturing Census, 1850.

processing mill, Grant's manufactory measured "120 feet on Franklin [Street] and back on 19th street 50 feet . . . [and] four stories in height, with 115 windows [and] require[d] more than two thousand panes of glass to fill them." Grant's spacious facilities did not stand alone in the city skyline; flour mills built during these same years were of increasingly large dimensions as well. Warwick and Barksdale's mill, rebuilt in the 1850s after a devastating fire, measured 94 by 164 feet at ground level and was 127 feet high. It housed twenty-three "run of burrs" and about eighty flour workers.[7]

Even more impressive than Grant's or Warwick and Barksdale's factories was the Tredegar Iron Works. Spread across five acres overlooking the James River, Tredegar consisted of rolling mills, heating furnaces, spike-making machines, and living quarters. On one end of the compound stood the armory rolling mill formerly owned by the state (acquired by the company during the 1840s and merged with the other parts of Tredegar), containing nine puddling furnaces and four heating furnaces to process pig and scrap iron into merchant bar iron and rails. On the opposite side of the compound stood the Tredegar mills consisting of nine puddling furnaces, seven heating furnaces, and three trains of rolls, in addition to a spike factory and a cooper shop where railroad and ship spikes were cut and packaged. A third set of buildings housed the foundry and forge used to cast, cut, and bore guns and cannons, the machine room to build and refine railroad car wheels, and the engine and carpentry shop where locomotives were built and "Tredegar workmen completed woodwork for sawmills, sugar mills and freight cars."[8]

What made Richmond's economic prosperity most impressive, however—and unique in the antebellum South—was the thousands of slave laborers who pressed the tobacco, forged the iron, and ground the wheat. Statistics compiled by Ira Berlin and Herbert Gutman give some sense of the importance of slave labor to the city's economy during the late antebellum era: according to their study, slaves constituted 48 percent of the city's adult male working class (between the ages of fifteen and sixty) by 1860. No city had as many male slave workers, and only Charleston and Lynchburg had higher percentages (tables 11 and 12).[9]

Richmond male slave residents came to dominate the workforces of key industries and were an indispensable part of most others. The tobacco-processing industry, for example, would have collapsed without slave workers. The predominance of slave labor in the industries is even more surprising given that the slave presence in the city was shrinking in proportion to the white population. In 1840 slaves constituted 37 percent of the population; by 1860 they represented just 31 percent. In

Table 11. Workingmen by status, nativity, and race, 1860

City	Number	Percentages		
		Slave	White	Free black
Richmond	9,557	48	44	7
Charleston	7,887	51	42	7
Mobile	7,002	35	63	2
Lynchburg	1,623	60	34	6

Source: Berlin and Gutman, "Natives and Immigrants, Free Men and Slaves," 1182.
Note: Workingmen include all male workers between the ages of 15 and 60, both skilled and unskilled labor. White workers include all southern, northern, and foreign-born males.

Table 12. Workingmen in Richmond by status and race, 1820, 1840, and 1860, in percentages

Year	Slave	White	Free black
1820	36	55	8
1840	43	49	8
1860	48	44	7

Source: U.S. Census, Population, for year cited.
Note: Workingmen include all males between 15 and 60, skilled and unskilled.

spite of this decline, slave workers remained crucial to nearly all large businesses, thus giving the appearance—to at least one visitor—that "all the work in Richmond is done by slaves."[10]

To typical visitors it would have appeared that slaves did do all the work. If they arrived by rail, a slave porter would have greeted them and stowed their luggage, and had they looked out the train windows, they would have seen crews of slave workmen maintaining the crossties and lines. Once in the city, visitors could have hailed a hack driven by a slave, or if they chose to walk, they would have crossed paths with a number of slaves running errands, going to the market, selling goods, or delivering shipments. At the hotel visitors' every demand would have been attended to not by a hotel manager but by the slave porter, waiter, cook, and chambermaid. And if visitors went searching for a new pair of boots, a suit, or a shave, they might have noticed that the shoemaker, tailor, and barber were either assisted by a slave or were slaves themselves. After a brief stay visitors could say with confidence that there were few jobs slaves did not perform.

The number of slave workers who had contact with visitors, however, was only a small fraction of the population. A greater portion of the slave workers, particularly the men, would not have crossed paths with a traveler unless the latter inspected one of the city's many factories. As slave employment patterns during the late antebellum era indicate, slave laborers were concentrated in the large mills rather than small craft shops. This is partly because industries such as tobacco manufacturing were expanding at a much faster rate than smaller businesses and therefore required a greater number of workers. Furthermore, there were few labor alternatives to obtain the hundreds of hands required for tobacco processing. As a result, slave workers continued to dominate the tobacco industry through the late antebellum era, constituting between 80 and 90 percent of the 3,000-plus workforce from 1840 to 1860 (table 13).[11]

Slave workers also were indispensable to the railroad industry. By leveling the land and laying down the track, slave rail workers helped advance communication with, and transportation to, the outside world. These slaves continued the work of the generation of laborers before them, who had dredged the James River and dug the Kanawha Canal. Though complete employment records do not exist, the number of workers hired to build and lay track for the five different railroads (Richmond and Petersburg; Richmond, Fredericksburg and Potomac; Virginia Central Railroad; plus two additional lines by the 1850s) must have

Table 13. Tobacco workers, 1840–60

Year	Total no. of workers	Total no. of slaves	%
1840	981	(689)	70
1850	2,062	2,196	106
1860	3,325	(2,761)	83

Source: Virginia, Manufacturing Census, 1840 and 1860. Figures in parentheses are from Green, "Urban Industry," 314.
Note: The total number of slave tobacco hands for these years is based on samples of various factories. The number of firms sampled in 1840 was seventeen, for 1850 it was forty-nine, and for 1860, thirty-nine.

been staggering. The Virginia Central Railroad, for example, employed several slave work crews as general laborers in the workshops and depots and as newly appointed brakemen and firemen. The largest group, however, was the maintenance crew consisting of "1 timber and wood inspector, 1 master carpenter, 1 principal overseer, 1 extra overseer, 9 section overseers, and 100 negro men."[12] This was a single crew at one rail company; the number of slave hands for all the companies must have been in the thousands.

Slave workers remained crucial to the flour industry as well. During the late antebellum years, the number of slave employees at the Gallego and Columbia mills—the city's largest—increased steadily to meet growing market demand. The Gallego mills employed approximately 80 slave hands during the 1840s and 140 by 1860. The Columbia mill reported a similar increase in workers from 30 in 1840 to 108 two decades later. On the eve of the Civil War, 248 slave hands worked in the two mills, comprising nearly 70 percent of the mills' total workforce.[13]

Nonindustrial businesses also sought slave labor. The city government, for example, employed slave workers to provide essential city services, including street paving and cleaning, maintenance of the Capitol grounds, and trash removal—jobs that white workers frequently shunned. Between 1840 and 1860 as many as thirty-six slaves worked as full-time sanitation laborers, and even more were hired during health emergencies, such as the 1849 cholera epidemic. During this crisis the city hired extra slave hands to clean the streets with lime, nurse the sick, and bury the dead.[14]

Slavery in Richmond had all the hallmarks of a successful and prosperous system. Richmond's slave community reached an all-time high of 11,699 in 1860, up from 7,509 in 1840. This increase is even more dramatic when compared with the corresponding figures for other cities (table 14). In several of the largest southern cities, slave populations decreased during the late antebellum era, but not in Richmond.

Interest in hiring out slave workers appeared quite strong as well. Throughout the late antebellum era, the pages of the *Daily Dispatch* and the *Richmond Enquirer* were filled with notices such as these: "Negroes for hire—Two house servants—1 Driver—3 Likely Men. . . . Wanted—One or two good hands (slaves) for Engineering service. A Liberal hire will be given and the slaves will be well treated. . . . Wanted—thirty laboring hands on the line of the R.F. and P. R.R. [Richmond, Fredericksburg and Potomac] about 12 miles from Richmond, to lay track."[15]

The annual slave-hiring period immediately after Christmas became a chaotic time with thousands of potential employers and employees roaming the streets in search of one another. According to one local

Table 14. Change in slave population in various southern cities, 1840 and 1860

Year	Baltimore	Charleston	New Orleans	Richmond
1840	3,199	14,673	23,448	7,509
1860	2,218	13,909	13,385	11,699
Total change	− 981	− 764	− 10,063	+ 4,190

Source: Wade, Slavery in the Cities, 325–27.

newspaper description, during the week between the Christmas and New Year holidays Richmond became a frenzied marketplace for human labor: "Saturday the streets were thronged with negroes, hirers, owners and buyers, as is the annual custom. Thousands of dollars exchanged hands, thousands of negroes changed homes and masters. During the remainder of this week the streets will be filled with negroes brought in from the country for hire."[16]

Small increases in slave-hiring rates also suggest that demand for slave labor was growing; between 1840 and 1860 the average cost of hiring a slave hand rose from $90 to $120 for men and from $34 to $45 for women. Although these estimates—compiled from newspapers and court records—differ slightly from those of other studies, such as Goldin's, all of the figures demonstate an increase in the rate of hire.[17]

Another sign of the success of urban slavery was the rapid increase in the number of professional slave agents who negotiated hiring contracts and supervised slaves on behalf of the owners. In 1845 there were seventeen agents; by 1860 the number had risen to forty-nine.[18] These figures would be significantly higher if they included lawyers, who acted as agents when hiring out slaves on behalf of individuals and estates.

An additional indication of urban industrial slavery's growing popularity was the emergence of a more accommodating attitude toward the unusual slave system. Although white residents' fear of a slave rebellion never dissipated, it was overshadowed during the 1850s by a philosophy that linked southern nationalism to the urban and industrial slave system. As fears of northern economic aggression and antislavery sentiment mounted, local businessmen and politicians began publicly advocating the use of slaves in factories as a way to achieve southern self-sufficiency and to "counteract the incessant and vexatious attacks of the North."[19] As one commentator stated, "If . . . the Southern people [were] to employ their slaves in the manufacture of such articles as are now made almost exclusively in the northern states . . . the slave labor of the south will, instead of contributing to the wealth of the north, as it has heretofore done, become the successful competitor of northern white labor in those departments of industry of which the north has in times past enjoyed a monopoly."[20]

These advocates received additional support from other southerners who believed employing slaves in industries not only was good for owners and individual businesses but would lead to a strong regional economy:

> In regard to the advantage of employing slave labor in the construction of the rail-roads . . . there would be a great gain to the owners of slave property. Suppose, for instance, that enough slaves were employed upon rail-roads to make 300,000 bales of cotton per annum. That would cause a decrease in the amount of cotton crop to that extent, and the decrease in the amount raised would be more than made up by the increase in the price which would result from the diminished amount of the crop. The cotton would really bring as much money to the planters as if there had been no slaves employed upon rail-roads.[21]

It appeared, then, that most residual doubts about employing slaves in urban industries had disappeared and that slavery no longer seemed at odds or inconsistent with the city and factory environment. By 1860 there were few jobs that slave workers were not performing. Their contribution to the tobacco and other industries was obvious and essential. Furthermore, industrial demand for slave workers continued to grow, particularly as attitudes toward factory employment of slaves were shaped by rising southern nationalism. Although occasionally an employer here or there would raise some concerns about using slaves, most industrialists and slave owners believed it was neither economically possible nor desirable to end urban industrial slavery.

Privileges and Punishments

Although Richmond could boast of high production rates and record sales of tobacco, flour, and iron, the city's economy was far from infallible. During the late antebellum era, Richmond became further entrenched in the larger national and global markets, and as a result, its businesses became more vulnerable to fluctuating market demand, rising labor costs, and economic downturns. Between 1840 and 1860 there were no fewer than four recessions (1838–43, 1851, 1854, and 1857) that wreaked financial havoc on Richmond industries.[22]

The panic of 1857 is a good example of the devastating impact that economic downturns had on city businesses. During that crisis nearly all tobacco manufactories closed down, and more than 2,000 hired slave hands were released, thereby jeopardizing the futures and fortunes of the businessmen involved, including tobacconists, local shippers, box and hogshead makers, local tobacco growers, and slave owners.[23]

Because the market was in constant peril of saturation, particularly in the tobacco industry, industrialists had to be extremely vigilant to hold down production and labor costs or make a wide margin of profit. The fact that hundreds of businesses (roughly 800 businesses and individuals in the three wards in 1860) continued to hire slave workers rather than employ free wage laborers clearly demonstrates not only their reliance on slaves but their satisfaction with urban slavery as a labor system.[24] This satisfaction is the result of at least five factors, including the possibility that slave labor may have been cheaper than free wage labor. In terms of yearly wages, this appears to be true; one study indicates the annual cost of hiring a free skilled artisan was $197 in 1840 and $179 in 1860— much higher than the amount for skilled slave workers ($120–$150) during the same time.[25] These figures, however, are somewhat deceptive because they do not take into account the additional costs of policing, feeding, clothing, boarding, and providing medical care that employers often paid out for slave workers. As a result, these maintenance costs could have easily raised the total costs for hiring a slave to match, if not excel, the wages of a free laborer.[26] Furthermore, the proportion of white adult workingmen increased during the 1850s, which depressed free wage levels, driving them downward near slave employment costs. Accordingly, a few employers did replace some of their slave workers with free wage laborers.

Before exploring that change, however, it is important to understand why so many employers continued to hire slaves rather than free workers. Public debates aired in the pages of *DeBow's Review* reveal that some employers were not convinced that bond labor was more expensive than free wage labor. One proponent trying to persuade the James River and Kanawha Company and the Virginia and Tennessee Railroad Company of the economic advantages of maintaining slave workers offered detailed estimates of the differences between slave and free labor costs:

> The cost to a company owning slaves who are masons, and to contractors who hire them, will approximate to the following calculation:
> Interest on $600 [estimated cost of purchasing
> a slave mason] $36

Insurance on life	$10
Clothing, &c.	$10
Bacon per year	$15
3 barrels corn d[itt]o	$ 7.50
Vegetables	$ 2.50
	$81.00

Eighty-one dollars per annum, allowing 250 working days, are equal to 32½ cents per day; whereas the hired mason will cost the contractor $2.50 per day, more than seven times as much as the mason costs the company who owns him. In this estimate there is no allowance made for tools and overseeing, as both use the former; and the hired mason, though white, requires as much overseeing as the slave.[27]

According to his calculations, a slave mason would cost only 32½ cents per day—including interest payments, insurance, clothing, and food—a tremendous savings compared to the $2.50 a free mason generally charged. Although these costs were calculated based on purchasing a slave worker, hiring slave masons no doubt provided equally attractive savings.

This was not the first nor the last article in *DeBow's* comparing slave and free labor costs. A year later another author made a similar argument that the former was economically more effective than the latter and compared railroad workers to demonstrate his point.

The usual hire of a prime negro man in the country, to work upon the railroads, is about $180 per annum. If the company would purchase slaves at the present price, say $1,000., the annual expense compared with the hired slave will be about as follows:

Interest upon $1,000 at 7 per cent per annum	$70
Insurance on life at 2½ per cent	$25
	$95

which is a fraction more than half the sum paid for a hired hand.[28]

Because railroad companies employed hundreds of workers, hiring slave rather than free labor would have saved thousands of dollars.

Evidence proving one labor force to be less expensive than the other, however, is sketchy and at times contradictory. Charles Dew's study of J. R. Anderson and the Tredegar Iron Works, for example, offers evidence that slaves were not cheaper than free laborers. Although initially slave workers in the rolling mill did reduce the cost of labor per ton of rolled iron from $12.02 between 1844–46 to $10.59 between 1850–52, as slave costs increased during the 1850s (due to high demands for slave workers), such savings decreased.

Monetary consideration did motivate some employers, but a sizable number believed slaves to be more efficient than free labor because they produced a higher output under noncoercive conditions than free workers. In fact, so many employers believed this that they hired 60.9 percent (4,929) of all slave working men and women in 1860 for their factories and workshops. In the employers' minds the efficiency of slave workers offset the high labor costs. Moreover, employers remained convinced that they could "squeeze every ounce of [slaves'] productiveness" and could make them work harder than free laborers. These intangible factors motivated employers most to maintain slave workers as the "better" of the two labor forces.[29] Indicative of such sentiments, one proponent of slave labor argued that slave workers were "cheaper, can be kept under better discipline, worked both in summer and winter, and the planter be relieved from those annoyances which always accompany the introduction among our plantations of contractors with hireling white labor from the north and foreign parts."[30] For this employer the merits of rigid social relations between employer and bondmen convinced him of the superiority of slave over free labor.

At least three other factors persuaded Richmond slave employers to maintain bond labor forces. In the case of the tobacco industry, the stigma that the work was for blacks only mitigated against white men and women from seeking employment in that field. This racial stigma helps explain why so few white Richmonders worked in the factories and why so many slave workers (as much as 90 percent of the tobacco workforce between 1840 and 1860) manufactured tobacco.[31]

Another factor concerns the prestige and status that slave owners and employers believed they derived from utilizing slave labor. Like planters, industrialists may have felt that possessing bond men and women was an outward sign of their financial independence and success and their overall social importance within the city.[32]

Other Richmond employers shunned white workers for fear of labor militancy. The experience of the James River Company and its efforts to limit the number of white immigrant workers after a series of strikes is a prime example. The replacement of white metalworkers with slave laborers after the 1847 strike at the Tredegar Iron Works is another good example. In fact, the Tredegar strike served to unify the local press in opposition to potentially militant free white laborers and the threat they posed to Richmond's social order. The "principle . . . that the employer may be prevented from making the use of slave labor . . . strikes at the root of all the rights and privileges of the master, and, if acknowledged, or permitted to gain a foothold, will soon wholly destroy the value of slave property," gravely warned the *Richmond Times and Compiler.* The *Richmond Enquirer* echoed this sentiment by calling for the "whole community" to "condemn" the actions of the striking Tredegar workers on the basis that they threatened the power of slave owners and employers.[33] The press's loud condemnations of the white strikers suggest that more than economic forces influenced employers' hiring considerations.

While contradicting evidence on slave and free labor costs continued to fuel the public debate, ultimately the maintenance of the social order in addition to economic considerations drove most employers to utilize bond workers. Although a few notable businesses did switch from bond to free labor, city employers for the most part continued to hire slave workers and never fully converted to free labor. Their interest in hiring bond workers during this period is clear; census and manufacturing statistics show that by 1860, 71 percent (4,844) of slave workingmen (between the ages of ten and fifty-five) and 46 percent of slave workingwomen (1,490) were hired to factories and homes.[34]

High demand for hired slave workers reflected not only the expansion of factories in size and output but also the changes in the type of tasks that slaves performed. At the Tredegar Iron Works, for example, the number of slave hands grew in part because of increased access to the positions of puddlers, heaters, and rollers. Slave workers were promoted to these skilled positions following a recommendation made by company agent Joseph R. Anderson (later president of the firm), who calculated that if Tredegar hired twenty-two slaves as puddlers, it would save $11,181 per year, and even more if it purchased the workers.[35]

The placement of slaves in these highly skilled positions was unprecedented at Tredegar. Before the 1840s only white workers had performed these jobs, maintaining a racial monopoly by teaching their skills only to selected white mechanics—generally their sons or apprentices of their own choosing.[36] This apprenticeship system allowed white mechanics to protect their jobs by barring slaves (that is, less expensive workers) from the positions and by thwarting industrialists' efforts to select their own workers. Such tactics did not escape industrialists' attention; Anderson was fully aware that "certain operations [such] as puddling, heating, rolling &c are known only to foreigners and a few Americans who have been from interest opposed to imparting this knowledge to negroes." To break the white mechanics' grip on the workforce and circumvent the apprenticeship system, Anderson hired an outside iron craftsman to "instruct such men or boys whether white or colored in the said Branch of the said manufacture of iron."[37] To guarantee a steady supply of slave ironmakers, Anderson continued to hire new slave workers through the

1840s specifically to be trained in the art of puddling. White mechanics protested the presence of slave puddlers and rollers at the mill by calling a strike. Anderson's response was swift and harsh: he fired the strikers and filled their positions with slave ironmakers. He notified the strikers of their new status with a letter that opened with these words: "To my late workmen at the Tredegar Iron Works."[38] By the mid to late 1840s, slaves worked in all phases of ironmaking (table 15).

Not all employment changes were so dramatic. In some cases, such as the rail lines and the canal company, changes in slave jobs were much smaller and done with far less fanfare. In the Virginia Central and the Virginia and Tennessee railroads, a small of number of slave laborers— in some years as many as seventy and in others as few as ten—left their backbreaking jobs laying track and boarded the trains as firemen, brakemen, and cleaners as a way to reduce costs.[39]

Canal officials similarly promoted slave workers to the positions of stonemasons, stonecutters, and quarrymen in an effort to reduce costs, but also to end white labor difficulties. As the chief engineer explained, "In the Southern country, where mechanics are scarce, the contractor

Table 15. Slave Ironworkers at Tredegar, 1847–60

Year	Tredegar	Armory	Total
1847	41	—	41
1848	78	39	117
1849	63	42	105
1850	66	34	100
1851	57	5	62
1852	57	5	62
1853	47	—	47
1854	64	3	67
1855	72	26	98
1856	62	23	85
1857	60	21	81
1858	54	20	74
1859	67	—	67
1860	80	—	80

Source: Dew, Ironmaker to the Confederacy, 27.

is often compelled to pay exorbitant wages for those of inferior grade, and of bad character and habits, men who war against our institutions, and refuse to work with our slaves. The contractors on the canal estimate the superiority of slave labour over white labour, in cost of wages, as one to two, and in physical endurance and efficiency, in the ratio of three to two." Persuaded by the chief's proposal, the company's board of directors arranged to start training slaves in the art of stonemasonry. Within several months about thirty slave men had learned to "quarry, drill and cut stone quite as well as the majority of the white men passing about on the line offering their services as journeymen."[40]

In the tobacco factories it was not slave promotions so much as new steps added to the production process that helped increase the number of workers. One new step was the addition of flavors to the plugs. Tobacconists had hoped to attract more chewers by sweetening the leaves with a mixture of licorice and sugar to give tobacco a "sweetish taste which renders it not perfectly abhorrent to those who chew it," as one ex-slave noted.[41] Flavoring the leaves added several steps between the stemming and lumping stages. While one group of workers moistened the leaves and removed the backbone, a second group prepared the licorice and sugar in large cauldrons over a slow, steady fire.[42] Once the mixture reached the correct consistency, the tobacco leaves were immersed in the liquid by a group of "dippers." After the dunking, the tobacco was laid out to dry and to absorb the flavoring. It was then seasoned with rum or spice before being lumped and twisted into plugs. Finally, the plugs were shaped, pressed several more times by other workers, wrapped with tin strips, and boxed for shipping. Altogether, the new process for producing chewing plugs required six or seven steps performed by as many groups of workers.

High industrial demands for bond labor had a tremendous impact on slaveholding and employment trends by raising the costs.[43] Even though slave workers were touted as being cheaper than free labor, the cost of slave laborers increased and most likely precipitated the decline of bond labor in smaller businesses between 1840 and 1860. It was during these years that the small shop run by an owner and a slave assistant—a common working arrangement of the early nineteenth century—rapidly became a relic. In an 1840 sample of ninety-two households identified as craft shops—a category that included carriage and chair makers, wheelwrights, and tanners—forty-nine (53.2 percent) employed or owned slaves. Twenty years later, however, only 24 out of 113 shops (21 percent) held slaves.[44]

The high cost of slave workers persuaded even some larger businesses to use alternative forms of labor. Milberger Smith, proprietor of the

American, a popular hotel, for example, began hiring Irish women as dining room servants, "positions earlier held by slave men."[45] A competing hotel in Richmond retained slave dining room servants but began hiring Irish women as chambermaids. Apparently these employment changes were dramatic enough to attract the attention of visitors such as William Chambers. He recalled: "[Having] arrived at Richmond . . . I was transferred to a hotel, which proved to be no way inferior to the establishments in the states further north. The whole of the waiters were negroes, in white jackets; but among the female domestics I recognized one or two Irish girls—the sight of them helping to make good what I had everywhere heard stated about the Irish dispossessing the coloured races."[46]

The changes occurring in small-sized businesses and those Chambers noticed at his hotel apparently were happening across the city at various establishments. The increased slave labor prices led some industrialists like J. R. Anderson, president of Tredegar, to reconsider his threat of replacing all white workers with slaves. Although he did purchase and hire a number of bondmen, he never converted his entire workforce from free to slave. The number of slave ironmakers widely fluctuated, reaching a high of 117 in 1848 to a mere 47 in 1853.

In spite of these notable labor changes, substituting free laborers for slave workers was not a popular trend among large businesses even though immigrants constituted the fastest-growing portion of the laboring class; between 1850 and 1860, foreign-born workingmen increased 166 percent.[47] The tobacco industries, for example, continued to hire predominantly slave laborers regardless of increasing costs.[48] Furthermore, it appears that the labor switch occurred in industries "which had traditionally been the preserve of white workers."[49] Therefore, the switch from slave to free labor, particularly in the case of Tredegar, must be viewed not as a rejection of slaves but as a continual switch between the two labor forces whenever it suited the employer. Anderson, for example, continued to hire and purchase bond workers in spite of increasing costs throughout the antebellum era, which indicates that he found benefits to using a mixture of slave and free labor that went beyond costs.[50]

Although slave employment practices did not significantly change within the large industries as it did in the small-sized businesses, the changes that did occur had a significant impact on the working and living conditions of bond men and women. Figures based on the 1840 census and a sample taken from the 1860 slave schedule indicate that a significant percentage of slave laborers worked and lived not in small households with one or two other slaves but in groups ranging from four to ninety-nine other bond workers—a trend that increased over time (table 16).

High slave labor costs additionally affected bond men and women in terms of their demographics. Census data indicate that between 1840 and 1860 the male slave population was overwhelmingly concentrated between the ages of ten and thirty-six. The percentage of slave men in that age bracket increased from 63 (2,490) to 76 (5,043) (table 17). Among slave women an opposing trend can be observed. The percentage of slave women of childbearing ages (who generally commanded higher prices because of their childbearing capabilities) declined while the figures for young girls and older women increased. Women between the ages of ten and thirty-six constituted 54 percent of the female slave population in 1840 and only 43 percent by 1860 (see table 17). Girls younger than ten years old, however, rose from 20 to 22 percent between 1840 and 1860, while women older than thirty-six increased from 25 to 34 percent during the late antebellum era.

These demographic shifts were not the result of natural population changes. Obviously the slave workers who remained in the city were chosen on the basis of their capabilities and their hiring and purchasing costs. Industries overwhelmingly chose young men because of their skills and physical abilities, while households found young girls and older women to be as able to cook, clean, and act as personal maids as young

Table 16. Slaveholding patterns, 1840 and 1860

No. of slaves	Year	No. of households	%	No. of slaves	%	Total
1	1840	286	29	386	9	983
	1860	99	39.6	99	7.3	250[a]
2	1840	238	24	476	11	1.0
	1860	41	16.4	82	6.0	.91
3	1840	161	16	483	11	4,237
	1860	25	1.0	75	5.5	1,354
4+	1840	298	30	2,892	69	1.0
	1860	85	34.0	1,098	81.0	1.0

Source: U.S. Census, Population, 1840; Slave Schedule, Richmond, 1860.
[a] The 1860 figures are based on a sample of 250 slaveholding households.

Table 17. Age and gender distribution of slave community, 1840 and 1860, in percentages

Age	1840		1860	
	Male	Female	Male	Female
0–10	17	20	5	22
10–24	33	34	44	26
24–36	30	20	32	17
36–55	16	19	12	24
55–100	3	6	3	10

Source: U.S. Census, Population, 1840 and 1860.

women, but at lower costs. These hiring decisions affected the slave community by creating an imbalance in both the sex and age distributions.

The growing city economy had important ramifications for bond workers beyond demographic shifts. It altered living and working conditions in ways that made their lives harder. But at the same time it created some new opportunities for slaves to minimize their oppression.

The maturation of Richmond's urban industrial economy brought growth and wealth, but also significant financial ups and downs, which affected some city residents far more than others. For owners and employers, sluggish sales or reduced production typically meant a temporary drop in revenue. For slaves the consequences were more painful: an economic downturn could cause them to lose cash payments, suffer a reduction in privileges, be sent back to the countryside, or, perhaps worst of all, be sold farther south.

While changes in the economy affected urban male slave workers most visibly, the ups and downs also affected a sizable minority of the female slave workforce. By 1860 nearly 6 percent (300) of city slave workingwomen were employed by industries (in "female" jobs) and would have felt the effects of a market glut or economic downturn just as much as their male coworkers. Even slave women domestics (both hired and directly owned) in private households were vulnerable to the vicissitudes of the economy. Failed businesses frequently took a toll on the households of employers and industrialists and threatened to disrupt the working and living arrangements of about 4,500 slave women domestics. It appears that an increasing number of white families found themselves unable to support a large staff of household slave workers and chose to sell them or hire them out. The figures given earlier on the percentage of slaveholders and the high number of hired slave women strongly suggest that many owners were unable to maintain slaves in their homes, and that many non-slave-owning households did not want to purchase workers during the late antebellum era because of costs.

For the thousands of slave tobacco workers, fluctuations in the economy appear to have made their lives particularly hard. Gluts in the market, bad crop years, natural disasters, and fires were a constant threat to their jobs and living conditions. The 2,000 slave tobacco hands who lost their positions during the panic of 1857, for example, faced either returning to their owners' homes or being sold.[51] Meanwhile, slaves who kept their jobs in the tobacco factories also faced new problems. With the expansion of the tobacco industry and its facilities and the new steps added to the manufacturing process, tobacco slave hands of the late antebellum era experienced a severe loss of autonomy and control over their labor as well as increasing tension and violence in the workplace.

As the number of tobacco slave hands climbed and factory structures grew during the 1840s and 1850s, the industry began to use professional managers on the company floors to oversee the hundreds of workers. These managers usually were white males between sixteen and twenty-six, who were given license to discipline slave workers. Though these men may have considered themselves different from plantation overseers, they were perceived in much the same light, as "low, miserable, cruel, [and] barbarous."[52] Like overseers, managers commonly resorted to striking, cuffing, and whipping slave workers. In his memoirs Henry "Box" Brown recalled witnessing an incident between a fellow worker and their manager that obviously left an impression on him. One morning the slave hand arrived at Barrett's tobacco factory and was confronted by the manager, John Allen, who asked, "What are you so late for, you black scamp?" The slave hand replied, "I am only ten minutes behind the time, sir." Dissatisfied with this answer, Allen struck the slave in the face with his fist.[53] A separate incident involving a slave tobacco stemmer, Jordan Hatcher, and his manager resulted in a struggle that destroyed both of their lives.

It appears that nearly all tobacco hands became vulnerable to this kind of brutality by the late antebellum era as tobacconists increasingly depended on managers to help maintain discipline and quality control within the factories. Tobacconist William H. Grant, for example, turned to Martin Grasswith, D. W. Weisiger, and Henry Snyder to help oversee the sixty slave hands at his manufactory. Fellow manufacturer Joseph H. Grant apparently felt more confident in his abilities to manage his workers and hired only two managers to oversee the 135 hands employed.[54] Although there are no company records to indicate how many managers were hired throughout these years or their length of employment, one study estimates there was one manager for every thirty-four hands in Richmond.[55]

The incidents of abuse at the hands of managers suggests other ways that factory working conditions changed and placed workers at greater risk. Punctuality, as the Brown incident suggests, and the efficient use of time became of greater importance during the mid–nineteenth century. During the 1840s and 1850s, tobacconists had become concerned with making the factories more productive in response to growing competition and volatile sales. With fifty-two different firms producing chewing plugs in Richmond alone and numerous other competing manufactories in Petersburg, Lynchburg, and Danville, tobacconists constantly sought new ways to stimulate sales, reduce overhead costs, and offset rising slave labor costs.[56] The addition of flavoring helped reach new customers, while costs were held down by pushing slave workers harder. The length of the working day, for example, was changed. Whereas early accounts about tobacco factories suggest the workday followed the pattern of the sun, late antebellum descriptions by ex-slaves and travelers indicate that shifts were dictated by clocks. During the summer months this change was not so noticeable because both shifts (timed and untimed) lasted about fourteen hours. During the winter months, however, the switch significantly increased working hours; on the shortest days of the year, a shift from sunup to sundown would last about ten hours, whereas a timed shift would last at least fourteen hours and as much as sixteen.[57]

The start and end of the workday were not the only times governed by the clock. In many of the factories, meal hours were now signaled by loud bells or whistles at which time, according to the visiting British writer Charles Dickens, the workmen quickly "poured forth into a building on the opposite street for dinner," hurriedly ate and returned to work. A range of other activities, such as singing while working, also were strictly regulated. Though slaves could still sing, some employers began to limit the amount of music, believing that it slowed the pace of production, which to some extent was true. Workers used singing as a way to relieve boredom but also to set a particular work pace. If the hands cared to slow the pace of work, they would sing a slower song. Accounts written by visitors including Dickens attest to this new singing policy: "Many of the workmen appeared to be strong men, and it is hardly necessary to add that they were all laboring quietly then. After two o'clock in the day they are allowed to sing, a certain number at a time." Alexander McKay from Scotland noted a similar singing policy in the manufactory he toured during his stay: "In all the departments of the factory the labour was performed by slaves. . . . the utmost silence was observed amongst them, except within the certain hours of the day, when they were permitted to relieve their toil by singing."[58]

The emphasis on productivity affected other aspects of tobacco processing, such as overtime bonuses. In addition to the increase in working hours, the amount of tobacco that laborers were expected to process also appears to have increased. Statements made by ex-slaves, including Henry "Box" Brown, suggest that stemmers, dippers, and pressers were required to process at least forty-five pounds of tobacco a day before they could earn cash bonuses. Extra work more than the forty-five pounds, however, was hardly voluntary as slaves were forced to remain on the premises the full fourteen or sixteen hours even if they had processed the minimum amount.[59]

With these work changes in the tobacco factories, many tobacconists achieved their aims and "realized consistently higher profits as the 1850s advanced." According to one study, 80 percent of the tobacco firms saw a median rate of return of 15 percent in profits. This rate is fairly high (and widespread) in comparison to the 4.5 percent median rate of return (spread across only 58 percent of the tobacco manufactories) in Lynchburg—a major competitor of Richmond.[60]

From the perspective of tobacco hands, the maturing economy and increased tobacco profits potentially held only bleak prospects. The introduction of managers effectively ended laborers' ability to supervise themselves or to make decisions about their tasks—privileges they had previously enjoyed and come to expect. The hands also lost a great amount of control over the pace of production as they were increasingly regulated by clocks and quotas, and rules about singing were put into place. Such changes must have angered slave workers who watched their limited but important powers slip away.

In addition to such unpleasant changes, however, the new economy brought some positive things to the slave community. Most visibly, the increased number of slaves working in the industries—under all conditions—meant that more members of the community enjoyed the benefits that accompanied the hiring-out system. By 1860, 60.9 percent (4,929) of all slave working men and women (between the ages of ten and fifty) worked outside of their owners' homes and received—to a varying degree—benefits including living apart, cash payments, and bonuses.

Another promising development was the increase in slaves promoted to higher skilled positions. For the men who had gone from laying crossties to cleaning boxcars—a seemingly small step up—the new job held great potential: larger cash payments, release from gang labor, and better working conditions during inclement weather.[61] For the slave iron hands, the promotions presented tremendous opportunities to gain leadership skills, increase their earning power, and have greater control over their working conditions. This was particularly true for slaves in the positions of forge hands and stevedores who for the first time were placed in charge of making bar iron, which required an enormous amount of skill and responsibility. In this process slave ironmakers had to melt pig iron to release carbon and remove impurities without burning the metal. Once the iron reached the right consistency, puddlers reached into the furnace with long rods to slowly shape the metal until it formed a "pasty ball of about 150 pounds."[62] The puddlers then removed the ball from the furnace, pounded it, and fed it through squeezers and puddle rolls until it took the shape of a long bar called a "muck bar." Slave heaters and rollers cut the cooled muck bars into pieces, bundled and melded them together in a second heating process, and then fed the product through a finishing mill, which shaped it into bar iron.

In spite of increasing mechanization in the process, much of the production depended on slaves' skills. Only puddlers, for example, could determine when pig metal reached the right consistency for shaping—no tool or machine could perform this function. Furthermore, what little supervision existed at these high-level positions was frequently in the hands of other slaves. Although white male managers (what Anderson called "boss men")[63] headed each group of workers, these managers had little time to monitor all the slave hands because they too were puddlers, heaters, and rollers. As a result, most discipline fell to the two slave assistants ranked immediately below each boss and to the slave hands themselves.[64]

Slave canal workers also saw some limited improvements. In addition to becoming stonemasons, a select group of slave canal workers were appointed to act as patrols, a position that offered greater pay and responsibilities. Like drivers or overseers, armed slave patrols were responsible for monitoring canal workers and preventing any "disasters," such as worker injuries or a rupture in the canal. The 1847 company annual report to the board of directors explained these new positions and the responsibilities they entailed: "A sufficient number of the slaves, possessing the requisite intelligence are employed as patrols, each of whom is required to travel over his beat everyday, with a proper implement in hand, to be ever on the look out for the first indications of breach or other casualty, and to prevent it. . . . this he does under the promise that in case no breach that could have been prevented by his exertions, thereof receive a stipulated reward which is sufficient to secure his vigilance. This arrangement, it is believed, has been very efficacious in preventing disasters on the line."[65]

The changes in the economy also held a few benefits for slave women. The high demand for hired slave domestics, for example, gave a sizable number of women some of the privileges their male counterparts had long enjoyed. With 46 percent of the slave workingwomen laboring for people other than their owners, close to 1,500 women could potentially negotiate their contracts, receive some form of payment, and choose their employer. Less visible than these benefits, however, were the opportunities for slave women (hired and directly owned) to earn extra cash by providing household services. It appears that along with the demand for hired workers there was a demand for the purchase of individual services such as laundering, ironing, repairing clothes, and preparing and serving food.

During the late antebellum era, demand increased dramatically for household services because of the growing number of boardinghouses, businesses that employed only men, and male households that lacked both the facilities and implements to cook or wash. Though documentation is scarce, there is evidence that slave and free black women provided these services to black and white Richmond residents for cash payments.[66] The Reverend Amasa Converse's household records indicate that he regularly paid a slave laundress twenty-five cents for washing, even though he held two servants in his household.[67] Eventually the demand for laundering services became so great that slave women were allowed to leave private households to become full-time, independent laundresses. Curetta and her daughter Betty, for example, worked solely as hired washerwomen during the early 1860s and were allowed to live apart from their owner. Their papers—a rare find among court records—give some indication as to their living arrangements and the late hours they kept as washerwomen: "Curetta and her daughter Betty are the property of Mrs. Helen A. E. Briggs . . . they occupy a house on the lot of Mrs. Fisher on 9th street . . . they are wash women and may sometimes be employed in carrying home clothes to as late an hour as 9 at night."[68]

Female slave domestics also participated in the market economy by using their free time to bake foods that they would sell to fellow slave and free black residents near the marketplace and factories. Some women went so far as to transform their owners' kitchens into illegal cookshops offering slave workers cheap hot meals.[69] Others were paid to work in "snack shops" owned by free black proprietors.[70]

The benefits and opportunities of these extra jobs came at a great price, however. For many slave women laundering or catering was a third job, performed after a long day of working in the masters' or employers' households and taking care of their own families. The long hours women worked and the heavy burdens they shouldered make it reasonable to question whether the extra income gave many of them the sort of "mobility" and "autonomy" commonly enjoyed by slave men. For some slave women participating in the market economy clearly offered a way to improve their lives. For others, the extra work seems to have provided little discernible benefit.

Slave women who prospered by providing household services on a cash basis enjoyed unprecedented options, including the means to buy a range of goods such as fancy foods, clothes, small trinkets, and in some cases, their freedom. The point was, as one historian states, "that these decisions were theirs to make."[71] Having cash added to slave women's strength within the community by allowing them to contribute financially to the church, fund a support society, or help organize large social events. Most important, however, in seeking extra income slave women exercised a degree of control not found in the rest of their lives. They had the choice of accepting or rejecting certain jobs and had the ability to negotiate the terms of their work and wages.

Richmond's spectacular economic rise propelled by the tobacco, flour, and iron industries forced the rest of the country—and particularly the northeastern states—to take notice of this southern city. The type of products produced, its manufacturing output and annual profits, and the type of labor employed made the city a strong competitor with certain northern industries and a highly unusual but greatly valued asset to an overwhelmingly rural South. Richmond's success, however, came with a price: increased vulnerability to national and international competition, rising slave labor costs, and widely vacillating market prices.

Every economic fluctuation reverberated through Richmond's communities, slave and free, with frequent devastating consequences for the former. Certainly all slaves faced the possibility of being sold away from family and friends, but with crippling recessions and increasing labor costs, the potential grew dramatically. For many Richmond slave workers, however, particularly prime male hands, the chances were slightly more in their favor of remaining in the city because of high industrial demands.

For the thousands of slave laborers who remained in the city, economic change affected nearly every aspect of their working and living conditions. Increased labor costs, for example, encouraged the use of the hiring system; about half of all slave workingwomen and nearly three-quarters of slave workingmen labored for employers rather than owners. Those employed in the factories found themselves working under new forms of slave management. At the Tredegar Iron Works slave hands were promoted to highly skilled positions with greater responsibilities and control. In the tobacco manufactories, however, changes in supervision and production resulted in a loss of control for workers. With managers and longer working hours that resulted in greater output, fewer slaves had the ability to supervise themselves and determine the pace of production.

No doubt the thousands of slave women who went from household to household on a regular basis as hired hands found the changes stressful. Not knowing where they would end up the following year or if their children would remain with them made their lives tenuous and uncertain. Yet even under these tense conditions, the women were able to find a few opportunities that brought a small degree of control over their labor and some "autonomy" as consumers.

Ironically, as industrialists expanded their use of slave workers, they unwittingly made themselves more vulnerable to challenges from them. It appears that each new change either allowed bond men and women to maneuver into positions with greater leverage and control or threatened to rescind privileges, prompting a fight to preserve them. In either case the authority of the employer and owner was severely tested and in some cases undermined. It is ironic that the very success of the city's industrial economy relied on the widespread use of labor practices that helped slaves defy their masters.

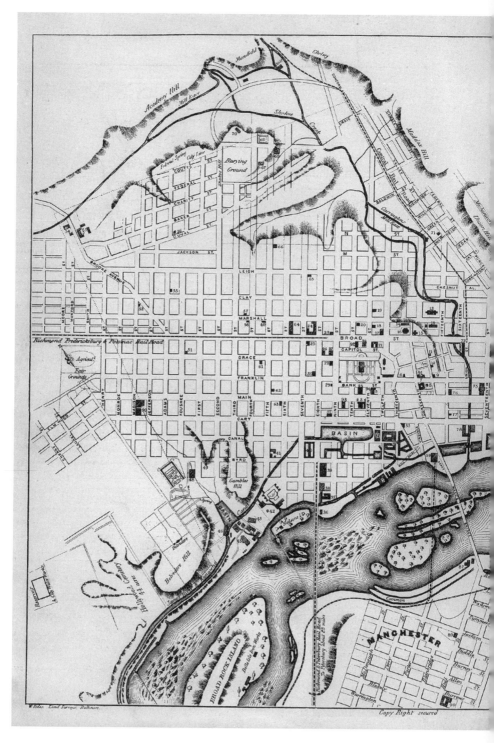

Map of Richmond, Virginia, 1859. (Courtesy of The Library of Virginia, Richmond, Virginia)

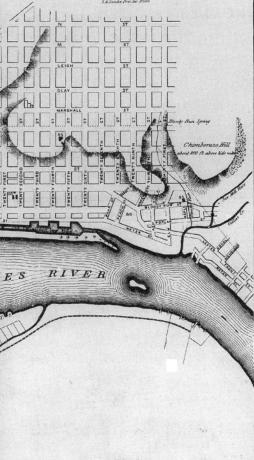

MAP
OF THE CITY OF
RICHMOND
HENRICO COUNTY
VIRGINIA.

*Prepared from actual Surveys, and published
expressly for Subscribers to the Richmond Directory*
BY W. EUGENE FERSLEW 1859

Scale 1100 ft. to an inch.

S. A. Sanders Prin'ter. Balt.

TABLE OF REFERENCES.

1. State Capitol and Public Square.
2. Farmers Bank of Virginia.
3. Bank of Virginia.
4. American Hotel.
5. Exchange Bank of Virginia.
6. Metropolitan Hall.
7. Exchange Hotel.
8. Trinity (Methodist) Church.
9. Odd-Fellows' Hall.
10. First Hebrew Synagogue.
11. Universalist Church.
12. City Jail.
13. Lancasterian (Free) School.
14. Medical College.
15. First African (Baptist) Church.
16. Monumental (Episcopal) Church.
17. First Baptist Church.
18. Sycamore Church, (Disciples.)
19. Second Hebrew Synagogue.
20. Richmond Athenæum. (Pulled down.)
21. Powhatan House.
22. City Hall.
23. Broad Street Hotel.
24. Depot of Richmond, Fredericksburg and Potomac Railroad.
25. Marshall Theatre.
26. St. Peter's (Roman Catholic) Cathedral.
27. Central Hotel.
28. St. Paul's (Episcopal) Church.
29. Mechanics' Institute.
30. United Presbyterian Church.
31. Bowers' Foundery.
32. Gallego Mills, (Warwick & Barksdale's.)
33. Columbian Hotel.
34. Shockoe (Tobacco) Warehouse.
35. Columbian Mills, (Haxall & Co's.)
36. } Virginia Steel and Iron Works.
37.
38. Franklin Paper Mill.
39. Richmond and Petersburg Railroad Depot.
40. Public (Tobacco) Warehouse.
41. Samson & Pae's Foundery.
42. State Armory and Iron Works.
43. Morriss & Tanner's Iron Works.
44. Tredegar Locomotive Works.
45. Stove Works.
46. Old Gauge-House and Boat-Yard.
47. State Penitentiary.
48. Lot belonging to the State.
49. Second African Baptist Church.
50. Penitentiary Spring.
51. Grace Street Baptist Church.
52. Clay Street (Free) School.
53. Clay Street Methodist Church.
54. Tan Yard.
55. Bacon's Quarter Branch Tavern and Spring.
56. Duval Street Presbyterian Chapel.
57. German Catholic Church.
58. St. Joseph's (Catholic) Orphan Asylum.
59. Depot of Richmond and Danville Railroad.
60. St. James' (Episcopal) Church.
61. Centenary Methodist Church.
62. Second Presbyterian Church.
63. Second Baptist Church.
64. Second Market and Watch-House.
65. Richmond Female Orphan Asylum.
66. Lutheran Church.
67. City Hospital.
68. Powder Magazine.
69. Hebrew Cemetery.
70. City Poor-House.
71. Wesley (Methodist) Chapel.
72. Depot of Virginia Central Railroad.
73. Seabrook's (Tobacco) Warehouse.
74. Christ's Church, (Episcopal.)
75. First Market, Watch-House and Public Hall.
76. St. Charles Hotel.
77. United States Custom-House, (old.)
78. Talbotts' Foundery.
79. Masonic Hall.
80. United States Hotel.
81. Old Stone House, (Headquarters of General La Fayette in the Revolution.)
82. Friends' Meeting-House.
83. Henrico County Court-House and Jail.
84. St. John's (Episcopal) Church and Cemetery.
85. New Gas Works.
86. Rocketts Old Warehouse, (burnt.)
87. Manchester Cotton Factories.
88. James River Cotton Factories.
89. Temperance Hotel, (Manchester.)
90. Methodist Church, (Manchester.)
91. Ballard House.
92. First Presbyterian Church.
93. Corinthian Hall.
94. Goddin's Hall.
95. New United States Custom-House and Post Office.

W. Gillespie, Sc.

"A Slave Auction in Virginia.—From a Sketch by Our Special Artist," *Illustrated London News* 38 (Feb. 16, 1861). (Courtesy of the Valentine Museum, Richmond, Virginia)

"The James River and Kanawha Canal, Richmond, Virginia," sketch by J. R. Hamilton, *Harper's Weekly* 9 (Oct. 14, 1865). (Courtesy of the Valentine Museum, Richmond, Virginia)

"Twist Room" from "In a Tobacco Factory, " *Harper's New Monthly Magazine* 47 (1873): 718. (Courtesy of The Library of Virginia, Richmond, Virginia)

"View of the Interior of the Seabrook Tobacco Warehouse at Richmond,
Virginia," *Harper's Weekly* 9 (1865): 709. (Courtesy of The Library of Virginia,
Richmond, Virginia)

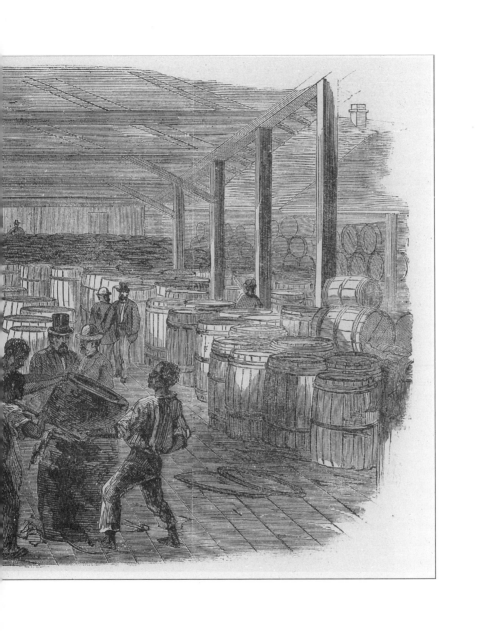

African-American laborers. (Photo War and Conflict no. 202, Brady Collection, National Archives, Washington, D.C.; courtesy of the Museum of the Confederacy, Richmond, Virginia)

Five

Formation of an Independent Slave Community

WITH THE EXPANSION of the industrial sector and the urban slave labor force, changes in slave living conditions were inevitable. Most notably, features of city slave life that had been considered irregular in 1820 and common in 1840 became ubiquitous by 1860. One such feature was separate slave housing. Whereas boarding out—or living apart—had been considered somewhat unusual in the early nineteenth century, by the late antebellum years it was deemed essential. Few businesses had the space or desire to accommodate the more than 5,000 male tobacco, iron, and flour workers and the few hundred female industrial laborers. As a result, industrial slave hands were free to seek lodging anywhere they could find it. In contrast to the previous period, however, slave housing in the 1840s and 1850s caused the widespread creation of racially segregated residential enclaves.[1]

During the late antebellum era, slave (and free black) residences became increasingly concentrated in two areas that bordered the edges of the city. The larger of these enclaves was in the extreme northwest corner of the city between Fourth and Belvidere streets from Broad to Leigh (later established as Jackson Ward in 1871).[2] Little is known about this early neighborhood except that it was primarily a residential section. There slave workers found housing by sharing homes or renting rooms from free black residents even though it was illegal for them to do so. Free blacks such as Lucy Moore willingly opened their homes to slave workers in violation of the law either to accommodate family members and friends or to make extra income.[3]

More is known about the second enclave down by Shockoe Creek near the docks, tobacco manufactories, foundries, and train depots. During the 1830s and 1840s this area housed workers of all races, classes, and ethnicities including German and Irish immigrants, native-born whites, free blacks, and slave city dwellers. By the 1850s, however, most of the European immigrants had moved to more comfortable residences on Union Hill and Oregon Hill. Black residents (free and enslaved) did not follow the immigrants into these new areas because white homeowners made it clear they were not welcome.[4] But the Shockoe Creek area remained open to poor workers of all backgrounds and colors and to small businesses owned by black and white residents, including cookshops, groceries, and grogshops. Though no legal barriers prevented different groups from living in the Shockoe Creek region (or in the Broad and Leigh Street area), white Richmonders began to view the neighborhood as exclusively for black workers and as a symbol of abject poverty and depravity. Evidence of this view came to light when Eliza Wilson, a white single mother of three children, was discovered residing in the neighborhood. Horrified that a white woman was living in a "large tenement filled with negroes," the *Daily Dispatch* pleaded with wealthy white residents to help this "family worthy of their sympathy."[5] The fact that women like Eliza Wilson who lived in other neighborhoods never received such attention from the local press strongly suggests that it was her residence in a black neighborhood, not her financial problems, that Richmonders found remarkable.

The earliest slave residents living in this waterfront area chose it because housing was fairly cheap, plentiful, and close to their jobs. Even though omnibus transportation was available after 1856, no lines went to the Broad and Leigh Street area. As a result, a slave hand living in this neighborhood would have had to travel by some other method or walk the mile or so to Thomas's or Grant's tobacco manufactory down by the docks.[6] Living in a tenement by Shockoe Creek, however, placed laborers within minutes of work. No doubt this advantage persuaded William and Fleming to live in a tenement on Cary Street just five blocks from their jobs at Poitiaux Robinson's tobacco factory. Moses and Jack lived even closer to their jobs at Quarles's brickyard, having to traverse only three blocks every morning and night.[7]

Slave housing in the factory area ranged from nearly uninhabitable to tolerable, at best. Slave workers lived in shacks and tenements located in alleyways that were unpaved, filled with open sewers and garbage, and considered "breeding grounds of disease."[8] The fact that the highest number of deaths from cholera occurred in this area attests to the poor sanitary conditions.[9] The tenements were of the most "miserable kind" with "fences unrepaired [and] walls crumbling into ruinous heaps."[10] Yet limited funds, the need to live near the factories, and "white pressures to keep blacks out" of other neighborhoods largely confined slave workers to these dilapidated and dangerous residences.[11]

While access, convenience, and cost initially drew—as well as pushed—slave workers to the Shockoe Creek area, family, friends, and economic and social institutions kept them there and encouraged other bond men and women to move in. In the midst of these poor housing conditions, slave residents managed to create a community that offered comfort, solidarity, protection, and entertainment.

The architecture of the Shockoe Creek area contributed much to the creation of this new community. Many of the tenements surrounding the factories were in alleys behind or beside businesses and could be accessed only through passageways.[12] Hidden from the public eye, these tenements provided slaves a physical and psychological space that allowed them a degree of separation from owners and employers that was not generally found in rural areas. Unlike most plantation and household slaves, tenement residents did not live within sight of the "Big House" and were not exposed to an overseer's prying eyes after work. Occasionally curious white residents would visit the alleys, and there were infrequent police raids; but generally this slave community was allowed to exist unmolested. No doubt the privacy that slaves enjoyed within these relatively isolated alleys gave them a sense of separation from the outside world and an opportunity to let their guard down, enjoy one another's company, or simply be alone.

The city's architecture brought black Richmonders closer together while the boarding system and financial pressures often forced them to share dwellings. Hired slave workers frequently roomed together or shared a house in order to reduce costs.[13] This was certainly the case for Moses, Jack, and Walker, who not only worked together at Quarles's brickyard but lived together in a nearby tenement.[14] Sharing residences was not limited to slave residents, however; slave and free black residents commonly roomed together as well. When Ann Eliza Ellis, a free black woman, found herself without a home, her friend John Sims, a slave, put her up in his boardinghouse room for several weeks.[15] Because of high rents and low cash payments, single free black and slave mothers frequently shared households. Although documentation is scarce, one study indicates that "taking in children or doubling up households" became an important method of making ends meet.[16]

Of greater impact on the development of the slave community than architecture or economic need, however, were the networks based on family and kin. United through marriage and by blood, family ties constituted an important part of the slave community and in many instances tied not only the slave but the slave and free black communities together.

Such bonds were possible because of the relatively large number of slave men and women in the city that resulted from urban and industrial labor demands. In 1850 the ratio of men to women was 115 to 100. By 1860 increased demand for male slaves pushed the ratio to 131 to 100. These figures differed markedly from those of other southern urban centers such as New Orleans, where female slaves outnumbered males 100 to 67 by 1860.[17] The age distribution of Richmond's slave community also points to a high potential for marriage and families. Census data show a significant number of men and women of compatible ages; in 1850 there were 2,333 slave men and 1,755 women between the ages of twenty-three and fifty-four, and by 1860 there were 2,852 men and 2,084 women within that age bracket.[18] A high birthrate among slave women offers additional evidence that there were many slave couples. Census materials indicate there were 368 slave children under the age of four for every 1,000 slave women between the ages of fifteen and forty-four in 1850. In New Orleans this figure was 271 children per 1,000 women. By 1860 Richmond's ratio increased to 393 per 1,000, while that of New Orleans remained static.[19] While high slave birthrates in Richmond do not prove the existence of many slave couples, it seems likely that the rates resulted at least in part from the relatively even numbers of adult men and women. (Other causes for the high birthrate also include the rape of black slave women by white slave owners).

Admittedly the presence of men and women of similar ages does not mean slave workers married. But evidence from church records, court documents, newspaper accounts, and slave owners' journals indicate that Richmond slaves frequently did join in matrimony. Parish registers from St. John's and St. James's churches indicate that clergymen often were called upon to perform slave marriages.[20] Slave Richmonders Edmund Watkins and Emily, for example, were joined together in 1857 by J. Peterkin, the officiating minister of St. James, as were a number of other couples.[21] Records from the First African Baptist Church show a good number of its slave congregants were married couples. In fact, much of the deacons' time was spent counseling married parishioners.[22]

Further evidence of slave marriages can be found in the legislative petitions that newly freed slaves filed to remain in the commonwealth. One of the most common reasons listed for wanting to stay in Virginia was family ties. Philip Robertson's petition filed in 1840 is a good example of these strong family bonds. In his plea to the court he explained that "he is connected by the strongest affection to a wife and children who are slaves, & that a separation from them would tear asunder some of the strongest ties which bind the human heart."[23] The existence of slave marriages is also evident in the records of the mayor's court. Of course, when a slave couple came "before His Honor," it was typically because relations were a bit rocky or even abusive. One married couple, Caroline and Henry, had to appear in court after the husband was arrested for beating his wife.[24]

Slaves married not only other slaves but free blacks. The potential for such relationships to develop was high because slave and free black residents lived in the same neighborhoods, frequently rented houses together or boarded with one another, and worked in the same factories. The opportunity for slave–free black households to develop was further enhanced by the growing discrepancy between the number of slave men and women. Even though Richmond's slave population was more evenly balanced in terms of sex than that of New Orleans or other cities, there were still many more men than women.[25] So it was not unusual for slave men and free black women to join together even though these relationships might be torn apart through sale or the loss of hiring privileges. Such risks did not deter slaves such as Henry Robertson, who found companionship with Caroline, a free black woman, during the year he was hired to a Richmond business. Nelly Hoomes, who was free, similarly threw caution to the wind when she married her slave husband Bartlett Hoomes and raised four children, in spite of the fact that Bartlett could not live with the family.[26] Such relationships grew stronger and more stable during the late antebellum years as an increasing number of free black residents became the legal owners of slave family members. In 1840 the personal property tax lists showed that only one free black Richmonder was able to purchase his family from an owner; but by 1850 there were thirteen free black slaveholders (nine men, four women) who purchased and retained ownership of their slave families so that they might stay together in Richmond, according to Virginia laws.[27]

Extended family networks also served to join the slave community as urban industrial labor demands occasionally brought siblings and other relatives from various counties and reunited them in the city. Minsey, a hired domestic slave, was able to rejoin her kinfolk when her uncle and aunt came to the city as hired household servants. Moreover, because of these family connections, Minsey's relatives were able to secure a position for her as a chambermaid in the same household.[28] A similar situation occurred for Michael Valentine when he was forced to move to Richmond with his owner. Although saddened to leave his wife behind, he was pleased to be reunited with his brothers and sisters, and their wives and husbands, whom he had not seen for years.[29]

Networks connecting city slave residents were further enhanced through social activities and business transactions played out within the tenements and alleyways, cookshops and marketplaces. Weekly gambling games played in the alleys continued to be an important social activity bringing together male slave residents. On Friday and Saturday nights, as many as a dozen bondmen came to a specified alleyway to play games such as faro for pennies and nickels.[30] Grogshops and cookshops hidden in the alleys or near the factories also served as forums for male community members to meet, talk, and develop friendships. One such location was Aaron Atkinson's snack house on Broad Street, a popular gathering place for slave and free black males until the police closed it for "selling ardent spirits."[31] Grocery stores owned by white and free black residents living in the area also became important social spots for local slaves. In these corner-store hangouts bondmen swapped stories, passed gossip, and played board games in their free time. During the 1850s a slave tobacco hand could always find conversation and a game of checkers at Barney Litman's grocery, for example. Going to the races became a popular group, if not community, activity. As the local newspaper pointed out, "Negroes from the city and county congregate in that vicinity [the Fairfield Course] every Sabbath to the number of one or two hundred, and spend the day in gaming and drinking."[32]

While alley gambling games and corner-store hangouts catered primarily to slave men, cookshops became a vital social institution for both sexes. There men and women met, discussed interests, debated issues, and voiced opinions without white supervision and outside the confines of church. Furthermore, cookshops served a particularly useful social and financial function for the slave women who ran them. While preparing and serving food, slave women (some of whom were domestic servants during other hours) were able to socialize, provide an important service to fellow slaves, strengthen neighborhood ties, and earn money.

Dinner parties and dances were important social events that brought slave men and women together and became an important part of courtship rituals. Generally these parties were small, informal gatherings (most likely to avoid detection by the night watchmen) in a slave's room or tenement, where neighbors would gather to sing and dance.[33] Other gatherings consisted of small dances in the evenings when single men and women, hoping to meet a potential marriage partner, would come together. Fields Cook met his wife, Mary, at one of these dances. In spite of the fact that there were eight to ten other comely women in the room,

Cook immediately spotted Mary because she had the "modesty of an angel," and "her winning coyness fire[d] my soul."[34] Some parties, however, were grandiose affairs that required planning and funds and brought together many community members. One such party was the grand "Subscription Ball" held in the basement of the Washington Hotel and attended by nearly one hundred slave and free black men and women "in full ball-room dress." Unfortunately, the party ended almost before it began; just as the dancing was about to start, a "posse of watchmen" entered the premises and began arresting the partygoers for meeting illegally. But if the ball failed to provide entertainment, the ensuing court trial certainly did, and it became a major community social event in itself. The next morning as the ninety or so arrested ballgoers were led to court, the streets filled with concerned friends, relatives, and curious neighbors. One newspaper account described the scene: "The trifling circumstances of removing from the cage a few blacks, accused of being in an unlawful assemblage the night before, called into the streets and around the Mayor's office, thousands of idle slaves who had been permitted to leave their homes, at a busy hour in the morning, merely to gratify their idle curiosity, and hundreds of them remained for hours, congregated around the City Hall."[35] With one exception, the partygoers were released because—much to the mayor's chagrin—they possessed passes from their owners and employers giving them permission to attend the ball.

Parties were not the only times the community came out. There were more solemn moments that drew them together as well. The regular baptismal services held in the James River to initiate new members of the African Baptist Church brought fellow congregants and friends to witness the rebirth and to give their blessings. This ritual was an extremely important event and was well attended, as this description suggests: "Within sight of the water, we beheld the banks covered with thousands of blacks of both sexes. . . . near the river [were the] numerous candidates for baptismal regeneration, clad in linen trousers and a shirt. They were led into the stream, and received by the officiating minister and his assistants, who . . . plunged them deep beneath the water. Before the immersion the assembled multitude sang at the top of their voices spirit-stirring hymns."[36]

The hundreds of black Richmonders who stood on the riverbanks came to show their support for the people emerging from the cool waters and to reaffirm the many ties that bound them together as family, lovers, coworkers, neighbors, and church members. While most of these bonds were formed without coercion, maintaining them under the system of slavery was never easy. Slave sales always threatened to tear apart friends and family. The unusual features of the urban slave system, however, allowed slave Richmonders to improve the odds that their relationships would remain intact. Through the development of alleyway housing, the rise of segregated residential enclaves, and the high demand for hired slave workers, urban industrialization and the unusual working and living conditions allowed slave residents to survive by enabling them to develop families, create crucial survival mechanisms (such as taking in children and boarding together), and form social institutions that provided camaraderie, entertainment, and ways to escape the pressures of slavery temporarily. All of these taken together played an important role in the formation of the city slave community.

Independence Won: The First African Baptist Church, 1841–60

Of all the organizations within the slave community, the independent black Baptist church was arguably the most important institution to emerge during the late antebellum era. Like segregated neighborhoods and social activities, the church was a unifying force, which provided emotional and financial support and offered opportunities for leadership and self-governance. But unlike the other institutions, such as the gambling games or cookshops, the church played a vital role in channeling the skills, experience, and knowledge of urban slaves into political and economic forms of resistance that helped them during slavery and after.

In fact, it was through the Baptist church that slave and free black residents jointly launched their first successful political and economic attack against white domination and control. During the 1840s black congregants vied for and won the right to establish a separate church. By pooling their financial resources, advancing their interpretation of the religious culture, and holding numerical superiority (2,000 blacks and 400 whites), black communicants pressured white church members into relinquishing control of the church facilities. After much negotiation (mediated by the Reverend Jeremiah Jeter) and generous contributions from prominent white Richmonders James Sizer, Archibald Thomas, and James Thomas Jr., the old church was purchased for $7,500, $4,500 of which was paid by black members themselves. Later, an additional $7,000 was raised by black congregants to pay off the debt.[37] By the winter of 1841 the First African Baptist Church was formally established.

The launching of the First African Baptist was a major event that had been twenty years in the making. As early as 1821 black Baptists had petitioned the local conferring association for a separate independent church. The Dover Association, however, rejected their petition, stating that "the formation of such a church [was] inexpedient." Undaunted, slave and free black congregants sent a second petition to the General Assembly in 1823 hoping that the state government would sanction such a move. That petition also was rejected.[38] Additional efforts made during the 1830s were thwarted by white residents disturbed by the implications of Nat Turner's Rebellion in 1831. Rampant fear that uncontrolled or unmonitored Christian teachings encouraged slaves to be rebellious led lawmakers to ban black preachers and to be generally unsympathetic to independent black institutions. The long history of this struggle made the creation of the First African Baptist Church enormously important to black Richmonders.

The modest "plain brick building" that housed the newly independent church did not look like a monument to black Baptists' efforts. But what went on inside the church certainly reflected their hard work. For the first time blacks had access to all areas of the church. No longer relegated to the galleries, black congregants quickly filled the 1,500 seats.[39] And they continued to do so as membership kept increasing; by 1842 the number of congregants had grown from 940 to 1,600, and between 1856 and 1859 membership exceeded 3,000.[40] More important, for the first time slave and free black congregants gained administrative control of their church and could elect their own deacons, committee members, and unofficial assistant preachers—subject to the pastor's approval, of course. There were, however, some significant limitations to their power. First, the pastor had to be white; Virginia law required that all-black assemblies be led by a white minister.[41] Second, a superintending committee from the parent, all-white First Baptist Church held authority over church affairs. The initial selection of the pastor and any changes made to the church's constitution, for example, were some of the committee's prerogatives. And if any major issue arose that could not be resolved by the congregation, the superintending committee could step in and make the final decision. It appears, however, that the committee generally allowed First African Baptist members to handle their own affairs, intervening only on rare occasions.

Of more immediate consequence to members of the new African Baptist Church was the new pastor, Robert Ryland. Although black congregants did get to vote on whether to accept the new minister, the candidate was selected by their old pastor, the Reverend Mr. Jeter. From the congregation's point of view, Ryland had been cut from the same cloth as Jeter. Like his predecessor, Ryland came across as "plain," "practical," and rational and did not care for theatrics or superstitions. In fact, one of his first tasks was an attempt to "correct the errors and to repress the extravagances into which his hearers were prone to run."[42] Also like Jeter, Ryland supported slavery. Both in his written work and spoken sermons, Ryland frequently directed slaves to "be obedient" to their owners, "with fear and trembling, in singleness of your heart, as unto Christ."[43]

Black congregants could expect no less. No preacher could retain a position in the South if he did not support slavery. Furthermore, black parishioners were used to hearing these kinds of messages and had learned long before simply to take what was meaningful to them and to reject the rest. What they did not expect, however, was the amount of latitude Ryland gave members in running the church. Even though Ryland had final say over church matters, the deacons held enormous power because he acted largely as a moderator. Church records suggest that Ryland rarely interfered with disciplinary actions and other similar decisions. In fact, he was known for frequently missing administrative meetings, allowing the deacons to act completely on their own.[44] Under these conditions the deacons along with the various committees assumed almost full responsibility for "all financial affairs, the admission and dismissal of members, social and charitable activities, and the regulation of the moral conduct of the members of the congregation."[45] The deacons became the de facto "permanent ruling power" in the church.[46]

Ryland's lenient administrative style allowed other members to take advantage of leadership opportunities as well. Individuals who felt the inclination to preach were given a chance to lead the congregation. Even though it was illegal for free blacks and slaves to preach—a response to Nat Turner's Rebellion—Ryland circumvented the law by allowing church members to "take the pulpit" and preside over funeral services. One way Ryland was able to evade the law was by inviting a member to open services with a prayer. The prayer, however, could be as involved as a sermon. This was certainly the case on the Sunday that Charles Weld came to visit. As Weld described: "The service was commenced by an extempore prayer from one of the congregation, uttered in a nasal tone. . . . As the negro proceeded, his eloquence and fervour increased, eliciting sympathy from the congregation, who accompanied every burst of enthusiasm by loud ejaculations and groans."[47]

It was opportunities like these that helped produce John Jasper, one of the most famous preachers of the nineteenth century and best known for his sermon "De Sun Do Move," which challenged the heliocentric view of the solar system. Jasper began his career as an assistant and as a funeral speaker in the church. From the 1840s until 1859—when Jasper left the city—he regularly preached at the First African Baptist Church in Richmond and at the Third African Baptist Church in Petersburg.[48]

Joseph Abrams also cut his teeth at the Richmond church and became so well known for his skills that at his funeral in 1854 some 8,000 mourners came to pay their respects. Deacon James Oliver regularly took the pulpit as well, though his appearances apparently did not please everyone; when Oliver rose to speak, fellow congregant Sophy Henderson would make loud "unkind remarks" and would "leave the house in a disorderly manner."[49]

The open environment of the church helped members assume leadership positions within the larger black (slave and free) community through the development of organizations that emphasized "collective self-improvement and mutual assistance."[50] Through these organizations congregants helped feed and clothe the poor, bury the dead, and raise funds to help slaves purchase their freedom. One such organization was the Poor Saints Fund (established in 1848) to assist the "needy, [and] helpless from disease or old age." The fund consisted of seventeen church trustees whose duties included collecting donations, visiting needy households, and attending to "all applications of aid."[51]

The assistance of the Poor Saints quickly proved too little to meet the needs of the black community, and soon a number of other mutual aid societies developed out of the church. Some of these groups were not so well known as the Poor Saints Fund because the members chose to keep their organizations and their identities a secret out of fear that the police would arrest them for illegally congregating. In fact, the scant amount of information that exists today emerged only after the Civil War. According to a recent study, one of these groups was The United Sons of Love, "a colored benevolent organization, whose principal features are to care for the sick, look after the poor and destitute, and bury their dead."[52]

This information is virtually all that is known about this and many other secret organizations during the antebellum era. Efforts to help needy people outside of the Richmond community, however, were better documented. According to treasury records, the church not only sent funds to the missionaries in Africa but also provided donations to groups such as the "suffering poor of Ireland."[53]

Other ways the First African Baptist Church helped the larger community included raising funds for a new separate all-black church. By the mid-1850s membership at the First African had reached such high numbers that a "colony" had to be sent out. In 1858 the "colony," aided by funds donated by the First Baptist Church, helped establish the Third African Baptist Church (later renamed the Ebenezer church).[54] By that year black Richmonders had three all-black independent churches to choose from: the First and the Second African Baptist (which was an offshoot of the integrated Second Baptist Church) and the Ebenezer.

Of all the committees and organizations that emerged in the First African Baptist Church, the most visibly powerful group was the deacons, thirty men "who constituted the ruling element of the Church."[55] Although there was some turnover among the deacons from retirements and deaths, many of the same names filled the roster throughout the late antebellum era, including Gilbert Hunt, Simon Bailey, Joseph Abrams, William Morris, John Kinney, Thomas Allen, and Richard Henderson. The overwhelming majority of the deacons were free blacks who possessed some wealth and property. A handful were "self-made men" such as Gilbert Hunt, who not only purchased his freedom but managed to open a blacksmithing shop and create a comfortable life for himself.[56]

Much of the deacons' power rested in their authority to discipline members for "disorderly" conduct and actions. While these duties had changed little during the transition from the First Baptist to the First African Baptist, there were no longer white deacons present to influence, or override, the black deacons' decisions. As in the past, deacons at the First African Baptist were concerned about adultery, fighting, lying, stealing, and gambling and attempted to deter such acts through swift and harsh punishments. John Bailor and Mary Johnson, for example, received no leniency when they were reported to have been fighting. At the next church meeting the deacons voted to exclude them from the church. Strabo Manning also was thrown out of church for having an affair with fellow congregant, Mrs. Morton. James Robinson met the same fate when several members caught sight of him dancing, which was considered a frivolous and immoral activity.[57]

While most problems were mundane and probably no different from those in white churches of the late antebellum era, black deacons also grappled with situations unique to the slave community. One such problem was remarriage. This was an extremely sensitive and painful issue because it exposed at once the cruelty of slavery and the moral limitations of the Baptist institution. The church and its leaders found slave remarriages to be problematic because often they did not meet its traditional prerequisites. Generally, the church allowed second marriages only if a person had lost a spouse, been abandoned by one, or had been granted a separation by the church. Slave couples, however, frequently were forced apart by slave sales, and many remarried when the prospects of reuniting with their partner grew dim. The deacons acknowledged the awkwardness of the situation yet even under these circumstances still demanded proof that a marriage had truly failed. As a result, church standards proved difficult for many slaves.

No doubt slave member Peter Kelly found the process of having his marriage sanctioned by the church a painful experience. The deacons had excluded Kelly because he married a woman whose first husband was still alive. Even after learning that Kelly's new wife had left her first husband six years earlier because of "the husband's mal-treatment of [her] and because he had gone off and married another wife," the deacons still questioned the validity of Kelly's marriage and only reluctantly sanctioned the vows. Slave congregant Archer Brown suffered an even more humiliating experience when he was excluded for "marrying a woman while his wife was living and for denying the fact."[58]

Although these punishments were harsh, it appears that slave and free black congregants did not view the church or the deacons as unreasonable or unfair. In fact, black residents came to view the church as a place where they could resolve disputes in a fashion deemed equitable and generally satisfactory to all parties involved. In such matters the church acted as a form of a community court for members to air both personal and financial disputes. When Gilbert Hunt and Thomas Griffin began fighting over an unpaid debt, both asked the church to step in. And when Richard Quarles felt he had been treated in a "discourteous" manner by a fellow congregant, Quarles sought redress through the church.

Records suggest that many free black congregants preferred to have their difficulties settled by the church because it was less costly, less time-consuming, and more sympathetic than the white-controlled Hustings Court system. Slaves preferred the church "court" because it was the only place they could seek justice without the assistance of their owner or employer. Although the mayor frequently heard cases involving slaves, generally it was the owner and employer of the slaves involved who brought the cases to court in hopes of receiving payment for damages done to their chattel. None of these cases, however, addressed the anger and humiliation that slave and free black defendants felt and the justice they sought. This certainly was one of the factors that motivated Betsy Holmes, a slave woman, to plead her case in church. Holmes reported that she chose the church "court" because she could speak for herself and fear no retribution in arguing that she had been unjustly accused of provoking a fight with a fellow slave.[59]

The community court, like the mutual aid organizations and the preaching opportunities, presented a radical challenge to white domination and control by allowing slave and free blacks to—among other things—govern themselves and to "take care of their own." In such capacities the church went far in politicizing black congregants by encouraging them to seek justice and equality. Not only did the church inspire, it also served as a forum for black residents to address issues of power, such as equal voting power and favoritism in elections, and to sharpen their political teeth. Little did Ryland and the deacons know that the church would become the focus of the earliest political battles among black parishioners.

In 1848, after six years of what seemed to be fairly routine business, Deacons Kinney, Morris, Henderson, and the others received a surprising letter from the congregation. It was a petition signed by thirty slave and free males demanding that they "change the Constitution of the church so as to allow all male members to vote."[60] While the deacons may not have seen this issue coming, these thirty (and possibly more) laymen believed it was long overdue. They noted that in spite of the overwhelming number of slave church members and these members' large financial contributions to the purchase of the church and the pastor's salary, slave (and many free black) congregants lacked equal rights within the church. Few, if any, deacons or committee members were slaves. Furthermore, church records indicate these key positions were awarded to free black males through elections in which only a portion of the free black male congregation could vote. In other words, all slave men, a portion of free black male members, and all black women were disenfranchised. Apparently the petition caught the deacons and pastor off guard. Lacking a proper response, they simply chose to ignore the demands of these men.

Two years later, however, the issue resurfaced. In May 1850 James Allison, Charles Feggins, and Stephen Brown, presumably slave men, sent a letter of complaint to the deacons decrying the "partiality to *free* persons in the administration of church affairs."[61] This time the letter was not ignored, and the deacons responded swiftly—by excluding all three men. The deacons' response stunned church members. Even the Reverend Mr. Ryland, who generally supported the deacons' decisions, suggested that their actions were too harsh and recommended that all three be restored as soon as possible. The deacons thought it over and consented to restore Allison, Feggins, and Brown but only if the men would agree that "the church had acted from a sense of duty in excluding them." In other words, the excluded members could return only if they agreed that the church's action had been correct. Brown agreed and was immediately restored. Allison and Feggins, however, steadfastly refused.[62]

The battle between the deacons and Allison and Feggins could not help but affect the congregation as tempers flared and members quickly took sides. Seeing how the issue had factionalized the church, the deacons and Ryland quickly sought to regain "harmony and fellowship" among the members by rewording their offer of restoration. Ryland explained "that he did not mean to require them [Allison and Feggins] to *justify* the act of exclusion, but only to acquit the church of *improper motives* in their late proceedings."[63] Allison and Feggins remained unmoved and still refused to return to the church.

The controversy festered for seven more months until November 1850, when the superintending committee from the all-white First Baptist Church, Ryland, the deacons from the First African Baptist Church, and "a large number of private members" met to resolve the issue. The proceedings were surprisingly calm and generally unemotional given how bitter the earlier battle had been. Once again Allison and Feggins were asked if they could "*fellowship* the deacons," while the deacons were asked if they could restore the two men. Both groups answered yes, and the two men returned to the fold.

While Brown, Allison, Feggins, and the thirty men who preceded them failed to alter the constitution or change voting policies, their actions did sow the seeds for future political battles by reminding constituents that the Baptist church was based on a liturgy of egalitarianism, that it was an institution of the congregation, and that its ruling hierarchy was created by the parishioners and not by an outside body. Because the deacons and committee members were elected, they were not above reproach from the congregation. It was this last point on which the next major political challenge pivoted.

Almost two years after Allison and Feggins returned, a new conflict arose that captured the attention of nearly all congregants. This conflict, however, concerned the deacons' power to regulate and discipline members and serve as mediators in the church "court." Suspecting that the power vested in the deacons gave them too much latitude, parishioners demanded and won the right to reprimand and remove any deacon for improper behavior. While no specific case seems to have prompted this change in policy, the battles that emerged thereafter suggest that the congregation had grown tired of the deacons' behavior and was in no mood to tolerate it. One of the earliest cases began in the spring of 1852 when Deacon Wilson Morris was brought up on charges of impropriety toward other church members.

Deacon Morris was accused of yelling, cursing, and directing "indecorous and abusive language towards two of his brother deacons" during a chance meeting on the street. The incident deeply bothered many of the church members, some of whom approached Morris and "presented to him a respectful request to resign."[64] Morris took no note of the letter and refused to leave office. The members who approached him, however, felt the matter needed to be addressed.

One month later, 336 church members signed a petition invoking their right to remove a deacon and demanded that Morris leave immediately. Morris still refused to resign, claiming that his actions were merely the "faithful discharge of official duties."[65] His position was backed by an opposition faction, which submitted a counterpetition signed by 255 of Morris's supporters. At this point the issue was referred to the deacons for a decision. A vote was taken, and fourteen deacons were opposed to Morris resigning, while ten were in favor and two abstained. Believing the issue to have been resolved, Ryland announced the vote and recommended that Morris remain and the matter be dropped. But Morris's opponents refused to drop the issue and went to the superintending committee of the First Baptist Church.

The following month the committee held a private meeting to discuss the case. No one was to learn of their decision until July 16, 1852. After church services that day, the committee announced that Wilson Morris had already resigned from his position, "at the suggestion of the committee." Although the committee members had written a report of their discussion, they refused to read it in public so as not to offend "the feelings of Wilson Morris." Their only comment was that "no officer ought ever to retain his place to the dissatisfaction of a respectable minority."[66] The congregation took the decision quite well; Morris's supporters did not demand his return or to know more about the committee's decision. The deacons, however, took the challenge as an affront to their power, and the next month Deacons Oliver, Kinney, Allen, Spriggs, and Price resigned in protest. If the deacons had hoped their resignations would scare parishioners into restoring Morris, their plan backfired. At the next church elections, they were simply replaced.

For white parishioners and churches, such political battles may have seemed mundane squabbles. But for black Baptists every controversy and decision-making process held tremendous significance. While many of the debates became powerful and emotional battles that occasionally threatened to divide the congregation forever, ultimately they served to help members work together and hone their negotiating skills. The incidents also provided opportunities for slave and free black members to participate in shaping and improving their institution. This process of shaping the church was critical in helping it meet the religious and secular needs of the black community, which had been ignored by the larger dominant society. Some of these needs included a theological interpretation that would "fit [the] peculiar experience of enslavement in America";[67] an institution that allowed members to look to God for spiritual guidance and to themselves for support to uphold those beliefs; and a physical and psychological space within which congregants could release emotions, express opinions, seek justice, advocate equality, be judged by peers, and better themselves—by themselves. The First African Baptist Church accomplished all these things and more.

"REARING WOLVES TO OUR OWN DESTRUCTION"

Although many Richmond residents felt confident about the future of industrial slavery, by the late antebellum era there was a growing sense among slave owners, employers, and other elites that the slave system was unstable and needed strengthening. Not only did they believe that acts of slave resistance against persons and property were increasing, but that slave workers had become more defiant. One slave owner claimed urban slaves had become more rebellious than their rural counterparts and recommended that they "be broken in like dogs and horses, in order to establish a power over them, and keep them in subjection."[68] A group of tobacconists seconded this belief, stating that there existed "a growing spirit of insubordination amongst the negroes of the city."[69] As proof, white residents pointed to incidents of violence committed by slave men and women against slave owners and employers—most notably the cases involving Jordan Hatcher and Jane and John Williams.

The first of these incidents began on a cold February morning at the tobacco factory of Walker and Harris, when seventeen-year-old slave stemmer Jordan Hatcher got into a scuffle with his white manager, nineteen-year-old William P. Jackson. The fight began when Jackson, who was displeased with Hatcher's work, began to beat him. After the first few blows, Hatcher caught hold of the whip to stop Jackson from hitting him. Jackson then ordered Hatcher to walk over to an open space on the floor near the stove. Hatcher complied, and when he came to the stove, Jackson resumed the beating. In response Hatcher picked up an iron poker that was lying nearby and struck the manager on the head, knocking him unconscious. Frightened, Hatcher immediately fled the manufactory.[70] When Jackson came to, it seemed that he had suffered only minor injuries from the blow, but the next day he unexpectedly collapsed and died. An autopsy was performed, and the results confirmed that Jackson's death was caused by the blow he had received the day before. The mayor immediately dispatched city watchmen to locate and arrest Hatcher. Eventually Hatcher was found and brought to trial. A month later, in March 1852, the court found Hatcher guilty of murder and sentenced him to be hanged.[71]

Not more than four months had passed after Hatcher's trial when new shock waves coursed through the white community following a second, equally dramatic incident: the murders of slave owner Virginia Winston and her child, allegedly at the hands of their slave servants, John and Jane Williams. According to court records, early Monday morning on July 19 the Williamses crept into the Winstons' private chambers, where Joseph and Virginia and their nine-month-old child slept in the same bed. The Williamses then began to strike all three repeatedly with a hatchet. Mrs. Winston and the child died, but Mr. Winston survived with severe cuts and gashes to his head.

The city sergeant and watchmen, who were among the first to arrive, immediately began inspecting the house and all the rooms. They also began questioning the four slave servants who lived on the lot: Joe and Nelly Scott and Jane and John Williams. During their investigation of the house, the city police discovered a hatchet with traces of blood in a bucket of dirty water, some hair and mucous membrane floating in the water, and a frock with spots of blood on the upper right-hand sleeve and on the bodice in Jane and John Williamses' sleeping quarters. On the basis of this evidence, the city watch arrested the Williamses on suspicion of murder.[72] In the following months the couple went to trial, and the Hustings Court found them guilty and sentenced them to die on the gallows.[73]

Of the two cases, the Jordan Hatcher incident evoked a more visible public response even though it was the less gruesome of the murders. This is largely because Hatcher's case did not end the way white residents expected: he did not hang. Twenty-four hours before Hatcher was to be executed, Governor Joseph Johnson delayed the hanging, and he later reduced the sentence to "sale and transportation beyond the limits of the U[nited] States" on May 6.[74] Johnson's action was not without precedent or prompting. Previous governors often had reduced slave sentences to sale and transportation. Only twenty-eight slave Virginians had been executed between 1804 and 1865, but 377 slave Virginians had been sold and transported from the state between 1816 and 1842, so Johnson probably did not think twice.[75] Furthermore, immediately following the trial, Johnson had received a petition urging him to grant Hatcher clemency because Jackson's death was neither premeditated nor desired. As historian Harrison M. Ethridge surmises, "Governor Johnson must have been impressed" by this petition which was endorsed by some of the most prominent residents in the city. Among the sixty signers were Joseph Anderson of Tredegar Iron Works, William H. Macfarland, president of the Richmond and Petersburg Railroad, and a number of lawyers and clergymen. Although Johnson also received a petition from a group of tobacconists demanding Hatcher's death, as an example to "all such offenders," clearly he was unmoved.[76]

Public response to Hatcher's reduced sentence was immediate and sharp. An angry crowd assembled outside of City Hall, and later Governor Johnson's mansion, to protest the lighter punishment. Participants in this "Indignation Meeting" accused the governor of "abat[ing] the trust confided to him by the Constitutions" by giving slaves "encouragement to insubordination and crime" and of secretly being a New York abolitionist, which he was not. The atmosphere in Richmond became so tense that the General Assembly briefly considered moving its meetings out of the city until the furor died down.[77] Eventually the commotion diminished, but only after Governor Johnson defended his actions in two separate speeches, was investigated by the Committee for Courts of Justice, and was maligned by both fellow Democrat and Whig opponents. Still, Hatcher was not executed, and on June 16 he and sixteen other slaves were purchased by Garland P. Ware and transported out of the United States.[78]

Public outcry against Johnson's decision reveals the deep fear that white residents had about slave resistance. What made white Richmonders particularly uncomfortable was the sense that urban industrial working and living conditions had helped produce Jordan Hatcher and the Williamses. All three were urban slaves who enjoyed a variety of privileges including hiring out, living apart, socializing without supervision, and cash bonuses. White Richmonders believed these privileges encouraged the slaves to be rebellious. Hatcher had been a hired tobacco hand who lived apart from both owner and employer. Although his employment may have been negotiated by Pamela Godsey, his owner, she had little knowledge of his comings and goings and little control over his activities because she lived in Chesterfield County.

John Williams shared some of the same working and living conditions as Hatcher. Although John belonged to the Winston household, he worked at the docks for John Enders during the day. Like most hired slave workers, John could move about the city before and after working hours with no supervision. He also probably received cash from his earnings and could earn extra by performing overtime work. John was not required to live in the Winstons' house but chose to in order to be with his wife. Jane, on the other hand, was directly owned by the Winstons and most likely did not enjoy the same privileges as her husband. But she was able to move about in the city making trips to the market, did socialize with other slaves and possibly free blacks, and was well aware of the privileges and expectations of hired slaves including her husband.

White residents came to believe that these factors encouraged slaves to act violently by planting within them "the germ of rebellion." One influential Richmonder, Joseph Mayo (who later became mayor), attributed the "glaring evils" of the slave population to "the system of board money . . . [and] the assumptions of equality exhibited by the blacks in riding in carriages contrary to law, and in dress and deportment." Increasingly, white city dwellers began to wonder if they had been—in the words of one resident—"rearing wolves to our own destruction."[79]

Elite Richmonders, however, were not sure which aspect of urban industrial slavery enabled slaves to resist and therefore called for different solutions. Some residents believed slave discipline to be too lax and asked for stricter laws, a larger police force, and the arming of officers with revolvers. Another group called for limiting the number of slave passes to prevent slaves from "going at large."[80] One person, seeing how bond men and women had "become corrupted by the vices of the city . . . [and by] associating indiscriminately with each other and the refuse of the white population," wondered if slaves should even remain in the city.[81]

Slaves workers were not sent out of Richmond, but immediately after the events of 1852 and during the next five years, they were bombarded by new restrictions including some that eliminated long-standing privileges. In addition to bans on smoking, carrying canes (symbols of wealth), and preaching in public, slaves could no longer drive or ride in carriages without their owners' consent, visit with free black friends for longer than several hours (this also eliminated living with free blacks), hire themselves out, or remain outdoors after eleven at night.

Slave homes and neighborhoods came under attack as well. Mayor Joseph Mayo (who held office from 1853 to the end of the Civil War) called on city property owners to close off or pave their alleyways to reduce the number of slave tenements and to end "all intercourse between slaves and free negroes." The mayor believed this step would affect slave activities by "stopping board money, cook shops and eating houses—the hiring of slaves by free negroes (a great evil) and the practice which prevails so extensively of standing masters for slaves."[82]

The capstone to these new restrictions, however, was the elimination of the unsupervised board system (living apart) in 1857. Slaves could still live apart from owner and employer but could no longer choose the location. Instead, owners were required to arrange room and board for slaves—as a way to keep tabs on their activities—a change that, in theory, would severely limit slave mobility.

For all the fears of Richmond's elite, there is no concrete evidence that the number of crimes committed by slaves increased during the late antebellum era. The high number of slave arrests for "going at large" in 1852, for example, could reflect the fervency with which the Richmond police executed the law rather than how frequently slaves violated it. Conversely, the significant drop in arrests for the same crime by 1854 might indicate the futility of enforcing this law, rather than a decline in the number of slaves "going at large." In addition, the assistance many slaves received from certain white Richmonders in evading the new regulations raised doubts about exactly who was challenging the law.[83]

As in the past, owners, employers, and shopkeepers continued to encourage and help slaves to break the law when it conflicted with personal and economic interests. Few free Richmonders were willing to give up practices that saved them money or encouraged slaves to work hard. The 1852 ban on "going at large" did little to change the behavior of slaves Alexander, Council, and Colin Scott or their owners. In fact, much to the horror of the city council and local newspaper, Alexander—who was among the first to be arrested under the newly enforced laws—had been "working at almost any place he chose for the last six months."[84]

Alexander was hardly an exception. Throughout the 1850s court records were filled with similar cases of slaves illegally hiring themselves out and living apart. One city resident told the newspaper there was so much widespread disregard for the laws restricting slave activities, it was not surprising that bond workers could escape from the city with ease. Urban slaves, he explained, "are enabled to effect their plans of escape more easily [by] being permitted to act as their own masters, and until the owners and hirers of slaves determine to comply with the law in relation to 'going at large,' they need never hope to put an end to their continual escapes."[85]

Although most owners and employers helped their slaves evade the law simply by ignoring the new legislation, a few such as owner Isaac Goddin aggressively fought the law. In response to charges brought against his slaves by officer Daniel Boze, Goddin lodged a complaint against the officer for harassing and threatening his bondmen. According to court records, Boze had been walking his beat one night when he spotted several slaves "cutting up shines in the street." Boze chased the men, but they ran onto Goddin's property and hid. The officer then knocked at the door and awoke Goddin, to inform him of his servants' activities, and then threatened to shoot the bondmen the next time he caught them. Rather than agreeing to discipline his slaves, Goddin reported Boze to the city council and demanded Mayor Mayo reprimand the officer for harassment.[86]

Slave owner J. S. Tinsley also challenged the law when his slave Albert Anderson was charged with "severely assaulting a free negress named Ellen Rebecca Ellett." Finding the defendant guilty, the court sentenced Anderson to receive twenty-five lashes. Tinsley, however, appealed this decision and hired four lawyers to defend his slave. The attorneys cross-examined witnesses and gave lengthy speeches until the mayor, exhausted and outgunned, rescinded Anderson's punishment.[87]

Newspaper accounts suggest that grocers and other small shopkeepers likewise showed little respect for the laws, even if it meant stiffer penalties. Henry Mangle, a grocer with a store on Brooke Avenue, ignored the ban on slave loitering rather than jeopardize sales to these customers. Willie Ann Smith, a free black woman, continued to run her "house of ill fame" and to sell liquor and food to free black and slave patrons because it was her only means of sustenance. Shopkeeper M. Francis broke several laws by continuing to sell cakes and liquor to slave and free black customers, even on Sundays.[88]

Since Richmonders, black and white, frequently ignored the new regulations, and city officials experienced great difficulty enforcing the law, there are not enough data to prove that slaves were committing acts of resistance at a higher rate. But an examination of the kind of acts committed suggests that tobacconists and other nervous white Richmonders were not entirely mistaken. It seems that a "spirit of insubordination"— or more accurately, a spirit of equality—did exist and became stronger and bolder over time. Incidents of domestic slaves boldly defying their employers and of slaves demanding their freedom were becoming more common. White residents were correct in their belief that urban industrial working and living conditions negatively affected the slave system. The board system, self-hiring privileges, cash bonuses, and crowded marketplaces did help slaves resist and rebel. Slave workers were able to slip away and meet with friends, drink, and trade fenced goods while ostensibly running errands for their owners and employers. But what white Richmonders did not realize was that city conditions helped slaves to challenge slavery in ways more damaging than drinking and gambling. Each successful challenge slaves launched against owners, employers, and authorities became the foundation for larger and more politicized forms of resistance. The cash that slave workers earned through the hiring and bonus systems, for example, frequently was used to fund institutions that emphasized self-reliance and confidence and to underwrite underground organizations that helped slaves escape. Local authorities saw the act of earning cash or trading goods for money as a threat but did not see that the way those funds were spent could present a much greater danger. Even if authorities had fully recognized how city conditions and privileges were undermining the slave institution, there was little they could have done; the very success of the industries and businesses based on slave labor depended on the unusual living and working conditions of urban slavery. In short, to end the "spirit of insubordination" would have meant destroying the urban slave system as it had developed in Richmond.

Nearly every aspect of the urban and industrial slave system encouraged or enabled slave workers to resist. Negotiating and terminating contracts and choosing an employer no doubt helped slave workers see the value of their work and develop a sense of self-confidence and self-worth. Slaves' emerging sense of their own value was most apparent in the workplace demands they began to make. During the late antebellum era, slaves began to view their privileges as "rights." Despite their legal status as property and the fact that they could be sold outside Richmond at any time, an increasing number of slave workers came to expect to choose their own jobs, have free time outside work, receive cash payments, socialize with whomever they chose, and take on extra work. These workers exercised their "rights" in defiance of laws at times and were prepared to defend them, even if it meant using violence.

One such slave was a hired domestic named Minsey. As was customary, she had permission to find a new job when her contract was finished at the end of the year. Minsey, however, chose to quit her job before then, at a time most inconvenient to her employer—in the middle of the Christmas party. During the festivities Minsey entered the parlor and announced to the household mistress and guests that she would no longer be serving them because she had found another position in a different home. Before her employer could say a word, Minsey turned and left.[89]

Fanny, another hired slave domestic, held similarly strong views about privileges and flew into a rage when her employer, Emanuel Seaman, did not provide them. According to court records Seaman revoked Fanny's ability to have visitors in her quarters—a practice considered a right by most urban slaves. In response, Fanny allegedly burned down Seaman's house.[90]

Slave John Williams felt his "rights" were being violated when his owner, Joseph Winston, began demanding work from him even though he had been hired to John Enders for the year. Williams was angry at having to use his own time to perform unpaid extra work, including polishing Winston's boots every day. Williams apparently found the situation intolerable and was moved to comment, in what was described as a threatening manner, "that he should put a stop to it—he could and would do it."[91]

Slave resistance also was fostered by the practice of living apart. The physical and psychological distance between slave and owner or employer allowed slaves not only to develop a semi-independent community but to acquire skills such as the ability to read and write. After working hours alleyway tenements became underground schools, among other things. It was in these hidden slave quarters that slave men and women sharpened their minds, raised their expectations, and gained greater self-confidence. In one impromptu tenement school, John Jasper freed his soul and mind by learning to read the Bible with guidance from fellow slave William Jackson.[92] Such a school also may have been where Beverly, a hired carriage driver, learned to "read Shakespeare."[93] And there is evidence that lessons occurred nightly in hundreds of slaves' rooms. One Richmonder proclaimed that literacy was so widespread among slave residents that "many of the whites have been taught to read by negro nurses."[94] The best evidence of these skills, however, can be found in the petition written by black Richmonders to President Andrew Johnson in 1865 in protest of poor postwar conditions. To prove that they were worthy of receiving equal rights and were as capable as white men, the petitioners stated that in spite of "the law of slavery [which] severely punished those who taught us to read and write . . . 3,000 of us can read, and at least 2,000 can read and write."[95]

In addition to literacy, urban slave living conditions helped bond men and women challenge slavery by encouraging—if not forcing—them to become "self-sufficient." Although few slaves, rural or urban, were ever fully dependent on their owners for their subsistence, Richmond conditions frequently required slave men and women to develop the skills to secure shelter, food, and clothing on their own. In order to manage their households successfully on the small cash payments they received, slave men and women had to plan carefully, conserve funds, pool earnings, and exercise great resourcefulness.

Such household management skills became more widespread as larger numbers of hired slaves settled in the city, and as more owners came to expect slaves to fend for themselves. This was particularly true in the cases where the owner was absent. Edward and James, two hired slaves in Richmond, had no one but themselves to depend on because both their owner and their appointed administrator paid little attention to them. The degree to which they were on their own is made clear in a letter from the administrator, Philip Lightfoot, to the slave traders: "Lieutenant Robert G. Robert of the United States Navy, left the country on a cruise to the Pacific Ocean, I [Philip Lightfoot] have been his agent here and have intended during the last 12 months, to address you concerning the amount due for the hires of his negro boys, Edward & James."[96]

It seems Robert had little idea what had happened to his slaves during his travels abroad, and Lightfoot was no more informed. William Fontaine of King William County similarly had little contact with his slave Aggy and did not seem bothered by this fact when he wrote, "I wished . . . to inform the person who hired Aggy, to keep her thro: the Christmas." S. L. Jones witnessed an even more distant relationship between a hired slave and owner during his visit to Richmond. According to his

journal the hired slave he met kept no contact with his owner except at
Christmas time when he "paid his hiring money, g[ave] an account of
his travels and successes, [and said] how well he was doing." Since contact between the two was so limited, all living necessities had to be handled by the hired slave himself.[97]

Even critical responsibilities of ownership such as health care frequently were administered by persons other than the owners. When employers did not provide medical services (and sometimes even when they
did), slaves often resorted to their own home remedies or consulted with
physicians within the community.[98] During the 1849 cholera epidemic,
city-appointed doctors, not owners, visited tenements to care for hired
slaves struck by the disease.[99] The ever-more-distant relationship between
slave and owner was further demonstrated in the aftermath of another
cholera epidemic in 1854. Information on the number of slave deaths
in the city—as published in the newspapers—came not from the owners
but from the slave traders. It appears that increasingly, owners' traditional responsibilities for their slaves were either unmet or assumed by
other groups, including slaves themselves.

Another aspect of urban slave life that had a tremendous impact on
slave resistance was the income earned through the cash payment and
bonus systems. On the simplest level the cash gave slave workers a
degree of autonomy as consumers. Slave workers spent their money on
essential material goods or small luxuries and generally were not re-
stricted in their purchases except by the size of their earnings. As the
number of bond men and women with cash reached the thousands,
however, slave workers came to realize the tremendous potential power
their collective earnings held. Evidence of this power came to light with
the purchase of the First African Baptist Church and the opening of the
Second African Baptist and Ebenezer churches, which gave black Richmonders an enormous amount of control over their religion and their
institutions.

The cash earned through the urban slave system had another liberating effect: it enabled a few slave men and women to buy themselves
or collectively purchase someone else out of bondage. Although such
purchases required a formidable sum, a number of Richmond slaves
were able to raise it. And slave savings became more important during
the late antebellum era as a greater number of city owners began man-
umitting slaves in exchange for money.[100] Between 1830 and 1860, 225
slaves were able to pay for their freedom. That compares with just 27
self-purchases during the previous thirty-year period.[101] The cost of freedom was rarely low; Burrell Mann had to pay $500 for his freedom, while
Walter and Mary Brown handed over $900 to their owner. During the

Civil War inflation drove the costs even higher. In 1864 Robert Hucles paid more than $10,000 to free his wife and four children.[102]

The high cost of self-purchase often proved beyond the means of an individual. So family members, kin networks, coworkers, and neighbors often pooled their savings to purchase a member out of bondage. One source of assistance was the First African Baptist Church. Members occasionally donated funds to help purchase fellow slave congregants, especially those who intended to become missionaries or clergymen.[103] Brother Thomas Allen was one of the fortunate souls whom the church purchased out of bondage. Although he did not become a missionary to Africa as he originally intended, he did go on to become the pastor of a church in Boston.[104]

Some of the cash within the slave community went toward helping an even larger number of slaves liberate themselves by funding a variety of secret escape networks and organizations. Through these underground organizations slaves received assistance that frequently included disguises, transportation, and personal guides. The existence of these organizations became known when local authorities discovered some of them. The arrest of the "Norfolk Nine" by police in 1858, for example, exposed an escape network that extended from Norfolk to Richmond and included (among the nine organizers) three white ship captains. Further investigation revealed that two of the ship pilots, Captains Bayliss and Lee, had received payments in return for hiding slave runaways in the false bottoms of their schooners and then sailing northward.[105]

Another unsuccessful escape recorded in the Hustings Court papers suggests the existence of an elaborately organized and well-funded underground organization based in Richmond. This organization came to light when Abbey Ann Dixon, a free black woman, was arrested for encouraging the escape of Martha, a slave owned by John Enders. According to Martha's testimony, Dixon had told her that "if she wanted to go away, she . . . would make arrangements for her." On the appointed night, while Martha waited for her contact to arrive, Dixon and an unidentified man walked past her, presumably to make sure she was alone. A few minutes later a second man, a free black named Robert, approached her and led her to a street corner where a third man, who was white, was waiting. Martha followed the third man to Mayo's Bridge where they were suddenly arrested by a watchman. Apparently they had been betrayed by the ship captain hired to take Martha away.

The amount of planning and funds and the number of people involved in this escape suggest a large, if imperfect, network. Every detail of the escape had been painstakingly arranged by Dixon and her accomplices. Martha had received money, a disguise (she was dressed as a boy), and the promise of transportation out of Virginia. The only flaw was a poor choice of sea captain. The details of such escapes suggest that great organizational capabilities and substantial funds existed within the slave and free black communities.[106]

Access to education and money, the development of certain self-improvement skills, and increased awareness of their own worth undoubtedly helped infuse slave workers with defiance, determination, and a "spirit of insubordination." This spirit can be seen in the way "finely dressed" slave and free black women occasionally "elbowed" white residents off the sidewalks, and in the way Henry, a slave hand, proudly smoked a cigar and carried a cane in the street.[107] It was this same spirit that prompted black church members to leave abruptly in the middle of a lecture on temperance and abstinence being given by a white judge.[108] And it was this spirit that gave John Scott and his twenty-two coworkers the courage to protest their enslavement publicly in 1853. During that year Scott and the other slaves, belonging to the recently deceased John Enders, filed into the mayor's office and demanded "to ascertain from the records whether or not they had been emancipated by the will of their late master." Apparently Enders had informed his slaves that he intended to emancipate them when he died. After waiting two years for a response, Scott raised the issue with "white gentlemen of the city," and Enders's son, who had inherited the slaves. Scott said the group had "done every thing in our power to get our rights according to the Will of old Master." Scott described an attempt to find legal help that produced lawyers who "deceived us and got our money" by producing wills that "seem to contridicts the other."[109] Scott wrote to the Colonization Society asking for assistance and indicated that all of the bondmen and their families would gladly move to Liberia should they be freed. But Scott never received a response from the society, and the twenty-three bondmen remained in slavery.

No law short of sending all slave residents out of the city could have prevented John Scott, Henry, or Minsey from making their challenges. And there is little reason to believe that any law could have prevented Jordan Hatcher or the Williamses from responding as they did. The city's expanding economy and efforts to adapt slavery to new working and living conditions practically ensured an environment hostile to a tightly restrictive slave system. More important, however, urban industrial conditions allowed a growing web of slave resistance as complex and well organized as the system of slavery itself.

Although the use of slaves in Richmond's industries and businesses helped create one of the most lucrative slave labor systems, it was one filled with problems and tensions. Money-saving tactics such as hiring

out and living apart threatened to replace the paternalistic bond between slave and master with one based only on market relations. Cash
payments and other financial incentives used to increase production
raised expectations among factory slaves and helped them see the value
of their labor. In fact, nearly all efforts to increase profits and maximize
production served to strengthen slave resistance. Taking advantage of
urban industrial conditions, bond men and women were able to gain a
degree of control over their labor and free time, transform privileges
into "rights," sharpen bargaining skills, and accumulate funds for goods
or self-purchase. Furthermore, slave resistance both strengthened and
drew strength from a strong community that helped educate and politi-
cize residents and aided their efforts to become self-reliant and self-
sufficient. Through strong kinship networks, segregated neighborhoods,
separate churches, and secret fraternal and financial societies, slave
residents maintained their own values, beliefs, and ideas and to some
degree defied efforts by owners, employers, and local authorities to control their lives. The successful struggle for a separate Baptist church
demonstrated slaves' determination to escape white authority. Once established, the African Baptist Church became a vehicle for slave defiance
by giving emotional and financial support to members and by becoming
the judicial center of the community. In the church "court," legally
silenced groups had a voice and were recognized as equal citizens.

Still, urban industrial conditions, lax discipline, and strong slave resistance did not amount to a step toward freedom, nor was the line
between slavery and freedom ever blurred. Though the conditions of
city slave life differed greatly from those in the countryside, the oppression of slavery was always present; no urban industrial slave was shielded
from the threat of being separated from his or her family, sold farther
south, or beaten by an owner. But urban industrial working and living
conditions did allow the Richmond slave community to severely test the
boundaries of its bondage.

Six

The War Years, 1861–1865

DURING THE SPRING of 1861, Richmond underwent a series of rapid, sweeping changes that dramatically and irreversibly affected the character of the city, its society, and its slave system. During the early months of the new year, Richmond dissolved its bonds with the Union, established an alliance with the Confederate States of America, and became the capital of the newly established Confederate government. While some ardent secessionists—such as John Moncure Daniel, the editor of the *Richmond Examiner*—had long anticipated these events, most Richmonders were taken aback as the changes engulfed them during a breathtaking two-month span. Just before the firing on Fort Sumter on April 12, Richmond was largely a pro-Union city with only a few vocal residents calling for secession.[1] Even after the inauguration of Lincoln—which seemed to cast a dark shadow over the city—and the secession of South Carolina, members of Richmond's ruling elite continued to call for sensible thinking and less impulsive action. Virginia's Governor John Letcher, a strong Unionist, exemplified this wait and see attitude through his many efforts to calm city and state residents. In several instances Letcher encouraged Richmonders to spend a day fasting and praying, hoping that the absence of rich foods and ardent spirits, combined with pious thoughts, might diminish the emotional furor. The governor, along with the state convention's moderate majority, endorsed a Washington "Peace Conference" between federal and Virginia state delegates, hoping for an eleventh-hour sectional compromise.[2] Letcher's efforts proved futile, however, as the events of Fort Sumter unfolded. When news of the incident reached the city, white Richmonders took to the streets claiming the surrender of the fort by Federal troops as the first Southern victory. Thousands of people filled the streets and gathered at the Capitol to hear speeches by local politicians on the significance of this victory. To celebrate, a few hardy Richmonders climbed to the top of the Capitol, tore down the United States stripes and raised the Confederate flag. Although Virginia was still officially a part of the Union, the crowds that cheered the new flag seemed to believe otherwise. It appeared only Letcher remembered that the state had not yet seceded; he quietly had the flag removed and the Virginia state colors placed in its stead.[3]

Letcher's action did little to dampen the pro-secessionist spirit as Richmonders continued to mill through the streets as if the entire city were an open-air market. Confederate flags acted like beacons calling forth crowds for more speeches and discussion over the next few days. One local raised the flag in front of his home on Church Hill and immediately a horde assembled at his doorstep eager for more talk.[4]

Within five days talk became action. On April 17 the Virginia State Convention, which had been in session for two months, quickly became the Virginia Secession Convention and voted 88 to 55 to dissolve the state's ties to the Union.[5] Virginia voters, however, were to be the ultimate arbiters of the state's future. On May 17 voters were to decide by referendum whether the state should secede. But Jefferson Davis, president of the newly formed Southern Confederacy, did not want to risk either Virginia not seceding or Federal troops storming Richmond. Two days after the state convention vote, he dispatched Vice-President Alexander Stephens to Richmond to create a military alliance between Virginia and the Confederacy.[6] Davis believed such an alliance would both protect Richmond from Federal invasion and bring the city into the Confederacy without a voter referendum. He was right. State voters appeared to welcome the alliance and were largely unconcerned by the lack of legal procedure. By April 27 Richmond's fate became inextricably tied to that of the Confederacy as representatives of Virginia took their seats in the Confederate Congress.

Virginia contributed more than its elite sons to the new government; it also gave one of its illustrious cities—Richmond—to the cause. During the month of May, at the invitation of the Virginia Secession Convention, President Davis, his cabinet, and the various departments of the Confederacy moved from Montgomery, Alabama, to Richmond.[7] Although Montgomery's location afforded better military protection, Davis was

intent on protecting the Richmond's war industries, such as the Tredegar Iron Works.[8]

Rapidly the city transformed from the capital of Virginia into the
capital of the Confederacy and command post for the Southern military
forces. Thousands of army personnel, newly elected Confederate con-
gressmen, and their families poured into the city, filling up hotels and
boardinghouses and greatly stimulating local businesses including "res-
taurants, bars and bawdy houses." It had taken Richmond nearly eighty
years to reach a population of 38,000, but it took only a few weeks of
war to double or triple that number. The most noticeable portion of the
city's new residents were the "ten to fifteen thousand troops" dressed
in uniforms ranging from the "butternut of the Georgia private" to the
red scarlet pants, "broad blue sash, white gaiters, a low-cut blue shirt . . .
and a jaunty fez" of the Zouaves, New Orleans Tigers.[9] With the presence
of the soldiers and their war departments, the city had become, in the
words of one observer, "one great camp."[10]

Because Richmond possessed industries vital to the Southern military
and because of the capital's proximity to enemy lines, efforts to secure
the city began almost immediately. Richmond's city council and the Virginia General Assembly quickly appropriated funds to build fortifications, garrison the city, and stockpile arms.[11] Although city and county
officials had toyed with the idea of building up its defenses earlier in the
year, it appears little had been accomplished before the events of April
and May. In fact, it was not until the Confederate capital relocated and
fears of a Northern invasion mounted that Richmond made significant
progress in fortifying the city defenses. The Northern battle cry "On to
Richmond" proved to be a great incentive to the Virginian corps of
engineers and other military and civilian personnel in charge of protecting the city.[12]

Plans for city defenses were straightforward: build batteries on the
outskirts of the city to repel land forces and fortifications along the bluffs
of the James River to fire on Federal gunboats. Initially the Virginia and
Confederate governments employed several hundred white men from
the local military units to accomplish these and other war-related tasks.[13]
But it soon became clear that far more workers were needed. To supplement its military workforce, the Confederate government turned to
city and county residents. Over the next four years, the Confederate and
Virginia state governments would become increasingly dependent on
the civilian population for their labor. The armory, for example, hired
as many as 300 white women and girls to make pistol and rifle cartridges,
and other ammunition for the war.[14] Besides the white male population
who either volunteered or were conscripted, however, the city residents

most affected by the war were Richmond's black residents. Even before the Battle of Manassas in July 1861, local and military authorities strongly urged free black residents to "enroll their names as operatives on the fortifications." In return, according to the local *Dispatch*, "at the conclusion of each day's work [the laborers] could come to the city if they saw fit. If they answered promptly to the roll-call, they would get fed and paid; if they did not, they would get something else." The General Assembly acts of July 1861 and February 1862 ensured that the "something else" was no idle threat. Free black males between eighteen and fifty who did not enroll would be fined, jailed, and placed on the fortifications' workforce—in chains, if necessary.[15]

The Confederate cause affected city and county slave workers in even greater numbers. Thousands of slave residents performed many, if not most, of the noncombatant tasks throughout the four years. Initially many became involved in the war effort through the hiring-out system. Later, impressment laws kept them working. Like their predecessors during the American Revolution, slave workers became full-time employees of the government through the newly created Quartermaster Departments, commissaries, and various wartime projects and industries. Nearly 100 slaves manned the canalboats, bateaux, steamers, and towing barges bringing goods to Richmond for the army. More than 280 slaves worked as teamsters for the Confederate warehouses. The state-run saltworks hired 110 slave workers and mechanics experienced in saltmaking, blacksmithing, and carpentry, as well as a handful of women "to make up clothing for the hands employed in the service of the state and to make the sacks necessary to pack salt in." Slave workers also manned local hospitals as attendants, ambulance drivers, cooks, and washers. General Hospital Number 8, for example, hired seventy-one slave workers between 1862 and 1863, most as laundresses, cooks, and nurses. Records for other army hospitals indicate equally high numbers of slave employees in similar occupations.[16]

While most noncombatant workers toiled in relative safety behind the battle lines, a number were in close proximity to the fighting, and more than a few ended up among the casualties. These were the hundreds of cooks, washers, nurses, personal servants, teamsters, and general laborers who either were servants of the officers or were attached to a unit. Commissioned officers, for example, often took their slave servants with them to battle or hired a personal valet to tend to their needs while in camp. Erasmus, nicknamed "Colonel," spent two years as a hired hand at the front lines cleaning the uniforms and boots, shaving, and securing supplies for two officers, Major McClellan and Colonel Chaburnum.

Since Erasmus had no choice but to follow his employers to each new camp, dodging bullets became a part of his job description.[17]

Another portion of the slave community participated in the war effort but in the factory setting. The number of industrial slave employees increased as factories were refitted for military production. The Manchester Cotton and Wool Manufacturing Company, which had not employed slaves since the 1840s, suddenly hired 122 slaves in 1863 to make the cloth for uniforms and blankets. That same year Virginia Central Railroad increased its holdings of hired slave hands from 224 to 322.[18] Joseph R. Anderson steadily increased the number of slave employees at Tredegar Iron Works over the war years as well. In 1860 there were 80 slave ironworkers; by 1862 there were 175, and by 1864 more than 200.[19]

In spite of the large numbers of hired slave workers and a relatively modest number of free black recruits, the Confederate government still needed more workers. As a result, the Confederacy began to commandeer slaves from nearby farms and plantations to dig trenches in key areas.[20] This proved to be an inefficient method of securing labor, however, because slave owners often refused to relinquish their field hands or demanded their slaves be returned almost immediately in order to continue farming activities. Evidence of slave owners' unhappiness with these temporary impressments is clear in this 1861 petition from Shenandoah Valley residents to Governor Letcher: "As you are advised, there are only 443 slaves in this county over twelve years of age of both sexes, and only about 150 working negro men. The labor is performed in a great measure by those who are in the militia, and if they be continued in service at this critical time, when they should be employed in preparing the land for a fall crop this vast productive agricultural region, instead of being the Egyptian granary whence our armies may be fed in the coming year, will scarcely support our own population in the aggregate."[21]

Resistance from planters and a continuing shortage of laborers for the war effort prompted the Virginia assembly to enact more formal measures to guarantee a steady supply of workers. In February 1862 the assembly passed the first impressment law, requiring all free black males between eighteen and fifty to register and be prepared to enter noncombatant service for 180 days. Even this, however, failed to raise an adequate number of workers. So in the following fall the assembly made provisions to force slave laborers into service. On October 3, 1862, the state legislature ordered a census of slave males between eighteen and forty-five, from whom the Confederate government would select workers. Under the new law no more than 10,000 slave males (or 5 percent of the slave population) would be impressed from each city and county, and each slave worker would be detained for no more than sixty days.[22] Although the October act obtained a number of slave workers, many slave owners defied the law, largely because they felt the compensation was too low—$15 per month per worker—and the army worked their slaves too hard. Owners frequently received reports that slave laborers worked in the "rain . . . in the trenches and rifle pits in mud and water almost knee-deep, without shelter, fire, or sufficient food."[23]

If harsh working conditions worried owners, the rumors of smallpox terrified them. Reports of an outbreak of the infectious disease in Richmond (which were accurate) induced slave owners not only to withhold slave workers but to demand the return of those already impressed by the government. Such fears prompted one entire county, Brunswick, to petition the governor for the return of its slaves. Letcher flatly rejected the request, stating, "We have no contagious diseases here[,] as I am informed the law requires the slaves to be sent, & I have no power to release them."[24]

Owners' complaints and refusal to comply prompted the assembly to draft a third impressment law in March 1863 to correct the flaws of the previous acts. This law exempted certain agricultural counties from the slave labor draft and increased payments from $15 to $20 per month, per slave. It also guaranteed adequate housing, food, clothing, and medical care for all bondmen to allay any concerns about their treatment.

Changes in the laws, however, did little to end slave owners' fears or to encourage them to hand over their slave workers. Furthermore, these fears were fairly widespread and not limited to a handful of distraught owners. The majority of the slave owners in the second Confederate congressional district, encompassing Greensville, Southampton, Sussex, and Surry Counties, refused to send their slaves for fear that they would "immediately run off to the Yankees."[25] Even owners in Richmond—those who possibly feared a Northern invasion the most—generally refused to comply.[26] Governor Letcher, exasperated by such recalcitrant behavior and the failure of the Richmond Hustings Court to enforce impressment laws, eventually sent word that if the court did not force compliance, he would make an example of the justices by "first impressing the slaves of members of the Court."[27]

Throughout these early years the Confederate government allowed the Virginia assembly to control efforts to secure workers. By 1863, however, the Confederate Congress had become frustrated by the state's lack of success and passed its own slave draft law, which superseded all previous state legislation. This law made all counties open to impressment, including agricultural counties. Slaves in those counties, however, were to be impressed only if the need for labor was deemed urgent. Impressment would last sixty days, and the government could detain workers for another thirty days if necessary. Owners would receive $20 per month per slave worker if they complied voluntarily, but only $15 if forced to comply.[28] This was the first of several impressment laws passed by the Confederate government between 1863 and 1865. Each law sought to correct problems such as inadequate pay, but none reduced the number of slaves impressed from each county or the length of their term.

With each new impressment law, more slaves and free blacks found themselves involved in war work. Even prisoners could not escape toiling for the Confederacy. Prisoners—slave and free, male and female—were regularly assigned to work on the public defenses in lieu of languishing in the penitentiary or being sold to a slave market outside of the United States. To maintain a steady supply of forced labor, Letcher frequently commuted slave sentences from "sale and transportation" to "labor on the public works for life." This was the fate of a number of slaves including Ann, a slave woman convicted of arson in Amherst County. Rather than being removed beyond the limits of the country, she found herself facing a lifetime of hard labor working for the state and the Confederacy.[29]

Between hiring and impressing workers, the Confederate government, the Virginia General Assembly, and the city council drew hundreds of Richmond's male slaves and a smaller number of female slaves into the Confederate cause. The October 1862 law, for example, initially impressed close to 600 male slave residents. Additional measures raised this figure into the thousands by 1865. Slave workers at various inner-city industries were affected by the impressment laws as well. Joseph R. Anderson of the Tredegar Iron Works sent twenty-one slave hirelings to work on the fortifications between 1863 and 1865 and later sent the same group to Drewry's Bluff for the army.[30] But many slave workers managed to avoid the backbreaking labor of digging trenches and building forts. Most slave women, for example, escaped public defense work and remained in private homes and businesses performing domestic chores. Slave men not claimed by the government found jobs in the few remaining factories and in trades not directly under Confederate control. Still outside the Quartermaster's Department control were a handful of tobacco manufactories, small shops such as bakeries, confectioneries, and milliners, small foundries, and businesses within the service industry including hotels, boardinghouses, taverns, and barbershops.

Hiring out to local businesses proved highly attractive during the Civil War. Not only was it safer for slave workers, it was more lucrative for owners, who raised rates in response to high demand for any sort of labor. Manufacturers who normally did not hire slave workers found it increasingly difficult to man their factories as white males joined the services and free black laborers were forced into public service. Purchasing slave labor was hardly an option as the value of Confederate banknotes spiraled downward and the prices of workers skyrocketed. By 1863 prices for young slave males reached as high as $5,000.[31] One Richmond slave owner, Andrew Ellett—obviously intrigued by the inflated wartime prices—carefully noted in his papers some of the vast changes in slave costs between 1860 and 1865 (table 18).

Hiring costs, in comparison, were far more manageable, ranging from $100 to $400.[32] But even hiring costs were not immune to inflation, and by 1865 it was not uncommon for skilled slaves to command as much as $1,000 or $1,500 for the year.[33] In spite of these increases, however, Richmond businesses clearly preferred hiring to purchasing in most cases. Surveys of slaveholding households and businesses during the war indicate hired slaves (between the ages of eighteen and forty-five) outnumbered those directly owned by a ratio of up to four to one.[34]

The massive changes to the government, the population, and industries greatly contributed to a kind of military excitement that pervaded Richmond; parades, drill exercises, and grand military balls filled the

Table 18. "Costs of slave hands in Andrew Ellett's household, 1865"

			Value ($)	
Name	Sex	Age	1860	1865
George	M	70	100	400
Rachel	F	40	400	1,850
Lucy	F	35	600	2,200
Daniel	M	23	1,300	4,000
Abram	M	22	1,300	5,000
Agnes	F	21	1,200	3,800
Cora	F	2	100	200
Jack	M	20	1,300	4,500
Thomas	M	19	1,300	4,500
Henry	M	19	1,300	4,500

Source: Andrew E. Ellett, Accounts, 1865, Newton M. Lee Papers, VHS.

streets and halls with music, excitement, and a feeling of anticipation.[35]
Richmonders showered soldiers with gifts and flattered them through
imitation. Young women would wait for the units to march by and hand
out sweets and delicacies to them, while young boys and even male slaves
incorporated elements of the military uniform into their everyday clothing by sewing yellow stripes to their outer pants seams.[36] Hundreds of
women happily gathered in church basements and formed sewing
groups to supply the troops with socks and bandages.[37] Most of the war
years, however, were filled not with flag-waving but with deprivation and
loss punctuated by housing and food shortages, increasing crime, and
civil riots. It was these circumstances that gradually gave Richmond the
look of a "beleaguered city."[38]

The increase in population with the arrival of military personnel,
refugees from border states, and their slave servants, placed enormous
pressure on the city's structure and services.[39] Hotels and boardinghouses were filled beyond capacity with guests bedding down in every
nook and cranny including on top of billiard tables.[40] Food shortages
and high costs—as a result of the Union blockade of the Virginia coast,
smaller harvests, and unscrupulous merchants purposely withholding
goods to inflate prices—forced residents to improvise or simply do without staples. Meals made without fat, butter, or sugar were quickly dubbed
"blockade inventions."[41] Theft of food, clothing, and fuel quickly increased as prices soared. Punishments became more severe. With mounting caseloads the Hustings Court had little time or room for compassion.
Bent on deterring further theft and vice, the court severely punished
transgressors as lessons to the larger populace. This new attitude
brought harsh justice to souls such as Albert Rush, a slave resident who
was sentenced to thirty-nine lashes for stealing three Confederate dollars' worth of coal. Anthony Bradley, a white man, served three months
in prison for stealing five Confederate dollars' worth of lumber.[42]

Richmond residents responded to the shortages in ways other than
petty theft. Midway through the war, in what became known as the Bread
Riot of April 1863, a group of white women angered by rising food costs
and by the governor's refusal to standardize prices marched down Main
Street and proceeded to smash and loot food and clothing stores. Within
a short time the women, along with some thieves who took advantage of
the situation, seized goods worth $13,000 in Confederate money includ-
ing 310 pounds of beef from government wagons. Clearly the women's
immediate purpose was "to get food," but their protest suggested
deeper and broader social and economic ills plaguing the city. The
mayor, the governor, and the president of the Confederacy, however,
were in no mood to hear or address the problems that their citizens

faced; they merely demanded that the women stop. When the demonstrators refused to back down, Davis ordered the militia to shoot.[43] After several tense minutes, the demonstrators dispersed and left.

While the hardships suffered by white residents were great, those endured by slave and free black Richmonders were even greater. With rampant inflation and a much-devalued currency, slave laborers working outside the war effort found themselves working harder for less money (or payment in kind) than in previous years. Richmond slave women were probably the first to notice this shift, which was unusual because in the city's history it was generally the men who first felt the impact of any broad labor and economic change.

Slave women found themselves burdened with more tasks and responsibilities. During the war years it was not uncommon for the cook to also act as the chambermaid, washer, ironer, and nurse. Families seeking domestic help often would list in newspaper advertisements a multitude of roles they expected a single slave worker to fulfill as basic qualifications for employment.[44] This was largely because many Richmond families could no longer employ servants for each job and therefore depended on the one or two slaves who remained to perform all chores for the same low pay.

Not only did employers hire fewer slave servants, they also shortened the contract terms. Although most domestics still negotiated yearly contracts, it was not uncommon for slaves to clean house "by the month."[45] This arrangement appealed to families staying in Richmond temporarily (such as refugee families moving south) or to those whose finances were rocky, but such contracts robbed slaves of any stability or assurance of cash payments.

Equally damaging to domestic slaves' working and living conditions was employers' insistence on hiring single persons without children. With increasing frequency the words "without incumbrance" appeared in advertisements.[46] Employers no longer wanted workers with infants because of the high costs of feeding extra mouths. Such restrictions were devastating to slave mothers desperate for domestic positions that would allow them to remain in Richmond and keep their families together.

Slave men encountered similar problems when job hunting in Richmond's industries and factories. Job prospects in the private sector became rather slim. The tobacco firms, which traditionally had employed the greatest number of slave laborers, had largely closed their doors. By 1863 the number of manufactories declined from a high of fifty-two to as few as a half dozen.[47] This reduction is attributable to a number of factors including a decline in available capital and credit, increased labor costs, the Union blockade of the Virginia coast (which made shipping tobacco to Europe difficult), and high taxes on tobacco.[48] Furthermore, resources to manufacture tobacco became scarce as workers, and even the buildings, were commandeered for the war effort; free black and slave laborers were commonly assigned to the batteries, while the warehouses were refitted as prisons for Union soldiers and hospitals for wounded Confederates.[49] Growers and manufacturers not deterred by these factors were hobbled by the 1863 executive proclamation and General Assembly act limiting the production of tobacco as a way to encourage more grain cultivation.[50]

By 1862 the largest single employer of city slave workers was the Confederate government. In addition to the public defense projects, most of the major industries, such as the railroads, flour milling, iron foundries, shoemakers, saddlers, lumberyards, livery businesses, and even the firehouse, were under the direction of the Confederacy. Slave laborers working in these various businesses frequently reported to an officer or worked on a production schedule set by one of the government agencies. A slave looking for work in Richmond during these years would have been hard-pressed to find a job that was not connected to the government.

Slaves paid a high price for accepting such work. In addition to harsh conditions, bondmen suffered from the immediate loss of their working and living privileges. As government slaves, they could neither hire themselves out nor negotiate cash payments because all contracts were handled directly between the various war departments and slave owners. Although the amount of payment each slave received varied depending on the type of job and the level of skills he or she possessed, the scale of payments set by the government was fixed. The informality and flexibility of the hiring system, which had for so long given slaves the ability to choose employers, negotiate the pay, and receive the cash directly, was summarily replaced by rigid bureaucratic procedures. As a result, slave hospital workers Hannah, Joseph, and Henry, a laundress, a nurse, and a cook, could not expect contracts for more than $15, $20, and $25 (Confederate currency) per month, respectively.[51] Furthermore, they would not see any cash from those earnings until after the hospital paid the slave owners, and their owners paid them. In the midst of a war, timely payments were not always certain.

Overtime bonuses also were discontinued. Limited government finances and impressment laws eliminated opportunities to earn cash above the set work payments. Given the financial situation of the Confederate government, it could ill afford to pay for extra work performed by slaves. More telling, however, government officials unaware of the subtleties of urban industrial slavery saw little need to give slave workers any incentives beyond the threat of physical punishment and "life on the public works."

Richmond slaves faced difficulties beyond the loss of their working privileges. Escalating inflation and constant supply shortages affected bond men and women the same way it did other poor Richmonders. Like the women of the bread riot, slave workers found themselves unable to stretch the supplies or their board money to feed themselves and their families. Providing for a family became even more difficult without the usual opportunities to earn overtime bonuses. Staples such as butter, sugar, and salt doubled and quadrupled in cost during the war, elevating them from common household goods to nearly unattainable luxuries. Butter, for example, sold for 75 cents per pound in 1862. A year later it sold for $3.00 (Confederate money) per pound—a price well beyond the budgets of slaves and many other Richmonders.[52]

To supplement the meager cash payments and supplies given by owners, slave laborers continued to moonlight, or work second jobs, even though city and state governments greatly discouraged it. Hawking goods or providing laundry and cooking services were fairly typical extra jobs that brought small sums of money. David, who spent long days working for Turpin and Yarbrough's store tried to make ends meet by selling newspapers on the streets. Aaron made extra income by selling fruits near the railroad station to passing soldiers and visitors. One slave woman, Dicey, created an unusual position for herself by "selling various articles of clothing for different ladies in the city." It seems that the wealthier ladies of Richmond had begun to sell their silk dresses and shawls for extra cash, probably to buy groceries and other essentials. In order to spare these ladies the shame and humiliation of selling their own clothes at the local street market, Dicey hawked the clothes for them, for a small fee.[53]

If the pressures of daily life did not make slave and free black Richmonders weary, then the mounting legal restrictions probably did. With each passing year black residents saw their "freedoms" dwindle as "webs of restraint" were quickly spun around them in efforts to prevent slave rebellion and pro-Union activities.[54] Even though thousands of fully armed troops were stationed in and around the city and were prepared to meet any sign of danger, city council officials felt it necessary to tighten the reins of slavery, if only to help white Richmonders sleep easier at night. Wartime regulations were hardly new; most reiterated the restrictions laid down in the codes passed in 1852 and again in 1859.[55] Slaves were prohibited from purchasing, trading, or drinking liquor, keeping a cookshop or any other store, selling newspapers, and hiring themselves out.[56] They also were prohibited from renting rooms or houses, carrying a cane at night, or smoking in public. Watchmen constantly patrolled the streets and alleys to break up any illegal assemblies of black residents at local grocery stores or cookshops. Free black visitors were not allowed to enter the city without a certificate of "good character and loyalty" from a county judge. Those who tried to enter without such papers were summarily pressed into service. Slaves confiscated as runaways also were sent to work for the war with no hope of relief.[57]

These wartime regulations surprised few slave and free black residents. They were already familiar with the restrictions against carrying canes, buying medicine, or standing on sidewalks. What probably did surprise them, however, was the fervency with which the laws were enforced. In the past city slave workers had little to fear when looking for work because arrests were so rare. But with Richmond in a state of war and martial law, authorities were quick to execute the new regulations. Between 1849 and 1851, for example, only three slaves had been arrested for self-hiring. But between 1862 and 1864, eighty-five slave workers spent time in jail for this crime.[58]

The zeal with which the public guard and night watchmen enforced the codes was matched only by the fervor of the court judges in punishing transgressors. Albert Rush was one of many slave residents automatically sentenced to thirty-nine lashes regardless of the crime. Although "39" was a common punishment for crimes such as larceny or assaulting a fellow slave in the prewar era, the chances of receiving a lighter sentence were fairly good. Confessing to a crime in the prewar era, for example, often resulted in lowering the sentence to twenty-five stripes. Slave women also escaped the full "39" for crimes such as larceny, frequently receiving punishments of fifteen to twenty lashes. During the war, however, punishments became fairly standard in their severity for both men and women. Assaults on slaves or free blacks by either group automatically resulted in "39." The majority of slaves picked up for "going at large" spent time in jail until their owners paid the requisite fine of $10 (Confederate currency) and court costs. For major offenses, such as attacking a white person or grand larceny, slaves received two to three sentences of "39" to be administered over several weeks. The harshest punishments, however, were reserved not for slaves but for free blacks. The common sentence for stealing, remaining in the commonwealth without the court's permission, or assaulting a white person was immediate and permanent enslavement.

City slave and free black residents did not have to participate in self-hiring or petty theft to court danger. Just living in Richmond, which was overrun by armed, drunken soldiers, proved fairly hazardous. Hardly a week went by without some tragic incident involving soldiers and civilians.[59] John S. Roane, a white tailor, was practically disemboweled by a soldier when he tried to break up a fight among the militia. According to the newspapers, Roane saw a group of soldiers fighting, "drew near and requested them to desist." In response one of them plunged a knife into Roane and slit his stomach.[60] Some residents did not even have to venture near the soldiers to become a target. Frequently soldiers full of rum would shoot their pistols in the streets trying to hit signs, lampposts, or even each other. And alarmingly often these stray bullets would hit civilians in the street or even in their own homes.

Although all city residents were vulnerable to this disgraceful behavior, slave and free black Richmonders were particularly at risk. Belief in white superiority and black inferiority emboldened many Confederate soldiers to take out their frustrations on black workers and brutalize them. Stories of black hack drivers being shot or servant girls cut up by drunk soldiers frequently made the newspapers. Slave resident Henry Cooper nearly lost his life one evening when he picked up a soldier in his hack. Because soldiers were notorious for not paying for goods or services, Cooper demanded the fare up front. The soldier responded by drawing his pistol and shooting the driver. Luckily one of the buttons on Cooper's coat deflected the bullet, probably saving his life.[61]

Life during the war for slave and free black Richmonders was brutal. No doubt the harsh working conditions, food shortages, restrictive laws, severe penalties, and random violence made black Richmonders feel extremely vulnerable. Slave residents faced the additional hardship of severe reductions in the working and living privileges that earlier had brought some relief and comfort. Even their ability to move through the streets unmolested—one of the hallmarks of urban slave life—had been eliminated. Slaves needed passes signed by owners for safe passage throughout the city. Although passes were required in the prewar era, such laws were never strictly enforced. Now, failure to get such documentation could result in immediate impressment for public defense work.[62]

Because of the dangers of traveling or working without a pass, slave laborers were forced to seek out their owners to obtain the proper papers. For slaves who worked and lived with their owners, such contact was not unusual. For hired slaves, however, who saw their owners only sporadically except for the times they handed over their cash payments, this was a marked change. Suddenly slave workers had to inform their owners of their activities and whereabouts, a major departure for those used to working and living apart.

Slave owners, at the same time, sought to reestablish relationships with their slaves in order to comply with local laws, monitor slaves' activities, and prevent them from escaping, being impressed, or encountering bad treatment when working for the Confederacy. Some owners may have genuinely cared about the welfare of their slaves; but most viewed a closer relationship with hired bond men and women as a good way to protect their property. The loss of a hired slave and the cash income they brought during the war years would have been devastating to most slave owners' households. As a result, owners felt it was financially beneficial to keep close tabs on workers.

Together the new restrictions, martial law, and wartime conditions appeared to do what state and local government efforts could not: suspend the eroding effect of urban industrialization and market relations on the slave system and gain greater discipline and control over the slave population. By constraining slave working and living conditions, forcing slaves and owners to establish relationships, and disrupting the slave community through impressment and strict regulations, the Confederate government seemed to have strengthened the slave system, if only temporarily. There was plenty of evidence supporting such a belief: the number of slaves arrested for "going at large" had significantly increased, slaves convicted of crimes were being punished harshly and promptly, and the overwhelming number of notes and passes found on slaves arrested on the suspicion of self-hiring indicated a high level of contact between slave and owner. Furthermore, wartime restrictions helped to eliminate the twilight zone between slavery and freedom that urban slave working and living conditions had created—an issue that had greatly concerned many elite Richmonders years before the war. During the 1850s white city residents had expressed fears that the benefits gave slaves too much control over their lives, which they believed encouraged slaves to think and act more like free people. The wartime regulations did much to demonstrate the wide division between slavery for black Richmonders and freedom for white Richmonders by impressing free black residents into war service, hiring them out when they failed to pay their taxes, and reducing them to slavery in the courts.[63] Through these draconian measures, free black residents Lemmuel Bower, James Carter, James Harris, and Samuel Yancy, among others, were treated like slave workers and auctioned for hire in front of the courthouse.[64] The Confederate government made it abundantly clear that freedom did not exist for black Richmonders.

While wartime regulations certainly made slave and free black life bleak, there is some doubt as to whether the system was as well under control as the government agencies liked to believe. The very fact that eighty-five slaves were caught "going at large" or self-hiring suggests that wartime laws could not completely stop these practices.[65] Also undermining claims of control was the outpouring of incidents of slave resistance, treason, and illegal black and white alliances—all indicating that the new restrictions did not subdue urban bond men and women, nor did they dampen their desire for freedom or for the comforts that made their lives less oppressive. Regardless of the laws, it appeared, according to the Virginia attorney general John Randolph Tucker, that "the negroes [were] dangerous members of society."[66]

Slave residents still found ways to celebrate life, entertain, and socialize in spite of the restrictions. The hosts and guests of the "colored fancy ball," complete with elaborate gowns, a fiddler, refreshments, and even several members of the white community, appeared unworried by the curfew and "illegal assembly" laws—that is until the nightwatchmen raided the party. But neither the laws nor the shocking raid of the fancy ball seemed to have a lasting impact on the slave community; only a month later a second similar party was held at the Columbia Tavern.[67]

Smaller, less formal activities such as cards, dice games, gambling, and drinking appear to have been unaffected as well. Men continued to gather in alleys and tenements for regular gaming and socializing.[68] "Kitchen parties," held in the kitchen of an "opulent citizen" where the "host" slaves worked and lived, continued to be a popular activity among slave women and men throughout the Civil War.[69]

Other evidence that the war regulations fell short of their aim includes the joint effort of slaves and their owners to continue the practices of self-hiring, living apart, and even avoiding war work. While the pass system forced slaves and owners to stay in closer contact, the law did little to reform their attitudes or behavior. Owners continued to reject laws and restrictions that negatively affected their income. According to the passes many owners did not know or seem to care about their slaves' activities or whereabouts as long as they produced a cash income. The instructions on the passes continued to be vague and open-ended, thus giving slaves a great deal of latitude. Stephen, a kind of traveling salesman, had one of these passes, which allowed him to find his market and live wherever was convenient. "Permit the bearer," Stephen's note began, "to sell and buy articles and sell them to anyone for one month[,] also pass him anywhere in the city until eleven o'clock PM."[70] Hannah's pass was only slightly more instructive. "Hannah," wrote owner Thomas Emett, "has permissun to rent a house and wash and do any kind of work she may chuse in the city and receive pay for the same."[71] Not everyone had so much license. Curetta and her daughter Betty, for example, shared a pass that specified where they lived, their occupation, and the hour they were supposed to reach home at night. Interestingly, the pass was written and signed not by the owner but by a slave agent.[72] This, of course, raises questions about how much Mrs. Briggs, the owner, actually knew about Curetta and Betty's activities.

Slaves often gained assistance from their owners in flouting the new requirements to perform war work, particularly when it was dangerous. Owners refusing to comply with impressment laws helped slaves avoid public defense work—a job notorious for its poor working conditions. In other instances, slave workers depended on their owners to shield them from the government even after being impressed. When a group of slave laborers ran away from the hospital where they were assigned to nurse victims of smallpox, few owners made them return to their jobs. A number of owners did not even wait for their slaves to escape, instead traveling to the hospitals to pull their workers from the premises. Although the chief surgeons complained, officials quickly found they could do little to prevent such actions.[73]

City slaves were able to circumvent wartime restrictions by continuing their relationships with free black and white store owners, landlords, and tavern keepers, among other businessmen. Slaves who continued to hire themselves out, for example, were still able to secure private lodgings apart from owner and employer, in direct violation of the law. White landlords willingly rented houses and tenements to slave workers with or without their owners' consent. Tavern keepers, cookshop proprietors, and store owners continued to sell ardent spirits, food, clothing, and any other goods that slaves desired, provided they paid in cash.

Richmond slaves developed a financial relationship with the non-business community as well; the "wealthy ladies" of Richmond, white women whose contact with slaves had been limited, suddenly became trading partners with them. Because of the numerous shortages, these ladies depended on slave hawkers to sell their silk dresses for extra cash or to buy hard-to-find rationed items, even if the goods were stolen.[74]

Another steady business that developed between enslaved and free Richmonders was forging passes. Slaves who possessed cash and wanted to escape could find Richmonders willing to sign papers for a fee.[75] One forger, William Thomas, built a rather extensive business and even employed "agents to bring slaves in want of passes" to him.[76] Some slave Richmonders found that their hard-earned cash could buy more than just a pass. Slaves Peter, William, Aaron, Lucy Richards, and Emma Maxfield, among others, made their escape by hiring a wagon, supplies, and an escort of three armed white men.[77]

During the war slaves were not the only fugitives who were harbored for money. According to a police report, a slave resident named Daniel helped white male residents avoid conscription. In the back of his house, hidden from the street, he secretly provided room and board for as many as six men at a time. In addition to these services, he acted as a warning sentry. When the police apprehended Daniel, he was throwing pebbles at the back bedroom window to warn the men of the "approaching danger."[78]

One of the greatest weaknesses of wartime regulations was their inability to sap slaves' desire to resist and survive. No law could have deterred the slave residents who escaped the armed city camp or the friends and family members who helped them leave. And such actions were not reserved for just a few bold individuals. In 1862 nearly 200 slaves "escaped to the enemy" while working on the city's fortifications. That same year eighty slaves working for the Virginia Central Railroad were reportedly "carried off by the enemy," although it is more likely they escaped to federally controlled areas nearby. A random sample of runaway advertisements featured in the local paper between 1861 and 1865 indicates that hundreds of slaves followed in their footsteps throughout the war years.[79]

Many of the runaways disappeared alone and without a trace. Clara, for example, left her position as a domestic servant one morning, never to be heard from again. Gilbert, who had recently been removed from North Carolina to Richmond, took advantage of the Christmas holidays to make his break for freedom. Gibby, who worked at the hospital, waited until the holiday festivities were over before she took leave.[80]

Wartime conditions made escape highly desirable but also quite difficult. With thousands of soldiers nearby, the city and ten miles surrounding it under martial law, and patrols combing the countryside for enemy spies, a lone slave making his or her way north would have been highly suspicious. As a result, a number of slaves decided the best way to avoid detection by Confederate soldiers was to mingle with them. With increasing frequency, slave workers hired themselves to officers as personal valets or cooks and then would leave the city with them when their units pulled out. This method worked for Sam and Washington who escaped their owner by hiring themselves to a volunteer company headed for Yorktown. Henry, a barber by trade, similarly had little trouble finding a position with an officer and promptly left the city. Edmund, another successful escapee, took more precautions and told soldiers he was a free black in order to avoid arousing suspicion.[81]

Joining the military and leaving the city, however, was only the first step toward freedom for many of these slave workers. Once the Confederate battalions moved closer to Union lines, many would head for federal camps. This was certainly the plan Caeser, a slave valet, had plotted. For eight months Caeser patiently waited and served Captain Robert

Abernathy of the Mississippi Volunteers until the battalion went north, close to the enemy's camps. When the battalion picked up to move on, Caeser was nowhere to be found.[82]

Wartime regulations not only failed to stem runaways, they also could not prevent activities that were seditious and even treasonous to the Confederate cause. One slave Richmonder, Allen, appears to have been unconcerned about the laws when he shouted in the streets that "Jefferson Davis [was] a rebel," and "no white man should be [my] master."[83] Another report indicates that groups of slave women openly taunted their mistresses by telling them that with the Federal victory at hand, "they will soon change conditions with them, and play upon pianos, and be ladies, while their mistresses will be compelled to cook and scrub."[84] A more subtle commentary about the Confederate cause made by slave Richmonders occurred on the morning of President Davis's inauguration. As Mrs. Davis rode in her carriage alone to the Capitol for the ceremony, "four sedate Negroes in white gloves" suddenly appeared alongside and accompanied the procession as if they were pallbearers. Alarmed, Mrs. Davis asked the driver what was going on. " 'This ma'am,' he said, 'is the way we always does in Richmond for funeral and sichlike.' "[85]

Some slaves took even greater risks: two slave workers in the Confederate army helped lead deserters "through the military lines to the enemy." Their activities became known when General Robert E. Lee's unit caught them in the act. Lee was horrified at the lack of loyalty the deserters and bondmen displayed. Clearly this act was illegal, but was it not an act of treason as well, General Lee and Governor Letcher asked the Virginia attorney general. After some thought John Randolph Tucker replied, "I am of opinion [it] may be." But Confederate law required more than Tucker's opinion; according to the various ordinances, two witnesses were required to prove the slaves committed an act of treason. As a result, the two bondmen escaped death.[86]

More damaging to the Confederate cause were the acts of treason that went undiscovered, such as spying and smuggling information. Documents produced after the war suggest a number of slave residents assisted Union troops by spying on Confederate officials. Elizabeth Van Lew, a local informant to General Benjamin F. Butler, apparently hired out several slave servants in Confederate president Jefferson Davis's home as spies. According to an article in the *Richmond Evening Journal*, "She [Van Lew] spied upon the Confederacy and all of its agents, both civil and military, installing her deputies in the household of President Davis as servants, and through them acquainting herself with his Cabinet conferences. The information thus obtained was put into cipher, and, concealed between an outer and inner sole of his shoe, was smuggled through the lines by a negro."[87]

Perhaps the greatest blow to Confederate efforts to control the slave population, and the greatest testimony to the weakness of the earlier restrictions, was President Davis's proposal to save the Confederacy: to recruit and arm slave and free black residents. In return for their loyal service, Davis proposed, slaves would be given their freedom, a goal "which is so marked a characteristic of the negro." Davis further added that such a reward would provide a "double motive for a zealous discharge of duty."[88] In this 1864 address to the Confederate Congress, Davis made two issues clear: the future of the Confederacy and of slavery was tenuous, and the labor and loyalty of slave residents needed to be secured through methods other than coercion.

By late 1864 Davis saw no other recourse. The number of slave runaways from plantations, the war industries, and public defense work was steadily rising. During the previous year nearly every county in Virginia had reported high losses in slave labor.[89] In addition to losing laborers, Confederate ranks were rapidly thinning, and without fresh recruits, the cause was doomed. Replacements from the white population, however, were not forthcoming; fewer and fewer men heeded the call for volunteers. In response to Davis's call for the elderly and the young to defend the Confederacy, officials such as Governor Brown of Georgia refused to comply and called the policy "usurping and despotic."[90] The combination of these factors made recruiting slaves the only choice.

The proposal to arm slaves met with fierce resistance from the Confederate cabinet and Congress. The loudest arguments quickly highlighted the contradictions inherent in such an act. "If slaves will make good soldiers our whole theory of slavery is wrong," Major General Howell Cobb wrote to Secretary of War James A. Seddon.[91] John Moncure Daniel, editor of the *Examiner*, reminded the president that rewarding slaves with their freedom was an abolitionist idea and that black residents were best off left as slaves.[92] The debate raged for months; but as the Confederacy suffered more political and military defeats, resistance softened. The deciding factor came when General Lee threw his support behind the measure. With the army now supporting slave recruitment, public opinion quickly changed.[93]

In the spring of 1865, the Virginia General Assembly responded and set up the proper agencies to recruit slave and free black residents. According to the March 13 act, it was now legal for black residents to be "organized as soldiers . . . for the public defense during the present war . . . to bear arms . . . and carry ammunition as other soldiers in the army."[94] Although the Virginia act did not guarantee freedom to those who volunteered (a concession to the dissenters), there was little doubt in the minds of the Confederate Congress, President Davis, and a good number of Richmond residents—black and white—that service in the military would be rewarded with freedom papers.[95] Even before the act had been passed, officials such as Secretary of State Benjamin were prepared to tell black Richmonders, "Go and fight—you are free!"[96]

Enough slave and free black Richmonders joined the Confederate army to create two companies. No doubt a few slave recruits saw that they had nothing to lose; if the Union army won, they would be free, and if the Confederacy won, they would be free. Sallie Putnam, who was living in Richmond during the war, described the atmosphere: "Recruiting offices were opened in Richmond, and soon a goodly number of sable patriots appeared on the streets, clad in the grey uniform of the Confederate soldier. Their dress-parades on the Capitol Square attracted large crowds of all colors to witness them, and infused a spirit of enthusiasm among those of their own race."[97] The sight of black troops—former slaves—dressed in the familiar gray uniform, marching in unison, and drilling with guns in the capital probably did not delight white residents and slave owners as much as it did black residents.

At any rate, these new Richmond recruits did not get a chance to prove themselves, nor did they have to earn their freedom. In fact, they never got to see a battle because just as they were ready to take their positions on the field, the war ended. On Sunday morning April 2 while President Davis sat at St. Paul's Church deep in prayer, he was suddenly called to attend a meeting. After a little while other government officials who were also sitting in the pews were called away. The handwriting was on the wall: General Grant's army was on its way, "on to Richmond." The next twenty-four hours were filled with confusion, terror, and then massive, uncontrolled fires. The city council quickly met and decreed that all spirits and liquor be destroyed. Simultaneously, a military order was passed to burn the major tobacco warehouses and the arsenal. Explosions accompanied the fleeing soldiers and government officials who filled the last trains pulling out of the city. On the morning of April 4, as the fires continued to rage and starving city residents helped themselves to the food supplies abandoned by the Confederate army, the first of the Federal troops arrived with official confirmation of what most Richmonders, black and white, already knew: slavery was finally over.[98]

Epilogue

WHEN THE UNION TROOPS entered Richmond, they found a city burning on both sides of the main boulevards and the "air . . . filled with sparks, mingled in places with exploding shells from the rebel ordnance stores." But the dangers presented by the fire and explosions did not keep hundreds of black Richmonders from shouting and dancing in the streets while welcoming the Federal soldiers with gifts of tobacco.[1] This was a day never to be forgotten in Richmond history, and one that was to become an important holiday within the newly freed black community. To underscore the importance of that day, black Richmonders celebrated the first anniversary of their freedom with a parade and rally. One newspaper described the festivities this way:

> An immense cavalcade of black horsemen led the van, preceded by a dusky son of Ham tooting on a worn-out bugle . . . then came a Patriarch with a stick, with a gourd on the top of it, all covered over with ribands; this individual was decorated in an apron of black and gold, and a gold stripe down his legs. . . . after the band there march a long string of unsentimental, unbleached, some with aprons, some with rosettes, and some with sashes. There were two banners in the line, one of which, composed of silk and bullion, was of commendable appearance; the other seemed to be but a piece of white domestic streaked all over with red letters. . . .

[The parade] finally climaxed with a parcel of field hands in
jeans walking in squads, without commander, uniform, or de-
corum.[2]

Two thousand black residents participated in the parade and were later
joined by an additional fifteen thousand observers when the group
reached the Capitol. Although the parade may have seemed a bit rag-
tag—as the newspaper disparagingly noted—in comparison to the Confederate military parades of earlier years, the event held great significance for black Richmonders and no doubt instilled in them a great deal
of pride. Each sash, scarf, and stripe reflected the strength and hard
work of the ex-slaves in their transition from slavery to freedom. As historian Peter Rachleff notes, these were no ordinary garments but the
"ceremonial garb" and "symbols" of the secret societies of which each
marcher was a member.[3] These societies included the Union Liberties
Protective Society, the Humble Christian Benevolents of the Chesterfield
Coal Pits, and possibly the Stevedores' Society, and the Independent
Order of the Messiah.

Although many, if not most, of these societies did not form until the
months following the end of the war, they played a huge role in helping
the recently freed black city residents fight for their rights, find jobs,
increase wages, improve working conditions, and accumulate funds.
Their appearance probably seemed sudden to Richmonders of that time.
But within the larger context of black Richmond history—particularly
in the antebellum era—the emergence of these societies after the war
was a natural continuation of events during slavery. The societies were
possible because of the political and financial skills that urban slave men
and women developed through living and working in the city. These
new organizations were merely the latest outgrowth of community efforts
that had helped Richmond slaves build an independent church, negotiate contracts and working conditions, petition for, purchase, or "steal"
their freedom, provide for their families, develop political alliances, and
maintain their humanity and dignity in the face of bondage. Not surprisingly, the black residents who led these organizations had been re-
spected members of the slave community and were prized for their ar-
tisanal skills, their power within the church, and their financial success.

In this brief work I have tried to sketch an image of slavery in Richmond that conveys the struggles that urban slaves faced, the strengths
they drew upon, and their steady growth as a community. Although it
will never be possible to fully understand the lives of enslaved black
Richmonders, I have tried to balance the presentation of historical
events with human stories: the anger and misery of Michael Valentine

when his owner forced him to move to Richmond without his wife; the satisfaction Minsey experienced when she quit her position as a house-maid in the middle of her employer's Christmas party; the determination that James Allison, Charles Feggins, and Stephen Brown showed when they demanded equal voting rights for free and enslaved members within the church; and the pride of black Baptists when they won their own church.[4]

I did not, however, want to focus on these victories and tragedies as isolated occurrences but rather as examples of a long tradition of resis-tance, hope, strong moral beliefs, and determination that fortified Rich-mond's black community then—and continues to do so today. To ac-complish this, I traced the development of Richmond's urban and industrial slave system, the architectural and landscape changes of the city, the unusual practices of self-hiring, living apart, and cash bonuses, and how bond men and women used all these factors to their advantage. By following these historical "threads" over an eighty-three-year period, I came to understand how the urban industrial milieu enabled slave residents to gain some control over their working and living conditions and subtly alter their relationships with owners and employers. It became clear that the city setting, and slaves' response to it, helped to create an unusually large and strong slave community.

I also came to understand how Richmond's slave system, in compari-son to Baltimore's, "succeeded" and yet became increasingly flawed with an infrastructure that weakened over time. Richmond's success de-pended on giving slave workers more control over their lives and labor, a practice that went against what antebellum southerners believed was necessary to maintain a strong system of bondage. The conditions cer-tainly allowed Richmond slaves to lead lives that were very different from what they would have experienced on plantations. But no matter how unusual the urban industrial slave system may have been, it was no less brutal, oppressive, or legally constraining than any other form of bond-age. Richmond's slave system did, however, create certain opportunities for slave men and women not only to survive—which in itself is extraor-dinary—but also to build a rich, complex community supported by strong family ties, the African Baptist Church, and mutual aid societies, among other institutions. The existence of these organizations revealed the limits of the city slave system and slave workers' ability to severely test those limits, during a time when slave owner control and the ide-ology undergirding slavery appeared absolute.

Notes

ABBREVIATIONS

FABC	First African Baptist Church, Richmond
FBC	First Baptist Church, Richmond
HL	The Huntington Library, San Marino, California
Hustings Deeds	Richmond, Hustings Court, Deeds
Hustings Suit Papers	Richmond, Hustings Court, Suit Papers
Hustings Wills	Richmond, Hustings Court, Wills, Inventories, and Accounts
LVA	Archives, The Library of Virginia, Richmond
Museum of the Confederacy	Museum of the Confederacy, Richmond
Valentine	Valentine Museum, Richmond, Virginia
VHS	Virginia Historical Society, Richmond
Virginia Baptist Historical Society	Virginia Baptist Historical Society, University of Richmond

INTRODUCTION

1. Wade, *Slavery in the Cities*, 48.

2. Eaton, "Slave-Hiring in the Upper South"; Schweninger, "The Free-Slave Phenomenon"; Green, "Industrial Transition in the Land of Chattel Slavery"; Egerton, *Gabriel's Rebellion*.

3. Douglass, *My Bondage and My Freedom*, 147–48.

4. Goldin, *Urban Slavery in the American South;* Fields, *Slavery and Freedom on the Middle Ground*, 7.

5. *Richmond Enquirer*, Sept. 13, 1831.

1. INAUSPICIOUS BEGINNINGS

1. Ward and Greer, *Richmond during the Revolution*, 8.

2. Charles de la Peña to John Adams Smith, Nov. 2, 1827, John Adams Smith, Esq., Papers, Valentine.

3. Albert, "The Protean Institution," 17.

4. Robert, *Tobacco Kingdom*, 90–91.

5. Goldfield, *Cotton Fields and Skyscrapers*, 16.

6. Peterson, "Flour and Grist Milling in Virginia," 105.

7. Lewis, "Darkest Abode of Man," 190–91.

8. Price, "Economic Function and the Growth of American Port Towns," 129–30.

9. Robert, *Tobacco Kingdom*.

10. Kulikoff, *Tobacco and Slaves*, 38.

11. Robert, *Tobacco Kingdom*, 197–208; Schnittman, "Slavery in Virginia's Urban Tobacco Industry."

12. Lewis, *Coal, Iron, and Slaves*, 181.

13. Eaton, *Growth of Southern Civilization*, 239.

14. John Harvie and William Foushee to Governor of Virginia, March 11, 1791, *Calendar of State Papers* 5:273.

15. Colonel Davies to the Governor, Feb. 2, 1782, ibid., 3:100.

16. Governor Harrison to Thomas Madison, Dec. 12, 1782, *Official Letters of the Governors* 3:399.

17. Dabney, *Richmond, the Story of a City*, 1.

2. THE ROAD TO INDUSTRIALIZATION AND THE
   RISE OF URBAN SLAVERY, 1800–1840

1. Dabney, *Richmond, the Story of a City*, 33; Tyler-McGraw, *At the Falls*, 72.

2. Wade, *Slavery in the Cities*, 325–30.

3. Richmond City Council, Minutes, Feb. 8, 1830, LVA.

4. *Statistics of the United States of America, Sixth Census; Compendium of the Enumeration of the Inhabitants, Sixth Census;* Green, "Urban Industry, Black Resistance," 334–42; Richmond, Personal Property Taxes, 1800–1840; *Richmond Direc-*

tory, Register and Almanac, 1819; *Ellyson's Business Directory and Almanac*, 1845, LVA.

5. Bureau of Census, Population, 1800–1840.

6. Freehling, *Drift towards Dissolution*, 137, 174–75.

7. Kulikoff, *Tobacco and Slaves*; Robert, *Tobacco Kingdom*.

8. Stampp, *Peculiar Institution*; Hughes, "Slaves for Hire."

9. Thomas Hicks Wynne, Journal, Jan. 2, 1843, HL.

10. Phillips, *Life and Labor in the Old South;* Gray, *History of Agriculture;* Fogel and Engerman, *Time on the Cross;* Goldin, *Urban Slavery;* "Estate of John Prosser in Account with Edmund W. Bootes, Executor," Jan. 28, 1812, Hustings Wills.

11. Bureau of Census, Population, 1800; *Virginia Argus*, 1800; *Virginia Gazette and General Advertiser*, 1800, LVA.

12. Pinchbeck, *Virginia Negro Artisan*, 54.

13. Richmond, Manufacturing Census, 1820 and 1840; Richmond, Personal Property Taxes, 1800–1840; *Richmond Directory, Register and Almanac*, 1819; *Ellyson's Business Directory and Almanac*, 1845; Green, "Urban Industry, Black Resistance," 334–42; Richmond, Manufacturing Census, 1840.

14. Robert, *Tobacco Kingdom*, 213–14.

15. Richard Carter v. William Patterson, Feb. 1824, Hustings Suit Papers.

16. Richmond, Manufacturing Census, 1820; Richmond, Personal Property Taxes, 1820, LVA.

17. Bureau of Census, Population, 1840; Richmond, Personal Property Taxes, 1840, LVA.

18. *Ellyson's Business Directory and Almanac, 1845;* Bureau of Census, Population, 1840; Richmond, Personal Property Taxes, 1840, LVA.

19. Dew, "Disciplining Slave Ironworkers," 399.

20. Fox-Genovese, *Within the Plantation Household*, 293.

21. Amott and Matthaei, *Race, Gender, and Work*, 146.

22. William Patterson v. Richard Carter, Feb. 1824, Hustings Suit Papers.

23. Bureau of Census, Population, 1840.

24. Bryant, *Letters of a Traveller*, 74–75.

25. Jones, *Life in the South*, 152–53.

26. Weld, *Vacation Tour*, 312–13.

27. Bureau of Census, Population, 1850; Richmond, Personal Property Taxes, 1845 and 1850, LVA.

28. Berry, "The Rise of Flour Milling in Richmond," 387–408.

29. Edgar, *Story of a Grain of Wheat*, 146.

30. Bureau of Census, Population, 1840.

31. Ibid., 1830 and 1840; Richmond, Personal Property Taxes, 1830, 1835, and 1840, LVA.

32. Green, "Urban Industry, Black Resistance," 413.

33. Buckingham, *Slave States of America*, 426.

34. Bureau of Census, Population, 1840; Richmond, Manufacturing Census, 1840 and 1850; Green, "Urban Industry, Black Resistance," 414–15.

35. James River and Kanawha Company, Second and Third Annual Reports, 1836–37, 93 and 246, VHS.

36. Ibid., Annual Report, July 17, 1835, VHS.

37. Eaton, *Growth of Southern Civilization*, 64.

38. James River and Kanawha Company, Annual Report, 1836, 93; ibid., 1839, 508, VHS.

39. Ibid., 1846, pt. 4, VHS.

40. Ibid., 330.

41. Ibid., 1838, 331–32, VHS.

42. George M. Cooke to John Henry Eustace, May 24, 1836, Benjamin Brand Papers, VHS.

43. Richmond, Personal Property Taxes, 1820, LVA.

44. *Richmond Compiler*, 1813–47; *Richmond Daily Mercantile Advertiser*, 1821–22; *Daily Dispatch*, 1852–65, LVA.

45. Genovese, *Roll, Jordan, Roll*, 343–44.

46. Mann, "Slavery, Sharecropping, and Sexual Inequality."

47. Chief Engineer to James River and Kanawha Company Directors, Nov. 18, 1850, Appendix to the 1850 Annual Report, VHS.

3. BEHIND THE URBAN "BIG HOUSE"

1. Estate of John Prosser, Nov. 10, 1810, Hustings Wills.

2. *Richmond Enquirer*, Jan. 2, 1806; Schnittman, "Slavery in Virginia's Urban Tobacco Industry," chap. 3.

3. Calderhead, "The Role of the Professional Slave Trader," 195–211; Bancroft, *Slave-Trading in the Old South*.

4. Stampp, *Peculiar Institution*, 72; Adams, *South-Side View of Slavery*, 76.

5. Commonwealth v. Bob, June–July 1800, Commonwealth v. Will, May–June 1814, Hustings Suit Papers.

6. Commonwealth v. Nancy Read, Aug. 1823, ibid.

7. Richmond, Personal Property Taxes, 1800, LVA.

8. Mutual Assurance Company, Records, 1800–1840, LVA.

9. Commonwealth v. Sam Payne, March 1818, Hustings Suit Papers.

10. Commonwealth v. Joseph Gray, Dec. 1861, ibid.

11. Commonwealth v. Lucy, Nov. 1819, Commonwealth v. Lavinia, Sept. 1862, ibid.

12. Ibid., Jan.–June 1830.

13. Starobin, *Industrial Slavery in the Old South*, 57–58, 60–61; James River and Kanawha Company, Annual Report, July 17, 1835, VHS.

14. Commonwealth v. Nancy Hicks, Dec. 1841, Commonwealth v. Daniel, Jan.–June 1830, Hustings Suit Papers.

15. Commonwealth v. Daniel, Jan.–June 1830, ibid.

16. Sterling, *We Are Your Sisters*, 16.

17. Charles Copland, Diary, 1820, LVA.

18. Hilliard, *Hog Meat and Hoecake*, 56.

19. Commonwealth v. Jack, March 1809, Hustings Suit Papers.

20. Richmond, City Council, Papers, Jan. 1, 1852, LVA.

21. Charles Copland, Diary, 1820, LVA.

22. *Daily Dispatch*, Aug. 20, 1853.

23. Hilliard, *Hog Meat and Hoecake*, 65; Fogel and Engerman, *Time on the Cross*.

24. Steckel, "A Peculiar Population," 721–42.

25. William Patterson v. Richard Carter, Feb. 1824, Hustings Suit Papers.

26. Commonwealth v. David Russell, April 1822, Commonwealth v. John Bailey, Sept. 1825, ibid.

27. Hill and Dabney Papers, HL; Hustings Suit Papers, 1830–60.

28. Elizabeth Richardson v. Etna Coal Company, Sept. 1840, Hustings Suit Papers.

29. Catherine Flood McCall v. George Ingles, March 1815, Catherine Flood McCall v. Josiah William, Jan. 1, 1811, ibid.

30. Starobin, *Industrial Slavery in the Old South*, 55; Mordecai, *Virginia Especially Richmond*, 355; Will of Nathaniel Dunlop, Aug. 13, 1838, Hustings Wills; Buckingham, *Slaves States of America*, 427.

31. Virginia General Assembly, Acts of the General Assembly, Jan. 28, 1843, LVA; Wall, "Medical Care of Ebenezer Pettigrew's Slaves," 450–70; Genovese, *Roll Jordan, Roll*, 223–29; Evey Jones v. Mrs. Taylor, March 1811, Hustings Suit Papers.

32. The Estate of Doctor William Foushee Sr., Feb. 28, 1825, Hustings Wills; James Currie v. Peyton Randolph, Aug. 1809, Hustings Suit Papers.

33. John Walker to Hill and Dabney, Jan. 1, 1839, Hill and Dabney Papers, HL; W. Wyatt (for James Martin) v. M. Sully and James Beale, July 1840, Hustings Suit Papers; Dr. Lewis Webb Chamberlayne, Account Book, 1835–36, VHS.

34. Estate of Charles Starr, Jan. 3, 1833, Hustings Wills; James River and Kanawha Company, Fourth Annual Report, 1838, 331, VHS.

35. Dr. William Foushee Jr., Records, LVA; Estate of Peter Copland, Dec.–Jan. 1832–33, Hustings Wills; "The Cholera," *Virginia Historical Register and Literary Advertiser*, 171–72, LVA.

36. Philip Nelson to Messrs. Hill and Dabney, Aug. 15, 1839, Hill and Dabney Papers, HL.

37. Frederick Winston v. James Brooks and Francis Markam, Aug. 1821, Hustings Suit Papers.

38. *Richmond Enquirer*, Feb. 4, 1806, Oct. 17, 1806.

39. Philip Nelson to Messrs. Hill and Dabney, Aug. 15, 1839, Edmund Taylor to Messrs. Hill and Dabney, Jan. 4, 1852, Hill and Dabney Papers, HL; Commonwealth v. Peter White, Oct. 1809, Commonwealth v. Nancy Read, Aug. 1823, Commonwealth v. Billy, July 1831, Hustings Suit Papers.

40. Commonwealth v. Lucy, Nov. 1819, Hustings Suit Papers; Will of Dr. James McClurg, July 17, 1823, Hustings Wills.

41. Edmund Taylor to Lewis Hill, Dec. 3, 1853, John Scott to Lewis Hill, Dec. 13, 1853, Hill and Dabney Papers, HL; Will of Isaac H. Judah, May 26, 1827, Hustings Wills.

42. Frederick Winston v. James Brooks and Francis Markam, Aug. 1821, Hustings Suit Papers.

43. Finkelman, "Slaves as Fellow Servants," 285–86.

44. Richard Blow to Samuel Proctor, Jan. 21, 1806, Richard Blow Letter Book, Dismal Swamp Company, VHS.

45. Davidson and Garnett (Co.), Daybooks, 1816–22, HL.

46. *Inventory of the Church Archives of Virginia*, 9.

47. Commonwealth v. Bob, June–July 1800, Hustings Suit Papers; Edward Garlick to Hill and Dabney, Jan. 4, 1838, Hill and Dabney Papers, HL.

48. Robert Brooke to John Clarke, Nov. 29, 1804, John Clarke Letter Book, 1804–8, VHS.

49. William Patterson v. Richard Carter, Feb. 1824, Hustings Suit Papers.

50. Curtis Carter v. William Bowles, June 1812, Thomas Stanton v. Meacon Green, May 1815, ibid.

51. James Hurt v. Francis Tyne (Tyree), May 1810, ibid.

52. Commonwealth v. Jamerson, Aug. 1819, ibid.; "Mrs. Mary Martin, 2nd Witness," Sept. 1800, *Calendar of State Papers* 9:162.

53. Commonwealth v. James Robinson, May 1823, Hustings Suit Papers; Phillips, *Life and Labor in the Old South*, 205.

54. Sernett, *Black Religion and American Evangelicalism*, 38–39; White, *First Baptist Church*, 10–11.

55. Ben Woolfolk's Confession, *Calendar of State Papers* 9:151; *Virginia Argus*, Oct. 14, 1800; Kimball, "The Gabriel's Insurrection," 154; Egerton, *Gabriel's Rebellion*, App. 1.

56. Sernett, *Black Religion and American Evangelicalism*, 24; Hughes, "History of Methodism in Richmond," 2–5; Raboteau, *Slave Religion*, 132.

57. Hughes, "History of Methodism in Richmond," 7.

58. *First Century of the First Baptist Church*, 86.

59. Magri, "History of the St. Joseph's Church, Richmond, Virginia"; Johnson, *A Special Pilgrimage; History of St. John's P.E. Church*; Blanton, *Making of a Downtown Church*.

60. White, *First Baptist Church, Richmond*, 14.

61. Raboteau, *Slave Religion*, 132.

62. *First Century of the First Baptist Church*, 255.

63. Ibid., 118.

64. Raboteau, *Slave Religion*, 133.

65. Jackson, "Negro Religious Development," 170.

66. Sobel, *Trabelin' On*, 160.

67. Pitts, *Old Ship of Zion*, 45.

68. Raboteau, *Fire in the Bones*, 24.

69. White, *First Baptist Church, Richmond*, 19.

70. Ibid., 27, 29; *Religious Herald*, Feb. 22, 1828.

71. White, *First Baptist Church, Richmond*, 28–29, 34–35; Colonization Society of Virginia, Second Annual Report, Virginia Baptist Historical Society; Slaughter, *Virginian History of African Colonization*, 11.

72. *First Century of the First Baptist Church*, 74.

73. FBC, Minute Book, 1825–30, vol. 1, LVA.

74. Ibid., Sept. 18, 1828.

75. Click, *Spirit of the Times*.

76. FBC Minutes, Aug. 14, 1827, June 5, 1829, LVA.

77. Ibid., Dec. 6, 1825, July 11, 1826, July 9, 1829.

78. Ibid., April 7, 1827.

79. *First Century of the First Baptist Church*, 247.

80. FBC Minutes, July 9, 1829, LVA.

81. Weld, *Vacation Tour*, 295.

82. *First Century of the First Baptist Church*, 259.

83. Jeter, *Recollections*, 209.

84. Sobel, *Trabelin' On*, 148.

85. Levine, *Black Culture*, 31.

86. Hopkins, "Slave Theology in the 'Invisible Institution,' " 5.

87. Sobel, *Trabelin' On*, 154.

88. Ibid.; Joyner, "Believer I Know," 25.

89. Sobel, *Trabelin' On*, 143.

90. Joyner, "Believer I Know," 18–46.

91. Jeter, *Recollections*, 102.

92. *First Century of the First Baptist Church*, 255.

93. FABC Minutes, Jan. 1, 1843, LVA; Jeter, *Recollections*, 103.

94. Jeter, *Recollections*, 105.

95. Sobel, *Trabelin' On*, 108–22.

96. Johnson, *God Struck Me Dead*, 151, 161–62; Bratton, "Fields's Observations," 80.

97. Sernett, *Black Religion and American Evangelicalism*, 84; Bratton, "John Jasper of Richmond," 34.

98. Hopkins, "Slave Theology in the 'Invisible Institution,' " 3.

99. Jeter, *Recollections*, 209.

100. Sobel, *Trabelin' On*, 187; *Inventory of the Church Archives*, viii.

101. Raboteau, "African-Americans, Exodus," 9.

102. Dover Association, Minutes, 1821, Virginia Baptist Historical Society; Virginia General Assembly, Legislative Petitions, 1823, LVA.

103. Egerton, *Gabriel's Rebellion*, 71; Kimball, "The Gabriel Insurrection of 1800," 153; Higginson, "Gabriel's Defeat," 339.

104. Major Mosby to Governor Monroe, Sept. 1800, "Slave Insurrection," Executive Papers, Sept.–Dec. 1800, LVA; Egerton, *Gabriel's Rebellion*, 69.

105. M. Carrington to Governor Monroe, Sept. 1800, "Information respecting Insurrection Received of John Foster," Sept. 9, 1800, Deposition of Gilbert, Executive Papers, Sept.–Dec. 1800, LVA.

106. "Slave Insurrection," ibid.

107. Mullin, *Flight and Rebellion*, 158; Confessions of Ben alias Ben Woolfolk, Sept. 17, 1800, *Calendar of State Papers* 9:151, 164.

108. Egerton, *Gabriel's Rebellion*, 111–13.

109. Saunders, "Crime and Punishment in Early National America," 33–44.

110. Duke and Jordan, *Richmond Reader, 1733–1983*, 28–29.

111. William Foushee to Governor of Virginia, Aug. 29, 1782, *Calendar of State Papers* 3:274; Ward and Greer, *Richmond during the Revolution*, 109.

112. Richmond, Common Council Minutes, 1796–1807, HL; "An Act concerning Hawkers and Pedlars," Jan. 18, 1798, Shepherd, *Statutes at Large* 2:94.

113. Shepherd, *Statutes at Large*, Jan. 19, 1798, 2:75–76; Ward and Greer, *Richmond during the Revolution*, 114.

114. Virginia General Assembly, Legislative Petitions, 1782, LVA; Hening, *Statutes at Large* 9:59; Shepherd, *Statutes at Large* 2:75–76; Ward and Greer, *Richmond during the Revolution*, 121.

115. Saunders, "Crime and Punishment," 35.

116. Guild, *Black Laws of Virginia*, 70; Virginia General Assembly, Acts of the General Assembly, Jan. 29, 1808, LVA; Shepherd, *Statutes at Large* 3:372.

117. Virginia General Assembly, Legislative Petitions, Dec. 17, 1834, LVA.

118. "An Act to Amend and Reduce into One the Several Acts of the General Assembly, for Regulating the Militia of This Commonwealth," "An Act Further Declaring What Shall Be Deemed Unlawful Meetings of Slaves," and "An Act Further to Amend the Act, Entitled, 'An Act to Reduce into the One Several Acts concerning Slaves, Free Negroes, and Mulattoes,' " Shepherd, *Statutes at Large* 3:17, 108, 123; Richmond, City Council Ordinances, May 10, 1830, LVA; Egerton, *Gabriel's Rebellion*, 164–65.

119. Testimony of Ben, Sept. 15, 1800, Executive Papers, LVA; Egerton, *Gabriel's Rebellion*, 148.

120. Linn Banks to Governor Floyd, Jan. 6, 1830, Executive Papers, LVA.

121. Virginia General Assembly, Legislative Petitions, Dec. 20, 1804, LVA.

122. Virginia General Assembly, "An Act to Amend the Act concerning Slaves, Free Negroes, and Mulattoes," April 7, 1831, "An Act to Amend an Act, Entitled an Act for Regulating the Navigation of James River, above the Falls of the Said River," Feb. 9, 1811, "An Act to Amend the Act Entitled, 'An Act Reducing into One the Several Acts concerning Slaves, Free Negroes, and Mulattoes,' " Feb. 24, 1827, LVA; Virginia General Assembly, Legislative Petitions, Dec. 17, 1834, ibid.

123. Commonwealth v. Morton, May 1820, Hustings Suit Papers.

124. Berkeley, "Prophet without Honor," 187.

125. Virginia General Assembly, "An Act to Amend the Act concerning Slaves, Free Negroes, and Mulattoes," April 7, 1831, March 11, 1834, "An Act to Amend

an Act, Entitled 'An Act Regulating the Manner of Granting Licenses to Retail Ardent Spirits, and for Other Purposes,' " Feb. 27, 1832, LVA.

126. "An Act concerning Free Negroes and Mulattoes," Feb. 4, 1806, "An Act to Amend an Act, Entitled an Act for Regulating the Navigation of James River, above the Falls of the Said River," Feb. 9, 1811, ibid.

127. Commonwealth v. John McKenna, Commonwealth v. Thomas W. Stubbs, Oct. 1839, Commonwealth v. Oakly Philpotts and Harry, Aug. 1820, Hustings Suit Papers.

128. Virginia General Assembly, "An Act to Amend the Several Acts concerning Slaves, Free Negroes, and Mulattoes," March 11, 1834, March 7, 1831, "An Act to Amend the Act Entitled 'An Act to Amend an Act to Reduce into One the Several Acts concerning Slaves, Free Negroes, and Mulattoes,' " Jan. 29, 1802, Jan. 31, 1805, "An Act to Prohibit the Owners of Ferries and Bridges from Allowing Slaves to Cross Certain Water Courses without the Permission of Their Owners," March 11, 1839, LVA; Richmond, City Council Minutes, April 8, July 17, 1834, LVA.

129. Richmond, City Council Ordinances, May 10, 1830, LVA.

130. Guild, *Black Laws of Virginia*, 71.

131. Virginia General Assembly, "An Act to Amend the Act Entitled An Act to Amend an Act to Reduce into One the Several Acts concerning Slaves, Free Negroes, and Mulattoes," Jan. 29, 1802, Jan. 31, 1805, "An Act to Amend an Act, Entitled 'An Act Regulating the Manner of Granting Licenses to Retail Ardent Spirits, and for Other Purposes,' Passed April 13th, 1831," Feb. 27, 1831, LVA.

132. Commonwealth v. Iris, and Commonwealth v. Titus, Jan. 1814, Commonwealth v. Will, May 1815, Commonwealth v. Nelson Hylton, Nov. 1829, Hustings Suit Papers.

133. Commonwealth v. M. P. Shop, Aug. 1819, ibid.

134. Commonwealth v. William Crane, March 1814, Commonwealth v. Pleasant Warren, Jan. 1822, Commonwealth v. John McDonough, Jan. 1823, ibid.

4. Maturation of the Urban Industrial Slave System, 1840–1860

1. *Richmond, Petersburg, Norfolk, and Portsmouth Business Directory, 1859–1860; Daily Dispatch*, Oct. 6, 1854.

2. Berlin and Gutman, "Natives and Immigrants," 1182.

3. Bureau of Census, Population, 1840 and 1860.

4. Dabney, *Richmond, the Story of a City*, 133.

5. Richmond, Manufacturing Census, 1860, LVA.

6. Ibid., 1850 and 1860.

7. *Daily Dispatch*, Aug. 21, 1852; Berry, "The Rise of Flour Milling in Richmond," 406.

8. Dew, *Ironmaker to the Confederacy*, 19–20.

9. Berlin and Gutman, "Natives and Immigrants," 1182.

10. Weld, *Vacation Tour*, 288.

11. Green, "Urban Industry, Black Resistance," 314; Robert, *Tobacco Kingdom*, chap. 10.

12. Virginia Central Railroad Company, Annual Report, Nov. 1853, VHS.

13. Bureau of Census, Population, 1840–60; Richmond, Personal Property Taxes, 1840–60, LVA; Berry, "The Rise of Flour Milling," 387–408; Green, "Urban Industry, Black Resistance," 395.

14. Richmond, City Council Minutes, 1849; Bureau of Census, Slave Schedules, 1860, LVA.

15. Goldin, *Urban Slavery*, chap. 5; Green, "Urban Industry, Black Resistance," 257–59; *Richmond Daily Whig*, Jan. 17, 1843; *Daily Dispatch*, July 3, 4, Sept. 12, 1854.

16. *Daily Dispatch*, Jan. 3, 1853.

17. Ibid., 1840–60; Hustings Suit Papers, 1840–60; Hill Papers, HL; Goldin, *Urban Slavery*, 72–74.

18. *Richmond Directory, Register, and Almanac*, 1819; *Ellyson's Richmond Directory*, 1845; *Richmond, Petersburg, Norfolk, and Portsmouth Business Directory, 1859–1860*.

19. "Employment of Slaves in Cotton Factories," *De Bow's Review* 8 (Jan. 1850): 75–76.

20. "Excessive Slave Population: The Remedy," ibid., 12 (Feb. 1852): 182–85.

21. "Slave Power on the Railroads" ibid., 11 (Dec. 1851): 638–39.

22. North, *Economic Growth of the United States*, 189–90, 212.

23. Bureau of Census, Population, 1860; Richmond, Manufacturing Census, 1860, LVA; O'Brien, "Factory, Church, and Community," 517.

24. Bureau of Census, Slave Schedules, 1860.

25. Margo, "Wages and Prices," 173–216.

26. Wright, "Cheap Labor and Southern Textiles before 1880," 851–70; Margo, "Wages and Prices during the Antebellum Period," 173–216.

27. "Slave Labor upon Public Works at the South," *DeBow's Review* 17 (July 1854): 77–78.

28. "Superiority of Slave Labor in Constructing Railroads," ibid., 18 (March 1855): 404–5.

29. Parish, *Slavery, History, and Historians*, 43–63.

30. "Superiority of Slave Labor in Constructing Railroads," *DeBow's Review* 18 (March 1855): 405.

31. Green, "Urban Industry, Black Resistance," 314; Robert, *Tobacco Kingdom*, chap. 10.

32. Cooper, *South and the Politics of Slavery;* Greenberg, *Masters and Statesmen*.

33. *Richmond Times and Compiler*, May 28, 1847; *Richmond Enquirer*, May 29, 1847, quoted in Schechter, "Free and Slave Labor in the Old South," 176.

34. Goldin, *Urban Slavery*, 36; Bureau of Census, Population, 1860.

35. Joseph R. Anderson to Board of Directors, June 1, 1842, Minutes of Directors and Stockholders, 1838–53, Tredegar Papers, LVA.

36. Wesley, *Negro Labor in the United States*, chap. 3; Bruce, *Virginia Iron Manufacturers*, 233–35; Dew, *Ironmaker to the Confederacy*, 23–24.

37. Joseph R. Anderson to Board of Directors, June 17, 1842, Minutes of Directors and Stockholders, 1838–53, LVA.

38. Bruce, *Virginia Iron Manufacture*, 224–27; Dew, *Ironmaker to the Confederacy*, 22–26.

39. Virginia Central Railroad Company, Annual Reports, 1850–53, Richmond and Danville Railroad Company, Annual Report, 1854, Virginia and Tennessee Railroad Company, Annual Report, 1852, VHS.

40. Chief Engineer to James River and Kanawha Company Directors, Nov. 18, 1850, Appendix to the 1850 Annual Report, VHS.

41. Brown, *Narrative of Henry "Box" Brown*, 41–42.

42. Weld, *Vacation Tour*, 313.

43. Dew, "Disciplining Slave Ironworkers," 399.

44. Bureau of Census, Population, 1840 and 1860; Richmond, Manufacturing Census, 1840 and 1860, LVA; *Ellyson's Business Directory*, 1845; *Richmond, Petersburg, Norfolk, and Portsmouth Business Directory, 1859–1860*.

45. Olmsted, *Journey in the Seaboard*, 53.

46. Chambers, *Things As They Are*, 271.

47. Berlin and Gutman, "Natives and Immigrants," 1183.

48. Schnittman, "Slavery in Virginia's Urban Tobacco Industry," 162–63.

49. Green, "Urban Industry, Black Resistance," 204.

50. Joseph R. Anderson to Harrison Row, Jan. 3, 1848, quoted in Schecter, "Free and Slave Labor in the Old South," 185.

51. Bureau of Census, Population, 1860; Richmond, Manufacturing Census, 1860, LVA; O'Brien, "Factory, Church, and Community," 517.

52. Brown, *Narrative of Henry "Box" Brown*, 41.

53. Ibid.

54. Elliott and Nye, *Virginia Directory*, 1852; Richmond, Personal Property Taxes, 1850, LVA.

55. Schnittman, "Slavery in Virginia's Urban Tobacco Industry," 113.

56. *Richmond, Petersburg, Norfolk, and Portsmouth Business Directory, 1859–1860*.

57. Brown, *Narrative of Henry "Box" Brown*, 41; U.S. Naval Observatory, Sun and Moon Data for Richmond, Va., Jan. 1, 30, June 25, 1997.

58. Dickens, "Where Slavery Was," quoted in Duke and Jordan, *Richmond Reader*, 80; Alexander McKay, "Another Traveler's View," quoted in ibid., 90.

59. Olmsted, *Journey in the Seaboard*, 114.

60. Schnittman, "Slavery in Virginia's Urban Tobacco Industry," 48.

61. Virginia Central Railroad Company, Annual Reports, 1850–53, Richmond and Danville Railroad Company, Annual Report, 1854, Virginia and Tennessee Railroad Company, Annual Report, 1852, VHS.

62. Dew, *Ironmaker to the Confederacy*, 23.

63. Joseph R. Anderson to Harrison Row, Jan. 13, 1848, quoted in Bruce, *Virginia Iron Manufacture*, 237.

64. Ibid., 248–49.

65. James River and Kanawha Company, Annual Report, 1847, VHS.

66. Bureau of Census, Population, 1860.

67. Converse, "How a Family Lived in the 1830s," 3–11; Tyler-McGraw and Kimball, *In Bondage and Freedom*, pt. 2.

68. Commonwealth v. Curetta and Betty, July 1862, Hustings Suit Papers.

69. *Daily Dispatch*, Nov. 9, 1852.

70. "Memoirs of Reverend Walter Brooks," Brooks Family Records, n.d., VHS; Chesson, *Richmond after the War, Daily Dispatch*, Dec. 24, 1852, Aug. 20, 1853; J. E. Bruce, "A Sketch of My Life," quoted in Lerner, *Black Women in White America*, 33–34.

71. Rachleff, *Black Labor in Richmond*, chap. 2.

5. FORMATION OF AN INDEPENDENT SLAVE COMMUNITY

1. Chesson, *Richmond after the War*, 15.

2. Rabinowitz, *Race Relations;* Scott, *Old Richmond Neighborhoods*.

3. *Daily Dispatch*, May 2, 1853.

4. Tyler-McGraw, *At the Falls*, 114; Chesson, *Richmond after the War*, 16, 98.

5. *Daily Dispatch*, Jan. 2, 1860.

6. Chesson, *Richmond after the War*, 7.

7. Board of Health, Minutes, 1849, VHS.

8. Rabinowitz, *Race Relations in the Urban South*, 114; Goldfield, *Cotton Fields and Skyscrapers*, 40.

9. Board of Health, Minutes, 1849, VHS.

10. Chambers, *Things As They Are*, 271–72; Dickens, "Where Slavery Was," quoted in Duke and Jordan, *Richmond Reader*, 80.

11. Rabinowitz, *Race Relations in the Urban South*, 98.

12. Borchert, *Alley Life in Washington*.

13. Chesson, *Richmond after the War*, 139.

14. Board of Health, Minutes, 1849, VHS.

15. *Daily Dispatch*, May 6, 1853.

16. Tyler-McGraw, *At the Falls*, pt. 4.

17. Bureau of Census, Population, 1850 and 1860; Wade, *Slavery in the Cities*, 330.

18. Bureau of Census, Population, 1850 and 1860; Goldin, *Urban Slavery*, 56–57.

19. Goldin, *Urban Slavery*, 62.

20. St. James Church, Records, 1800–1860, and St. John's Parish, Register, 1785–1879, VHS.

21. St. James Church, Parish Register, July 9, 1857, VHS.

22. FBC Minutes, LVA.

23. Virginia General Assembly, Legislative Petitions, Jan. 17, 1840, LVA.

24. *Daily Dispatch*, Jan. 16, 1852.

25. Bureau of Census, Population, 1850 and 1860.

26. *Daily Dispatch*, Jan. 16, 1852; Hustings Suit Papers, Jan. 25, 1833.

27. Richmond, Personal Property Taxes, 1840 and 1850, LVA.

28. Jones, *Life in the South*, 165–66.

29. Starobin, *Blacks in Bondage*, 71.

30. *Daily Dispatch*, Jan. 27, Sept. 6, 1852, Feb. 15, March 23, 1853.

31. Ibid., Dec. 24, 1852.

32. Ibid., Sept. 6, 1853.

33. Ibid., March 9, 1852.

34. Bratton, "Fields's Observations," 89–90.

35. *Daily Dispatch*, Nov. 10, 13, 1852.

36. Weld, *Vacation Tour*, 297–98.

37. Jeter, *Recollections*, 210–11; *First Century of the First Baptist Church*, 250.

38. Dover Association, Minutes, 1821, Virginia Baptist Historical Society; Virginia General Assembly, Legislative Petition, Dec. 3, 1823, LVA.

39. Weld, *Vacation Tour*, 294–95.

40. FABC Minutes, Sept. 30, 1859, LVA; O'Brien, "Factory, Church, and Community," 526.

41. Virginia General Assembly, "An Act to Amend and Explain an Act Further Declaring What Shall Be Deemed Unlawful Meetings of Slaves," Jan. 4, 1805, LVA.

42. Jeter, *Recollections*, 211–12; O'Brien, "Factory, Church, and Community," 525; *First Century of the First Baptist Church*, 83.

43. Ryland, *Scripture Catechism for Coloured People*, 139, LVA; O'Brien, "Factory, Church, and Community," 531.

44. FABC Minutes, Aug. 8, 1852, LVA.

45. O'Brien, "From Bondage to Citizenship," 45, 48–49; *First Century of the First Baptist Church*, 260–61.

46. O'Brien, "From Bondage to Citizenship," 38.

47. Weld, *Vacation Tour*, 295–96.

48. Bratton, "John Jasper of Richmond," 32–39; John Jasper, "De Sun Do Move," quoted in Miller, *BlackAmerican Literature*, 128–35.

49. FABC Minutes, Oct. 7, 1855, LVA.

50. Rachleff, *Black Labor in Richmond*, 25.

51. FABC Minutes, Dec. 4, 1848, LVA.

52. *Richmond Republic*, Jan. 22, 1866, quoted in Rachleff, *Black Labor in Richmond*, 25.

53. FABC Minutes, Feb. 14, 1847, LVA.

54. *First Century of the First Baptist Church*, 261; Ebenezer Church, Records, July 7, 1858, July 13, 1861, LVA.

55. *First Century of the First Baptist Church*, 254.

56. Tyler-McGraw, *At the Falls*, 95; Dabney, *Richmond, the Story of a City*, 91, 98, 156.

57. FABC Minutes, March 3, 1844, Aug. 1846, Jan. 1855, LVA.

58. Ibid., Jan. 2, Feb. 6, 1842.

59. Ibid., Jan. 2, 1842.

60. Ibid., May 6, 1848.

61. Ibid., May 5, 1850.

62. Ibid., July 20, 1850.

63. Ibid.

64. Ibid., May 2, 1852.

65. Ibid., June 13, 1852.

66. Ibid., July 18, 1852.

67. Raboteau, "African-Americans, Exodus," 9.

68. Jones, *Life in the South*, 149–50.

69. Ethridge, "The Jordan Hatcher Affair," 450.

70. *Daily Dispatch*, Feb. 28, 1852.

71. Ethridge, "The Jordan Hatcher Affair," 446–63.

72. Gov. Joseph Johnson, Oct. 7, 1852, Executive Papers, LVA; Commonwealth v. John and Jane Williams, Slaves, Hustings Suit Papers, Aug. 9, 1852; *Daily Dispatch*, July 20–22, 26, Aug. 2, 10, 13, Sept. 11, 15, Oct. 23, 1852.

73. Hustings Suit Papers, Nov. 1849; *Particulars of the Dreadful Tragedy in Richmond*, HL.

74. Gov. Joseph Johnson, April 22, 1852, Executive Journal, LVA; *Daily Dispatch*, May 15, 1852.

75. Auditor of Public Accounts, "Slave and Free Persons for Sale and Transportation at the Penitentiary, 1816–1842," LVA; Schwarz, "Forging the Shackles," 133–34.

76. Ethridge, "The Jordan Hatcher Affair," 449; Petitions to Gov. Joseph Johnson, April 3, March 26, 1852, Executive Papers, LVA.

77. *Daily Dispatch*, May 8, 10, 1852.

78. Ethridge, "The Jordan Hatcher Affair," 462.

79. *Daily Dispatch*, Dec. 22, Aug. 19, 1852; *Richmond Enquirer*, Sept. 13, 1831.

80. *Richmond Enquirer*, Dec. 22, 1852, Oct. 11, 1853, July 22, Nov. 8, 1854, June 8, 1855.

81. Ingraham, *South-West by a Yankee*, 253.

82. *Richmond Enquirer*, Aug. 9, 1853.

83. Goldin, *Urban Slavery*, 49.

84. *Daily Dispatch*, Jan. 3, 1853; Hustings Suit Papers, March–May 1860.

85. *Daily Dispatch*, June 8, 1855.

86. Ibid., April 26, 1853.

87. Ibid., Sept. 16, 1852.

88. Ibid., Sept. 6, 7, 1854, Sept. 8, 1853.

89. Jones, *Life in the South*, 165–66.

90. Hustings Suit Papers, Feb. 1849.

91. *Daily Dispatch*, July 20, 1852.

92. Bratton, "John Jasper of Richmond," 36.

93. *Daily Dispatch*, Aug. 9, 1861.

94. Lyell, *Second Visit to the United States*, 207.

95. *New York Tribune*, June 17, 1865, quoted in Rachleff, *Black Labor in Richmond*, 14.

96. Philip Lightfoot to Lewis Hill, July 19, 1844, Lewis Hill Papers, Brock Collection, HL.

97. William Spotwood Fontaine to Hill and Dabney, Dec. 11, 1840, Hill and Dabney Papers, ibid.; Jones, *Life in the South*, 150.

98. *Daily Dispatch*, March 19, 1853.

99. Board of Health, Minutes, 1849, VHS.

100. Jackson, "Manumission in Certain Virginia Cities," 304–6.

101. O'Brien, "From Bondage to Citizenship," 27–28; Hustings Deeds, 1800–1829.

102. Jackson, "Manumission in Certain Virginia Cities," 306; Hustings Deeds, Nov. 17, 1859, March 5, 1864, LVA.

103. FABC Minutes, April 6, 1845, LVA.

104. Ibid., April 6, 1845, April 3, 1858.

105. Green, "Black Resistance and Racial Restriction," 494–96.

106. Commonwealth v. Abbey Ann Dixon, "a free black woman," June 1849, Hustings Suit Papers, LVA.

107. *Daily Dispatch*, Jan. 24, 1860, May 21, 1863.

108. FABC Minutes, June 6, 1852, LVA.

109. Starobin, *Letters of American Slaves*, 107–10.

6. THE WAR YEARS, 1861–1865

1. Dabney, *Richmond, the Story of a City*, 159; Bill, *Beleaguered City*, 36.

2. Stanard, *Richmond, Its People and Its Story*, 161–62; Thomas, *Confederate Nation*, 85.

3. Bill, *Beleaguered City*, 40; *Daily Dispatch*, April 15, 1861.

4. *Daily Dispatch*, April 15, 1861.

5. Thomas, *Confederate Nation*, 93.

6. Jefferson Davis to John Letcher, April 19, 1861, quoted in Rowland, *Jefferson Davis*, 64.

7. John Janney, President of the Convention, to President Davis, April 27, 1861, quoted in ibid., 67; Dabney, *Richmond, the Story of a City*, 164.

8. Eaton, *Jefferson Davis*, 155; Thomas, *Confederate Nation*, 100–101.

9. Thomas, *Confederate State of Richmond*, 71; DeLeon, *Four Years in the Rebel Capital*, 86, 87–88; Bill, *Beleaguered City*, 50.

10. Varina Howell Davis, quoted in Jones, *Heroines of Dixie*, 60.

11. Dabney, *Richmond, the Story of a City*, 165.

12. *Daily Dispatch*, Jan. 8, Sept. 19, 1861.

13. Dabney, *Richmond, the Story of a City*, 165.

14. Auditor of Public Accounts, General Army Vouchers, Jan. 18–March 8, 1862, LVA; *Daily Dispatch*, Jan. 1, 1863.

15. *Daily Dispatch*, July 15, 1861; Virginia General Assembly, "An Act to Amend and Re-enact an Ordinance to Provide for the Enrollment and Employment of Free Negroes in the Public Service, Passed by the Convention July 1st, 1861," Feb. 12, 1862, LVA; "Messages of the Governor of Virginia," March 30, 1863, *Virginia House Documents and Annual Reports*, 163.

16. Brewer, *Confederate Negro*, 19, 20; "Documents Relative to the Subject of Salt," Jan. 23, 1865, *Journal of the House of Delegates, 1863–1865*; General Hospital No. 8, Account Book, 1862–64, Museum of the Confederacy; Confederate Surgeon General, Letter Book, 1862, HL; Chimborazo Hospital, Account Book Kept by Henry B. Gaines, 1864–65, Museum of the Confederacy.

17. Commonwealth v. Edward C. Epps, Aug. 8, 1864, Hustings Suit Papers.

18. Virginia Central Railroad, Annual Report, 1862, VHS; Richmond, Personal Property Taxes, 1862–63, LVA.

19. Dew, *Ironmaker to the Confederacy*, 23; Richmond, Personal Property Taxes, 1862, LVA; Brewer, *Confederate Negro*, 61.

20. Trexler, "The Opposition of Planters to the Employment of Slaves as Laborers by the Confederacy," 211.

21. Petition from Citizens in the Shenandoah Valley to Governor Letcher, Aug. 1861, quoted in *War of the Rebellion* 1/5:818.

22. Brewer, *Confederate Negro*, 6, 8.

23. J. Bankhead Magruder to Honorable George W. Randolph, Secretary of War, April 29, 1862, quoted in *War of the Rebellion* 1/11:475.

24. Report from Board of Health, Nov. 22, 1862, City Council Papers, 1862, LVA; Surgeon C. D. Rice to E. S. Gaillard, Dec. 13, 1862, quoted in Berlin, *Freedom: A Documentary History of Emancipation*, 703; Gov. John Letcher Papers, Jan. 5, 1863, Executive Journal, LVA.

25. John Randolph Chambliss to Jefferson Davis, Jan. 27, 1863, John Randolph Chambliss Letters, VHS.

26. Gov. John Letcher Papers, March 13, 1863, Executive Journal, LVA.

27. *Daily Dispatch*, Sept. 15, 1863.

28. Trexler, "The Opposition of Planters to the Employment of Slaves as Laborers by the Confederacy," 214; Brewer, *Confederate Negro*, 9.

29. "Ann, Slave, Punishment Commuted," Jan. 17, 1863, Executive Journal, LVA.

30. Tredegar Iron Works, Business Records, 1845–65, LVA.

31. "Profit and Loss to Negro a/c/ for the following Negroes ran off," Dec. 31, 1863, Tredegar Company, Records, LVA.

32. Virginia Central Railroad, Documents, 1850–68, HL.

33. "Certificate of Slave Hire to Mrs. Mary F. Brooks," Feb. 23, 1865, Midlothian Coal Mining Company, Letters and Documents, 1858–67, HL.

34. "Report of Male Slaves between the Ages of 18 & 45 Years, Employed in the City of Richmond," Hustings Suit Papers, 1863–64.

35. *Daily Dispatch,* Jan. 1, 1861.

36. Catherine Doyle McKenny Capston to Lt. James Logan Capston, May 22, 1863, McKenny Family Papers, 1814–64, VHS; Emma Mordecai, Diary, May 1864–May 1865, VHS; *Daily Dispatch,* Nov. 18, 1861.

37. Judith Brockenbrough McGuire, Diary, June 5, 1861, quoted in Jones, *Heroines of Dixie,* 42.

38. Mrs. Williams A. Simmons, March 23, 1865, quoted in Jones, *Ladies of Richmond,* 264.

39. Emma Mordecai, July 4, 1864, Diary, May 1864–May 1865, VHS; Tyler-McGraw, *At the Falls,* 138.

40. "An Inside View of Four Years in the Rebel Capital," *Cosmopolite* 1:111 (1866): 253.

41. Emma Mordecai, July 13, 1864, Diary, May 1864–May 1865, VHS.

42. "Albert Rush, Slave, an Appeal to the Commonwealth," Nov. 12, 1861, and Commonwealth v. Anthony Bradley, Nov. 15, 1862, Hustings Suit Papers.

43. Tyler-McGraw, *At the Falls,* 150–51; Thomas, *Confederate State of Richmond,* 119–20.

44. *Daily Dispatch,* Jan. 1–30, 1862, Jan. 1–30, 1863, Jan. 1–30, 1864.

45. Ibid., Jan. 2, 1862, Jan. 1, 3, 1863.

46. Ibid., Jan. 1, 2, 1862, Jan. 3, 1863, Jan. 1, 1864, Jan. 3, 1865.

47. "Report of Male Slaves between the Ages of 18 & 45 Years Employed in the City of Richmond, Districts, 1, 2 & 3," 1864, Hustings Suit Papers, Dec. 1863–June 1864, LVA; Richmond, Manufacturing Census, 1860, LVA.

48. Arnold, *History of the Tobacco Industry,* 20–21; Tanner, *Tobacco from the Grower to the Smoker,* 15; Brooks, *Mighty Leaf,* 235.

49. *Daily Dispatch,* Nov. 18, 1861; Manarin, *Richmond at War,* 210–13.

50. Gov. John Letcher Papers, March 16, 1863, Executive Journal, 1862–63, LVA.

51. General Hospital No. 8, Account Book, 1862–64, Museum of the Confederacy.

52. *Daily Dispatch,* March 24, Oct. 23, 1862, March 11, 1863.

53. Ibid., Jan. 1, 1863, Aug. 22, 1862, Sept. 19, 1863.

54. Wade, *Slavery in the Cities,* chap. 4.

55. The Richmond Black Code (1859), quoted in Duke and Jordan, *Richmond Reader,* 107–14.

56. City Council Minutes, July 13, 1863, Oct. 10, 1864, quoted in Manarin, *Richmond at War,* 346.

57. *Richmond Enquirer,* 1861–65; Hustings Suit Papers, 1861–65.

58. Hustings Suit Papers, 1849–51, 1862–64.

59. *Richmond Whig*, June 11, 18, July 11, 13, 16, 19, 21, 23, 1861.

60. *Daily Dispatch*, July 2, 1861.

61. Ibid., Oct. 28, Dec. 13, 1861.

62. Guild, *Black Laws of Virginia*, 92.

63. Auditor of Public Accounts, City of Richmond, Delinquent Tax Lists, 1861–62, LVA.

64. Ibid., Delinquent Free Negroes, Richmond City, 1862.

65. Hustings Suit Papers, 1861–65.

66. John R. Tucker to Gov. John Letcher, Dec. 20, 1862, Executive Papers, 1861–65, LVA.

67. *Daily Dispatch*, Oct. 20, Nov. 15, 1862.

68. Ibid., June 14, Nov. 17, 1862.

69. Ibid., Oct. 12, 1861, April 14, 1863.

70. Commonwealth v. A. W. Richardson, Dec. 8, 1862, Hustings Suit Papers.

71. Commonwealth v. Thomas Emett, Nov. 11, 1862, ibid.

72. Commonwealth v. Helen A. E. Briggs, July 17, 1862, ibid.

73. Berlin, *Freedom: A Documentary History*, 703.

74. *Daily Dispatch*, Sept. 19, 1863; Commonwealth v. Elizabeth Woodcock, Dec. 19, 1861, Hustings Suit Papers.

75. *Daily Dispatch*, Nov. 16, 1863.

76. Ibid., Nov. 19, 1863.

77. Ibid., Jan. 9, 1865.

78. Ibid., May 14, 1864.

79. "A List of Slaves That Have Escaped to the Enemy, circa 1862," HL; Virginia Central Railroad, Annual Report, 1862, VHS; *Daily Dispatch*, 1861–65.

80. *Daily Dispatch*, Aug. 26, 1861, Jan. 1, Jan. 16, 1862.

81. Ibid., July 15, 1861, March 24, 1862, Aug. 9, 1861.

82. Ibid., Feb. 6, 1862.

83. Commonwealth v. Allen, March 7, 1862, Hustings Suit Papers.

84. *Daily Dispatch*, July 29, 1862.

85. Dowdey, *Experiment in Rebellion*, 151.

86. Gen. Robert E. Lee to Gov. John Letcher, Dec. 30, 1862, John R. Tucker to Gov. Letcher, Dec. 30, 1862, Executive Papers, LVA.

87. *Richmond Evening Journal*, n.d., quoted in Elizabeth Van Lew, Miscellaneous Papers, 1862–1901, LVA; Dowdey, *Experiment in Rebellion*, 218–19.

88. Jefferson Davis to the Confederate Congress, Nov. 7, 1864, quoted in Rowland, *Jefferson Davis*, 394–97.

89. Auditor of Public Accounts, "Runaway and Escaped Slaves, 1863," Receipts and Reports, 1806–59, 1863, LVA.

90. Dowdey, *Experiment in Rebellion*, 260.

91. Howell Cobb to James A. Seddon, Jan. 8, 1865, quoted in Durden, *Gray and the Black*, 183–85.

92. Bill, *Beleaguered City*, 258.

NoTES TO PP. 143–147

93. Thomas, *Confederate Nation*, 296.

94. Act of General Assembly, March 6, 1865, *War of the Rebellion* 46:1315.

95. Thomas, *Confederate State of Richmond*, 189.

96. Bill, *Beleaguered City*, 259.

97. Putnam, *Richmond during the War*, 351–52.

98. Thomas, *Confederate Nation*, 300–301; Putnam, *Richmond during the War*, 366–67; Joel C. Baker, First Lieutenant 9th Vermont Infantry, "The Fall of Richmond," paper presented at the meeting of the Vermont Commandery of the Loyal Legion, 1892, 10–11, HL.

Epilogue

1. "Incidents of the Capture of Richmond," *Atlantic Monthly* 46 (1880): 24.

2. *New York Times*, April 4, 1866, and *Richmond Citizen*, April 4, 1866, quoted in Rachleff, *Black Labor in Richmond*, 39.

3. Rachleff, *Black Labor in Richmond*, 39.

4. Starobin, *Blacks in Bondage*, 71; Jones, *Life in the South*, 165–66; FABC Minutes, May 5, 1850.

Bibliography

U. S. Government

Coxe, Tench. *A Statement of the Arts and Manufactures of the United States of America, for the Year 1810.* Philadelphia, 1814.

U.S. Bureau of the Census. Census of Manufacturers. Richmond, Virginia. 1820, 1830, 1840, 1850, and 1860. LVA.

———. *Heads of Families, First Census of the U.S.: 1790, State Enumerations of Virginia: From 1782 to 1785.* Washington, D.C., 1907–8.

———. *The Second Census of the United States, 1800.* Population Tables for Virginia. Washington, D.C., 1800.

———. *Aggregate Amount of Each Description of Persons within the United States of America; and the Territories Thereof, Agreeable to Actual Enumeration Made according to Law, in the Year 1810.* Washington, D.C., 1811.

———. *Aggregate Returns for the United States, Census for 1820.* Washington, D.C., 1821.

———. *Fifth Census; or Enumeration of the Inhabitants of the United States, 1830.* Washington, D.C., 1832.

———. *Compendium of the Enumeration of the Inhabitants and Statistics of the United States as Obtained at the Department of State, from the Returns of the Sixth Census by Counties and Principal Towns.* Washington, D.C., 1841.

DeBow, J. D. B. *The Seventh Census of the United States: 1850.* Washington, D.C., 1854.

U.S. Bureau of the Census. *The Seventh Census of the United States, 1850.* Manufacturing Schedule, MSS. Virginia. Washington, D.C., 1865.

————. *The Eighth Census of the United States, 1860.* Manufacturing Schedule, MSS. Virginia. Washington, D.C., 1865.

————. Slave Schedules of Richmond, Virginia. 1850 and 1860. LVA.

U.S. Department of the Treasury, Bureau of Statistics. *Monthly Summary of Commerce and Finance of the United States, June 1903.* Washington, D.C., 1903.

VIRGINIA STATE GOVERNMENT

Auditor of Public Accounts. Accounts and Receipts. Box 1791. LVA.

————. Condemned Slaves. Box 1. LVA.

————. Records. 1783–1855. LVA.

Board of Health. Minutes. 1849. VHS.

Board of Public Works. James River Company. Records. 1794–1840. LVA.

————. James River and Kanawha Company. Records. 1834–78. LVA.

Calendar of Virginia State Papers and Other Manuscripts, 1652–1869. Ed. William P. Palmer et al. 11 vols. Richmond, 1875–93.

Confederate State of America. Papers. VHS.

Executive Journals. 1800–1865. LVA.

Executive Papers. 1800–1865. LVA.

Journals of the Council of the State of Virginia. Ed. H. R. McIlwaine et al. 5 vols. Richmond, 1931–82.

Personal Property Tax Records. Henrico County. 1800–1860. LVA.

The Statutes at Large; Being a Collection of All the Laws of Virginia, from the First Session of the Legislature in the Year 1619. Ed. William Waller Hening. 13 vols. Richmond, etc., 1809–23.

The Statutes at Large of Virginia . . . 1792 . . . 1806. Ed. Samuel Shepherd. 3 vols. 1835–36; rpt. New York, 1970.

Virginia General Assembly. Acts of the Assembly. 1800–1860. LVA. Also printed annually as *Acts Passed at a General Assembly of the Commonwealth of Virginia. . . .* Richmond.

————. Legislative Petitions. 1782–1860. LVA.

Virginia House Documents and Annual Reports, Session 1862 September 15 to Session 1863 March 30. Ed. William F. Ritchie. Richmond, 1863.

Virginia House Documents and Annual Reports, Session 1863 December 7 to Session 1864 March 3. Ed. William F. Ritchie. Richmond, 1864.

CITY GOVERNMENT

City Council. *The Charters and Ordinances of the City of Richmond with the Declaration of Rights and Constitution of Virginia.* Richmond, 1859.

————. Minutes. 1800–1860. LVA.

————. *Ordinances of the Corporation of the City of Richmond, and the Acts of Assembly Relating Thereto.* Richmond, 1831.

————. *Ordinances Passed by the Council of the City of Richmond since the Year 1839.* Richmond, 1847.

————. Papers. 1800–1860. LVA.

City Sergeant. Register. March 13, 1841–May 8, 1846. VHS.

Common Council. Minutes. 1796–1807, Brock Collection, HL.

Common Hall. Ordinances. 1782–1800. LVA.

Hustings Court. Deeds. 1782–1860. LVA.

———. Minutes of the Court. 1800–1860. LVA.

———. Suit Papers. 1800–1860. LVA.

———. Wills, Inventories, and Accounts. 1782–1865. LVA.

Richmond at War: The Minutes of the City Council, 1861–1865. Ed. Louis Manarin. Chapel Hill, N.C., 1966.

NEWSPAPERS AND BUSINESS DIRECTORIES

Daily Compiler (Richmond), 1813–16.

Daily Dispatch (Richmond), 1852–65.

Daily Richmond Examiner, 1861–65.

Daily Richmond Whig and Public Advertiser, 1833–40.

Richmond Daily Mercantile Advertiser, 1821–22.

Richmond Daily Whig, 1842–61.

Richmond Enquirer, 1830–60.

Richmond Examiner, 1847–49.

Richmond Semi-Weekly Examiner, 1849–63.

Richmond Whig and Public Advertiser, 1833–67.

Virginia Argus (Richmond), 1796–1816.

Virginia Gazette and General Advertiser, 1790–1803.

Virginia Gazette and Richmond and Manchester Advertiser, 1794.

Virginia Gazette and Weekly Advertiser, 1790–1803.

Virginia Gazette or the American Advertiser, 1782.

Virginia Gazette or the Independent Chronicle, 1783–86.

Elliott and Nye. *Virginia Directory and Business Register, for 1852.* 1852.

Ellyson's Business Directory and Almanac (Richmond), 1845.

The Richmond Directory, Register, and Almanac. 1819.

Richmond, Petersburg, Norfolk, and Portsmouth Business Directory, 1859–1860. 1859.

MANUSCRIPT COLLECTIONS

Henry E. Huntington Library, San Marino, Calif.

    Baker, Joel C. "The Fall of Richmond." Paper presented at the Vermont Commandery of the Loyal Legion, Vermont, 1892.

    Burwell, William M. "Receipted Voucher of Work Done by His Slave Godfrey for the Confederate States of America." June 20, 1863.

    Confederate Surgeon General. Letter Book. 1862.

    Davidson and Garnett (Co.). Daybooks. 1816–22.

    Hill, Lewis. Papers. 1778–1857.

    Hill and Dabney. Papers.

    Midlothian Coal Mining Company. Letters and Documents. 1858–67.

    Peasants Family. Correspondence. 1785–1800.

    Richmond Dock Company. Memo Book. 1819.

Virginia Central Railroad. Documents. 1850–68.

Wynne, Thomas Hicks. Journal.

Library of Virginia, Richmond

Bailey, William. Accounts. 1813–62.

Bohannan, Dr. Charles. Business Records. 1845.

Clarke, John. Letters. 1821–24, 1828–29, 1831.

Copeland, Charles. Papers. 1788–1822.

Ebenezer Baptist Church. Records. 1858–1980.

First Baptist Church. Minute Book. 1825–30.

First African Baptist Church. Minutes. 1841–65.

Foushee, Dr. William, Jr. Records.

Mutual Assurance Company. Records. 1800–1860.

Richmond and Danville Railroad Company. Annual Reports. 1854–60.

Richmond and Petersburg Railroad Company. Annual Report. 1857.

Tredegar Iron Company. Records. 1838–65.

Van Lew, Elizabeth. Miscellaneous Papers. 1862–1901.

Virginia and Tennessee Railroad. Annual Reports. 1848–60.

Museum of the Confederacy, Richmond

Clopton Hospital. Register. 1861–65.

Gaines, Henry B. Chimborazo Hospital Account Book. 1864–65.

General Hospital No. 8. Account Book. 1862–64.

Valentine Museum, Richmond

Smith, John Adams, Esq. Papers.

Virginia Baptist Historical Society

Dover Association. Minutes. 1800–1860.

Virginia Historical Society, Richmond

Ambler Family. Papers. 1772–1852.

Asplund, John. *The Annual Register of the Baptist Denomination in North America.* 1792.

Blair, Reverend John D. Papers.

Blow, Richard. Letterbook. 1746–1833.

Booth, R. W. Receipt. 1863.

Branch and Company. Business Records. 1846–48.

Brand, Benjamin. Papers. 1790–1838.

Breckinridge Family. Papers. 1740–1902.

Brock, Robert Alonzo. Diary. 1858–61.

Brooks, William Benthall. Papers. 1862–67.

Cabell, William H. Commonplace Book. 1840.

Cardwell, Wyatt. Papers. 1853.

Carrington, Paul. Account Book. 1787–91.

Chamberlayne, Edward Pye. Account Books. 1821–77.

Chamberlayne, Dr. Lewis Webb. Account Books. 1798–1854.

Chambliss, John Randolph. Letters. 1863.

Claiborne, Herbert Augustine. Account Books. 1819–1902.

Clarke, John. Letterbook. 1804–8.

Colonization Society of Virginia. Annual Reports. 1833, 1838–39, 1851.

Committee of Vigilance. Records. 1813–14.

Confederate States of America. War Department Imprints.

Evans, James H. Papers. 1856–65.

Gooch, Philip Claiborne. Diary. 1845–52.

Harrison Family. Papers. 1786–1908.

Haxall, Bolling Walker. Account Books. 1851–83.

Haxall Family. Papers. 1835–1920.

Howlett, James C. Receipt. 1864.

James River and Kanawha Canal. Annual Reports. 1835–41, 1848–52, 1860.

Little, Dr. John Peyton. Commonplace Book. 1836–63.

Magri, Joseph. "History of the St. Joseph's Church, Richmond, Virginia."
    Typescript.

Mason, Lewis Edmunds. Account Book. 1849–63.

McCarthy and Mitchell. Account Book. 1862–67.

McKenny Family. Papers. 1814–64.

McRae, Sherwin. Accounts. 1837–81.

Mordecai, Emma. Diary. May 1864–May 1865.

Myers Family. Papers. 1763–1923.

Pitts Family. Papers. 1848–1926.

Richmond and Danville Railroad Company. Annual Reports. 1848–60, 1865.

Richmond, Fredericksburg, and Potomac Railroad Company. Annual Re-
    ports. 1834–65.

Richmond Mining Company. Accounts. 1836–37.

Sparrow, Caroline T. "Notes concerning the Case of the Slave Girl Virginia
    Who Was Tried before the Hustings Court of Richmond, Virginia, in Feb-
    ruary and March 1843 for Setting Fire to and Burning a Dwelling by
    William B. Rushmer and Belonging to Thomas Cowles and Sterling I.
    Crump." Typescript.

St. James Church. Records. 1800–1860.

———. Parish Register. 1855–89.

St. John's Parish. Register. 1785–1879.

St. Paul's Church. Vestry Book. 1845–55.

Tabb, Philip Mayo, and Son. Letters. 1846.

Talbott and Brother. Papers. 1831–80.

Tompkins, Christopher Quarles. Dover Mines and Tuckahoe Pits. Common-
    place Book. 1863–67.

Van Lew, Elizabeth. Album. 1818–1900.

Virginia and Tennessee Railroad Company. Annual Reports. 1848, 1850–52,
    1856, 1859.

Virginia Central Railroad Company. Annual Reports. 1836, 1851–53, 1862–
    63.

Virginia Commissioners of James and Jackson's Rivers. Letters. 1821.

Antebellum Works

Bagby, Dr. George W. *Selections from the Miscellaneous Writings of Dr. George W. Bagby.* Richmond, 1884.

Brockenbrough, William. *Cases of the General Court, 1786.* Philadelphia, 1815.

Brown, Henry "Box." *Narrative of Henry "Box" Brown: Who Escaped from Slavery, Enclosed in a Box Three Feet Long, Two Wide and Two and Half High: Written from a Statement of Facts Made by Himself with Remarks upon the Remedy for Slavery by Charles Stearns.* Boston, 1849.

Bryant, William Cullen. *Letters of a Traveller: Or, Notes of Things Seen in Europe and America.* New York, 1850.

Buckingham, J. S. *The Slave States of America.* 2 vols. London, 1842.

Chambers, William. *Things As They Are in America.* London, 1857.

Douglass, Frederick. *My Bondage and My Freedom.* New York, 1855.

Farley, Charles A. *Slavery; A Discourse Delivered in the Unitarian Church.* Richmond, 1835.

Ingraham, Joseph Holt. *The South-West by a Yankee.* 2 vols. New York, 1968.

Jones, S. L. *Life in the South: From the Commencement of the War by a Blockaded British Subject.* Vol. 1. London, 1863.

Mordecai, Samuel. *Virginia, Especially Richmond in By-Gone Days; with a Glance at the Present.* Richmond, 1860.

Olmsted, Frederick Law. *A Journey in the Back Country.* New York, 1863.

———. *A Journey in the Seaboard Slave States: In the Years 1853–1854.* New York, 1904.

Putnam, Sallie R. *Richmond during the War: Four Years of Personal Observation.* New York, 1867.

Ruffin, Edmund. *Slavery and Free Labor Described and Compared.* N.p., 1860.

Schoepf, Johann David. *Travels in the Confederation, 1783–1784.* New York, 1911.

Weld, Charles Richard. *A Vacation Tour in the United States and Canada.* London, 1855.

Secondary Works

Albert, Peter Joseph. "The Protean Institution: The Geography, Economy, and Ideology of Slavery in Post-Revolutionary Virginia." Ph.D. diss., University of Maryland, 1976.

Amott, Teresa, and Julie Matthaei. *Race, Gender, and Work: A Multicultural Economic History of Women in the United States.* Boston, 1991.

Arnold, B. W., Jr. *History of the Tobacco Industry in Virginia from 1860 to 1894.* Baltimore, 1897.

Bancroft, Frederick. *Slave Trading in the Old South.* Baltimore, 1931.

Bellamy, Donnie D. "Macon, Georgia, 1823–1860: A Study in Urban Slavery." *Phylon* 45 (1984): 298–310.

Berlin, Ira, et al., eds. *Freedom: A Documentary History of Emancipation, 1861–1865.* Ser. 1 and 2. New York, 1985.

Berlin, Ira, and Herbert G. Gutman. "Natives and Immigrants, Free Men and Slaves: Urban Workingmen in the Antebellum American South." *American Historical Review* 88 (1983): 1175–1200.

Berry, Thomas S. "The Rise of Flour Milling in Richmond." *Virginia Magazine of History and Biography* 78 (1970): 387–408.

Bill, Alfred Hoyt. *The Beleaguered City: Richmond, 1861–1865.* New York, 1946.

Brewer, James H. *The Confederate Negro: Virginia's Craftsmen and Military Laborers, 1861–1865.* Durham, N.C., 1969.

Brooks, Jerome E. *The Mighty Leaf: Tobacco through the Centuries.* Boston, 1952.

Bruce, Kathleen. *Virginia Iron Manufacturers in the Slave Era.* New York, 1930.

Calderhead, William. "The Role of the Professional Slave Trader in a Slave Economy: Austin Woolfolk, a Case Study." *Civil War History* 23 (1977): 195–211.

Campbell, John. "As 'A Kind of Freeman'?: Slaves' Market-Related Activities in the South Carolina Upcountry, 1800–1860." *Slavery and Abolition* 12:1 (1991): 131–69.

Campbell, Randolph B. "Slave Hiring in Texas." *American Historical Review* 93 (1988): 107–14.

Chesson, Michael. *Richmond after the War, 1865–1890.* Richmond, 1981.

Converse, Paul D. "How a Family Lived in the 1830s." *Current Economic Comment,* Feb. 1950, 3–11

Cooper, William J. *The South and the Politics of Slavery, 1828–1856.* Baton Rouge, La., 1978.

Cottrol, Robert J. "Comparative Slave Studies: Urban Slavery as a Model, Travelers' Accounts as a Source—Bibliographic Essay." *Journal of Black Studies* 8 (1977): 3–12.

Dabney, Virginius. *Richmond, the Story of a City.* Charlottesville, Va., 1976; rpt., 1990.

DeLeon, Thomas C. *Four Years in Rebel Capitals.* Mobile, Ala., 1890.

Dew, Charles. *Bond of Iron: Master and Slave at Buffalo Forge.* New York, 1994.

———. "David Ross and the Oxford Iron Works: A Study of Industrial Slavery in the Early Nineteenth-Century South." *William and Mary Quarterly,* 3d ser., 31 (1974): 189–224.

———. "Disciplining Slave Ironworkers in the Antebellum South: Coercion, Conciliation, and Accommodation." *American Historical Review* 79 (1974): 393–418.

———. *Ironmaker to the Confederacy: Joseph R. Anderson and the Tredegar Iron Works.* New Haven, 1966.

Dodd, Donald B., and Wynelle S. Dodd. *Historical Statistics of the South, 1790–1970: Compilation of State-Level Census Statistics for the Sixteen States of the South.* Tuscaloosa, Ala., 1973.

Dowdey, Clifford. *Experiment in Rebellion.* New York, 1946.

Duke, Maurice, and Daniel P. Jordan. *A Richmond Reader, 1733–1983.* Chapel Hill, N.C., 1983.

Dunaway, Wayland Fuller. *History of the James River and Kanawha Canal.* New York, 1922.

Durden, Robert F. *The Gray and the Black: The Confederate Debate on Emancipation*, Baton Rouge, La., 1972.

Eaton, Clement. *The Growth of Southern Civilization, 1790–1860*. New York, 1961.

———. *Jefferson Davis*. New York, 1977.

———. "Slave-Hiring in the Upper South: A Step toward Freedom." *Mississippi Historical Review* 46 (1959–60): 663–78.

Egerton, Douglas R. *Gabriel's Rebellion: The Virginia Slave Conspiracies of 1800 and 1802*. Chapel Hill, N.C., 1993.

Fields, Barbara J. *Slavery and Freedom on the Middle Ground: Maryland during the Nineteenth Century*. New Haven, 1985.

Finkelman, Paul. "Slaves as Fellow Servants: Ideology, Law, and Industrialization." *American Journal of Legal History* 31 (1987): 269–305.

The First Century of the First Baptist Church of Richmond, Virginia, 1780–1880. Richmond, 1880.

Fogel, Robert, and Engerman, Stanley. *Time on the Cross: The Economics of American Negro Slavery*. 2 vols. Boston, 1974.

Fox-Genovese, Elizabeth. *Within the Plantation Household: Black and White Women of the Old South*. Chapel Hill, N.C., 1988.

Franklin, John Hope. "Slaves Virtually Free in Ante-Bellum North Carolina." *Journal of Negro History* 28 (1943): 284–310.

Freehling, Alison Goodyear. *Drift towards Dissolution: The Virginia Slavery Debate of 1831–1832*. Baton Rouge, La., 1982.

Goldfield, David R. *Cotton Fields and Skyscrapers: Southern City and Region, 1607–1980*. Baton Rouge, La., 1982.

Goldin, Claudia Dale. *Urban Slavery in the American South, 1820–1860*. Chicago, 1976.

Gray, Lewis. *History of Agriculture in the Southern United States to 1860*. 2 vols. Washington, D.C., 1933.

Green, Rodney D. "Industrial Transition in the Land of Chattel Slavery: Richmond, Virginia, 1820–1860." *International Journal of Urban and Regional Research* 8 (1984): 238–53.

———. "Urban Industry, Black Resistance, and Racial Restriction in the Antebellum South: A General Model and Case Study in Urban Virginia." Ph.D. diss., American University, 1980.

Greenberg, Kenneth S. *Masters and Statesmen: The Political Culture of American Slavery*. Baltimore, 1985.

Guild, June Purcell. *Black Laws of Virginia: A Summary of the Legislative Acts of Virginia concerning Negroes from Earliest Times to the Present*. Richmond, 1936.

Higginson, Thomas W. "Gabriel's Defeat." *Atlantic Monthly* 10 (1862): 337–45.

Hilliard, Sam, B. *Hog Meat and Hoecake; Food Supply in the Old South, 1840–1860*. Carbondale, Ill., 1972.

Hopkins, Dwight N. "Slave Theology in the 'Invisible Institution.' " In *Cut Loose Your Stammering Tongue: Black Theology in the Slave Narratives*. Ed. Dwight N. Hopkins and George C. L. Cummings. New York, 1991.

Hughes, Sarah S. "Slaves for Hire: Allocation of Black Labor in Elizabeth City County, Virginia, 1782–1810." *William and Mary Quarterly*, 3d ser., 35 (1978): 260–86.

Hughes, William. "History of Methodism in Richmond." Typescript. 1937. Virginia Historical Society, Richmond.

Ingersoll, Thomas N. "Free Blacks in a Slave Society: New Orleans, 1718–1812." *William and Mary Quarterly*, 3d ser., 48 (1991): 173–200.

Inventory of the Church Archives of Virginia. Prepared by the Historical Records Survey of Virginia, Inventory of the Church Archives of Virginia, sponsored by the Virginia Conservation Commission: Negro Baptist Churches. Richmond, 1940.

Johnson, Clifford H., ed. *God Struck Me Dead: Religious Conversion Experiences and Autobiographies of Ex-Slaves.* Philadelphia, 1945.

Johnson, Nessa Theresa Basherville. *A Special Pilgrimage: A History of Black Catholics in Richmond.* Richmond, 1978.

Jones, Katherine M., ed. *Heroines of Dixie: Confederate Women Tell Their Story of the War.* New York, 1955.

Joyner, Charles. " 'Believer I Know': The Emergence of African-American Christianity." In *African-American Christianity: Essays in History.* Ed. Paul E. Johnson. Berkeley, Calif., 1994.

Kimball, William J. "The Gabriel's Insurrection of 1800." *Negro History Bulletin* 34 (1971): 153–56.

Kulikoff, Allan. *Tobacco and Slaves: The Development of Southern Cultures in the Chesapeake, 1680–1800.* Chapel Hill, N.C., 1986.

Lack, Paul D. "An Urban Slave Community: Little Rock, 1831–1862." *Arkansas Historical Quarterly* 41 (1982): 258–87.

Lerner, Gerda, ed. *Black Women in White America: A Documentary History.* New York, 1973.

Lewis, Ronald L. *Coal, Iron, and Slaves: Industrial Slavery in Maryland and Virginia, 1715–1865.* Westport, Conn., 1979.

———. " 'Darkest Abode of Man': Black Miners in the First Southern Coal Field, 1780–1865." *Virginia Magazine of History and Biography* 87 (1979): 190–202.

Margo, Robert A. "Wages and Prices during the Antebellum Period: A Survey and New Evidence." In *American Economic Growth and Standards of Living before the Civil War.* Ed. Robert E. Gallman and John Joseph Wallis. Chicago, 1992.

McDonald, Roderick A. "Independent Economic Production by Slaves on Antebellum Louisiana Sugar Plantations." *Slavery and Abolition* 12 (1991): 182–208.

Miller, Ruth. *BlackAmerican Literature, 1760–Present.* Beverly Hills, Calif., 1971.

Moore, John Hebron. "Simon Gray, Riverman: A Slave Who Was Almost Free." *Mississippi Valley Historical Review* 49 (1962): 472–84.

Morris, Richard B. "The Measure of Bondage in the Slave States." *Mississippi Valley Historical Review* 41 (1954–55): 219–40.

Mullin, Gerald W. *Flight and Rebellion: Slave Resistance in Eighteenth-Century Virginia.* New York, 1972.

North, Douglass C. *The Economic Growth of the United States, 1790–1860.* Englewood Cliffs, N. J., 1961.

O'Brien, John T. "Factory, Church, and Community: Blacks in Antebellum Richmond." *Journal of Southern History* 44 (1978): 509–26.

Parish, Peter J. *Slavery, History, and Historians.* New York, 1989.

Peterson, Arthur. "Flour and Grist Milling in Virginia: A Brief History." *Virginia Magazine of History and Biography* 43 (1935): 98–105.

Phillips, Ulrich B. *American Negro Slavery: A Survey of the Supply, Employment, and Control as Determined by the Plantation Regime.* Baton Rouge, La., 1916.

———. *Life and Labor in the Old South.* Boston, 1951.

Pinchbeck, Raymond B. *The Virginia Negro Artisan and Tradesman.* Richmond, 1926.

Price, Jacob. "Economic Function and the Growth of American Port Towns in the Eighteenth Century." *Perspectives in American History* 8 (1974): 123–88.

Quarles, Benjamin. *The Negro in the Civil War.* New York, 1953.

Rabinowitz, Howard N. *Race Relations in the Urban South, 1865–1890.* New York, 1978.

Raboteau, Albert J. "African-Americans, Exodus, and the American Israel." In *African-American Christianity: Essays in History.* Ed. Paul E. Johnson. Berkeley, Calif., 1994.

———. *Slave Religion: The "Invisible Institution" in the Antebellum South.* New York, 1978.

Rachleff, Peter. *Black Labor in Richmond, 1865–1890.* Chicago, 1989.

Randolph, Peter. *From Slave Cabin to the Pulpit; The Autobiography of Reverend Peter Randolph: The Southern Questions Illustrated and Sketches of Slave Life.* Boston, 1893.

Robert, Joseph Clarke. *The Tobacco Kingdom: Plantation, Market, and Factory in Virginia and North Carolina, 1800–1860.* Gloucester, Mass., 1965.

Rowland, Dunbar, ed. *Jefferson Davis, Constitutionalist: His Letters, Papers, and Speeches.* Vol. 5. Jackson, Miss., 1923.

Saunders, Robert M. "Crimes and Punishment in Early National America: Richmond, Virginia, 1784–1820." *Virginia Magazine of History and Biography* 86 (1978): 33–44.

Schechter, Patricia A. "Free and Slave Labor in the Old South: The Tredegar Ironworkers' Strike of 1847." *Labor History* 35 (1994): 165–86.

Schnittman, Suzanne Gehring. "Slavery in Virginia's Urban Tobacco Industry, 1840–1860." Ph.D. diss., University of Rochester, 1986.

Schwarz, Philip J. "Forging the Shackles: The Development of Virginia's Criminal Code for Slaves." In *Ambivalent Legacy: A Legal History of the South.* Ed. David J. Bodenhamer and James W. Ely Jr. Jackson, Miss., 1984.

———. "Gabriel's Challenge: Slaves and Crimes in Late Eighteenth-Century Virginia." *Virginia Magazine of History and Biography* 90 (1982): 283–309.

———. *Twice Condemned: Slaves and the Criminal Laws of Virginia, 1705–1865*. Baton Rouge, La., 1988.

Schweninger, Loren. "The Free-Slave Phenomenon: James P. Thomas and the Black Community in Ante-Bellum Nashville." *Civil War History* 22 (1976): 293–307.

———. "The Underside of Slavery: The Internal Economy, Self-Hire, and Quasi-Freedom in Virginia, 1780–1865." *Slavery and Abolition* 12 (1991): 1–22.

Scott, Mary Wingfield. *Old Richmond Neighborhoods*. Richmond, 1950.

Sernett, Milton, C. *Black Religion and American Evangelicalism: White Protestants, Plantation Missions, and the Flowering of Negro Christianity, 1787–1865*. Metuchen, N.J., 1975.

Sheldon, Marianne Buroff. "Black-White Relations in Richmond, Virginia, 1782–1820." *Journal of Southern History* 45 (1979): 27–44.

Stampp, Kenneth. *The Peculiar Institution: Slavery in the Antebellum South*. New York, 1956.

Stanard, Mary Newton. *Richmond, Its People and Its Story*. Philadelphia, 1923.

Starobin, Robert. *Blacks in Bondage: Letters of American Slaves*. New York, 1974.

———. *Industrial Slavery in the Old South*. New York, 1970.

———. "Privileged Bondsmen and the Process of Accommodation: The Role of House Servants and Drivers as Seen in Their Own Letters." *Journal of Social History* 5 (1971): 46–70.

Still, William. *The Underground Railroad: A Record of Facts Authentic Narratives, Letters, &c*. New York, 1968.

Tanner, Arthur Edmund. *Tobacco from the Grower to the Smoker*. London, 1937.

Thomas, Emory M. *The Confederate Nation, 1861–1865*. New York, 1979.

———. *The Confederate State of Richmond: A Biography of the Capital*. Austin, Tex., 1971.

Trexler, Harrison, A. "The Opposition of Planters to the Employment of Slaves as Laborers by the Confederacy." *Mississippi Valley Historical Review* 27 (1940): 211–24.

Tyler-McGraw, Marie. *At the Falls: Richmond, Virginia, and Its People*. Chapel Hill, N.C., 1994.

Tyler-McGraw, Marie, and Gregg D. Kimball. *In Bondage and Freedom: Antebellum Black Life in Richmond, Virginia*. Richmond, 1988.

Wade, Richard. *Slavery in the Cities: The South, 1820–1860*. New York, 1964.

Wall, Bennett. "Medical Care of Ebenezer Pettigrew's Slaves." *Mississippi Valley Historical Review* 37 (Dec. 1950): 451–70.

Ward, Harry M., and Harold E. Greer Jr. *Richmond during the Revolution, 1775–1783*. Charlottesville, Va., 1977.

War of the Rebellion: A Compilation of the Official Records of the Union and Confederate Armies. Ser. 1. Vol. 5. Washington, D.C., 1880.

Wesley, Charles H. *Negro Labor in the United States, 1850–1925: A Study in American Economic History*. New York, 1967.

White, Blanche Sydnor. *First Baptist Church, Richmond, 1780–1955: One Hundred and Seventy-five Years of Service to God and Man.* Richmond, 1955.

Wiley, Bell Irvin. *Southern Negroes, 1861–1865.* New York, 1938.

Woodson, Carter G. *The Mind of the Negro as Reflected In Letters Written during the Crisis, 1800–1860.* New York, 1926.

Wright, Gavin. "Cheap Labor and Southern Textiles before 1800." *Journal of Interdisciplinary History* 17 (spring 1987): 851–70.

Yetman, Norman R. *Life under the "Peculiar Institution": Selections from the Slave Narrative Collection.* New York, 1970.

Index

Carter G. Woodson Institute Series in Black Studies

Michael Plunkett,
Afro-American Sources in Virginia: A Guide to Manuscripts

Sally Belfrage,
Freedom Summer

Armstead L. Robinson and Patricia Sullivan, eds.,
New Directions in Civil Rights Studies

Leroy Vail and Landeg White,
Power and the Praise Poem: Southern African Voices in History

Robert A. Pratt,
The Color of Their Skin: Education and Race in Richmond, Virginia, 1954–89

Ira Berlin and Philip D. Morgan, eds.,
Cultivation and Culture: Labor and the Shaping of Slave Life in the Americas

Gerald Horne,
Fire This Time: The Watts Uprising and the 1960s

Sam C. Nolutshungu,
Limits of Anarchy: Intervention and State Formation in Chad

Jeannie M. Whayne,
A New Plantation South: Land, Labor, and Federal Favor in Twentieth-Century Arkansas

Patience Essah,
A House Divided: Slavery and Emancipation in Delaware, 1638–1865

Tommy L. Bogger,
Free Blacks in Norfolk, Virginia, 1790–1860: The Darker Side of Freedom

Robert C. Kenzer,
Enterprising Southerners: Black Economic Success in North Carolina, 1865–1915

Midori Takagi,
"Rearing Wolves to Our Own Destruction": Slavery in Richmond, Virginia, 1782–1865